D1594374

RARY

Spiritual Growth
with Entheogens

"A powerful testimony from pioneers of consciousness research, spiritual teachers, and scholars about the potential of psychedelic plants and their compounds to bring spirituality to modern society and help alleviate the dangerous alienation that has brought humanity to the brink of destruction."

Stanislav Grof, M.D., author of *LSD Psychotherapy,*
Psychology of the Future,* and *When the Impossible Happens

"A useful reference work that presents the current state of understanding from the relevant scientific, practical, and judicial perspectives."

Dennis McKenna, Ph.D., founding board member of the Heffter Research Institute and coauthor of *The Invisible Landscape*

"Explains all aspects of the psychedelic experience as a tool for spiritual evolution—from personal accounts to detailed information and practical instructions. A key book."

Dieter Hagenbach, president of Gaia Media Foundation

"*Spiritual Growth with Entheogens* is essential reading for people interested in humanity's efforts to experience the divine. This is an outstanding collection of essays and studies on mystical experience."

Michael Nielsen, professor and chair of psychology,
Georgia Southern University, and coeditor of
Archive for the Psychology of Religion

"A tour de force of the history of the Western reencounter with these perennial sacred plants, written by leading figures from many disciplines. The broad coverage exemplifies the importance of psychedelic plants for many disciplines and their diverse potentials for personal and social transformation."

Michael Winkelman, Ph.D., author of *Shamanism:*
A Biopsychosocial Paradigm of Consciousness and Healing
and editor of *Altering Consciousness*

"This essential collection forces a reexamination of the legal status of controlled substances in view of the benefit that mind-altering sacramental entheogens offer for psychotherapy and spiritual growth."

**Carl A. P. Ruck, professor of classical studies, Boston University,
and author of *Mushrooms, Myths, and Mithras***

"Tom Roberts is the keeper of the flame for the study of psychedelics, the chief librarian of the entheogenic archive. In this soul-nourishing book he's compiled the wisdom, humanity, and technical expertise the world just might be ready for now in order to provide us legally accessed soul-manifesting sacramental experience via psychedelics."

**Charles Hayes, editor of *Tripping: An Anthology
of True-Life Psychedelic Adventures***

"For those who value profound religious experiences and who wish to become increasingly well informed about how entheogens could become responsibly integrated into meditative practices and the offerings of spiritual retreat centers, there is much to be learned from the well-chosen essays in this book."

**William A. Richards, S.T.M., Ph.D., Department of Psychiatry,
Johns Hopkins Bayview School of Medicine**

"Some of the most serious, sustained, thoughtful, and mature voices on the subject of entheogens and religion. The contributors reflect on the historical trajectories of this conversation, address the common stereotypes and misconceptions, and offer new directions of thought and vision, reminding us again of what this conversation has always been about: the extraordinary cosmic being we so casually and carelessly call the human being."

**Jeffrey J. Kripal, professor of religious studies,
Rice University, and author of *Mutants and Mystics:
Science Fiction, Superhero Comics, and the Paranormal***

"Makes the case for primary religious experience through entheogens as a way to experience the sacred and realize personal transformation."

**Bruce Sewick, LCPC, RDDP, CADC,
therapist and addiction counselor**

SPIRITUAL GROWTH
WITH ENTHEOGENS

PSYCHOACTIVE
SACRAMENTALS AND
HUMAN TRANSFORMATION

EDITED BY THOMAS B. ROBERTS

Park Street Press
Rochester, Vermont • Toronto, Canada

Park Street Press
One Park Street
Rochester, Vermont 05767
www.ParkStPress.com

Text stock is SFI certified

Park Street Press is a division of Inner Traditions International

Originally published in 2001 by the Council on Spiritual Practices under the title
Psychoactive Sacramentals: Essays on Entheogens and Religion

Note to the Reader: The information provided in this book is for educational,
historical, and cultural interest only and should not be construed as advocacy
for the use of entheogens. Neither the authors nor the publisher assume any
responsibility for physical, psychological, legal, or other consequences arising from
these substances.

Library of Congress Cataloging-in-Publication Data
Spiritual growth with entheogens : psychoactive sacramentals and human
transformation / edited by Thomas B. Roberts.
    p. cm.
Proceedings of a conference held in 1995 in Menlo Park, Calif.
Includes bibliographical references and index.
ISBN 978-1-59477-439-3 (pbk.) — ISBN 978-1-59477-709-7 (e-book)
1. Hallucinogenic drugs and religious experience—Congresses. I. Roberts,
Thomas B. II. Title.
BL65.D7P78 2012
204'.2—dc23

2011040036

Printed and bound in the United States by Lake Book Manufacturing
The text stock is SFI certified. The Sustainable Forestry Initiative® program
promotes sustainable forest management.

10 9 8 7 6 5 4 3 2 1

Text design and layout by Virginia Scott Bowman
This book was typeset in Garamond Premier Pro and Gill Sans with Grajon,
Copperplate, and Gill Sans used as display typefaces

———— ◆ ————

This book is dedicated

to Susan—
with many, many thanks for putting up
with me while I worked
on the Vallombrosa conference and on this book.
I couldn't have done them without your patience
and understanding.
You are the foundation of my life.
Love, Tom

to Becca—
with hopes that you and your generation
will someday
legally be able to enhance your spiritual
development with entheogens.
You light up my life.
Love, Dad

Contents

On the sand I have abandoned my small boat.
Now with you I will seek other seas.

CESAREO GUBORAIN,
"TU HAS VENIDO A LA ORILLA,"
YOU HAVE COME DOWN TO THE LAKESHORE

Out of Society's Secret Corners

Thomas B. Roberts

Children of a future age,
Reading this indignant page,
Know that in a former time,
A path to God was thought a crime.

AFTER WILLIAM BLAKE

In 1995, the Chicago Theological Seminary and the Council on Spiritual Practices (CSP) invited a group of theologians, clergy, mental health professionals, transpersonal psychologists, and other professionals who shared an interest in entheogens to a weeklong conference-retreat at Vallombrosa Conference Center in Menlo Park, California. We asked the participants to reflect on the topics that were discussed. CSP gathered these reflections and published them under the title, *Psychoactive Sacramentals*. While some chapters closely follow the Vallombrosa talks, others were entirely new.

These essays ask profound questions about the meaning of being human, our place in the universe, and how we can explore our spiritual nature. No one knows the answers to these questions. But as the writings in this book demonstrate, entheogenic explorers at the end of the twentieth century have endowed the explorers of the twenty-first century with enlightening experiences, uplifting spiritual challenges, and, above all, more intriguing questions. We are lucky to live during a time when it is increasingly possible to explore such questions through entheogen-assisted primary religious experience.

The decade leading to this new edition of this book has moved entheogens out of society's secret corners through language, science, and law. Here are some of the significant shifts.

In language, the *Oxford English Dictionary* officially recognized the word "entheogen." Their September 2007 "release of new words" noted that

> this word, used to refer to a psychoactive substance employed for spiritual purposes, has an ancient Greek etymon, but is only attested from 1977. The word was apparently coined as an alternative to the words **hallucinogen n.** and **psychedelic n.**, which were strongly associated with recreational drug use.

In science, most spectacular is the work that CSP initiated at the Johns Hopkins University. Scientists there, headed by Prof. Roland Griffiths, have conducted studies of the effects of psilocybin given to healthy, normal volunteers (in contrast to patients seeking psychiatric treatment). Most of the study volunteers rated a psilocybin session as among the most spiritually significant experiences of their lives and reported subsequent increases in well-being. Links to the research and some of the extensive media coverage are at www.csp.org/psilocybin. Studies at Harbor-UCLA Medical Center, New York University, and Johns Hopkins are exploring the use of psilocybin with cancer patients to help alleviate end-of-life psychological struggles. Although that work is framed medically, it is coming to be understood that the most potent therapeutic factor in the treatment is the primary religious experience, rather than the drug per se.

In the law, two religious groups have received U.S. federal court recognition of their right to use a controlled substance sacramentally. The first such case was brought by the U.S. branch of a Brazilian church, the União do Vegetal (see udvusa.com). It reached the Supreme Court, which in 2006 issued unanimous guidance favorable to the church. Let us remember too the Native American Church, whose hundreds of thousands of members have long suffered persecution from federal and state authorities. Their right to use peyote was solidified in 1997 by an act of Congress. I discuss some broader issues about entheogens in an hour-long presentation at blip.tv/mjhhaven/psychedelic-4604065.

With these and other developments, the entheogens are coming into the light, but they are not in a bright spot yet. Will the next decade move entheogens into the sunlight?

The kingdom of God is within you.

LUKE 17:21

Thomas B. Roberts, Ph.D. (Stanford), is an emeritus professor of Educational Psychology now teaching *Psychedelic Studies* in the Honors Program at Northern Illinois University. His major publications include the reference-resource, *Religion and Psychoactive Sacraments: An Entheogen Chrestomathy* (www.csp .org/chrestomathy), *Psychedelic Horizons, Psychedelic Medicine* (2 vols), and *The Psychedelic Future of the Mind* (forthcoming 2012). He was the Program Chair of the Vallombrosa Conference that inspired this book. His home page resides at niu.academia.edu/ThomasRoberts.

Acknowledgments

Thank you, Rev. Kenneth Smith, retired President of Chicago Theological Seminary, and thank you CTS for co-sponsoring the Vallombrosa Conference-Retreat. By recognizing the social injustice being done to entheogen users and by expressing the spiritual courage to support an unpopular expression of religious exploration, your cosponsorship made it possible for the Council on Spiritual Practices to attract some of the best minds to this meeting. Personally, I am proud that CTS is a seminary of my denomination, and we are once again in the forefront of human rights as we were in the public schools movement, the founding of universities, abolition, women in the ministry, and sexual orientation. You make me proud to be a Congregationalist-UCC.

Thank you, contributors to this book, for the dedication and care you gave to your chapters. They show careful thought and precise wording. Thank you for putting up with the many revisions, tweakings, and editorial details. I hope you've experienced this as traveling a path of personal growth, as I have. While editing this volume, your writings have helped me over rough spots and around impediments in my path as well.

Thank you all participants at the Vallombrosa Retreat, both authors and nonauthors. Thank you for recognizing the importance of entheogenic religious expression by participating so avidly in our discussions, for asking insightful questions, for listening with open hearts and open minds, for taking time away from your families and jobs, and for being so dedicated that you even paid your own expenses. Thanks to you, this was one of the spiritually richest and psychologically most meaningful weeks of my life. I hope it was for you, too.

A special thank you to the conference benefactors: Jeffrey Bronfman and the Aurora Foundation, Eric E. Sterling and the Criminal Justice Policy Foundation, Melisa Richardson, E. A. (Sandy) Sandling, and M. and Peter Normal. Your support allowed us to organize the conference, and your ongoing funding of CSP helped us edit and polish the drafts and complete the thousands of tasks that go into producing a book. When you read this book, I hope you'll feel the satisfaction of proud accomplishment and human service that you deserve.

Thank you to the staff of the Vallombrosa Retreat Center. Your unobtrusive efficiency and friendly skillfulness are another aspect of Vallombrosa's beauty.

Thank you, Grey Six at the Council on Spiritual Practices, for taking up the ball and shepherding this book though to completion. Your calmness and attention to a snowstorm of details is neverending.

Thank you, Bara Bonnet, for a proofreader's sharp eye. I know this book and my chapter are enormously improved thanks to your editor's ear for words and finesse in phrasing.

Thank you, Sam Shirley, for turning words on disk into this book.

Thank you, Rae Erowid, for your help with the index. Not being able to find something in a book because there's no index is one of my pet aggravations. Your indexing makes this book more usable to readers and saves us all from that frustration.

Thank you, Dave Wilson and Craig Comstock, who are both tillermen and lookouts for CSP. Bon Voyage!

And an endless thank you, Bob Jesse, CSP's president, for your steadfast energy, devoted endurance, detailed focus, personal dedication, and exemplary standards—inspiring models we can all admire. None of this could have happened without you.

An institutional thank you to the College of Education at Northern Illinois University and my colleagues in the Department of Educational

Psychology and Foundations for providing time to work on this book and the years of your patience to see that it was done right.

Thank you especially to the unseen ones, the hundreds of thousands, perhaps millions, of people whose entheogenic experiences are landmarks along their spiritual paths. Whether you are clergy, members of religious orders and organizations, laity—churched or unchurched—it is a comfort knowing you are there. This book acknowledges you.

—TOM ROBERTS,
EDITOR

The Varieties of Mind-Enhancing Practices

Roger Walsh

How can we enhance our mental health and well-being? This is an ancient question to which we now have many answers. In fact, for the first time in human history we have all the world's answers. These answers cover an enormous range and include diverse lifestyles, relationships and communities, supplements, drugs and technologies, studies and psychotherapies as well as a variety of physical, mental, and spiritual disciplines.

This abundance of life-enhancing riches raises an obvious question: Can we cull from them to create effective programs for increasing psychological and spiritual well-being and maturity? In the early twenty-first century, we have begun to see the first attempts to create just such programs. Three specific examples are lifestyle programs, essential spiritual practices, and integral practices.

- *Lifestyle programs* point to the healing and enhancing power of therapeutic lifestyle changes (TLCs). Eight TLCs with proven benefits include nutrition, exercise, relationships, recreation, relaxation, time in nature, spiritual practices, and service to others.

    Considerable research demonstrates the benefits of all of these. TLCs can be just as effective as psychotherapy or medication for disorders such as anxiety and depression, while they can enhance psychological and spiritual well-being in people whose health is already good (Walsh 1999).

- *Essential Spiritual Practices:* The world's religious and spiritual traditions agree that a full life, let alone an enlightened life, requires a set of practices to cultivate specific qualities of heart and mind. In fact, the great religions all recommend seven kinds of practices to cultivate seven corresponding qualities. These practices are living ethically, transforming emotions, developing concentration, refining awareness, purifying motivation, cultivating wisdom, and engaging in service (Walsh 2011). When done together over sustained periods of time, these practices hold the promise of profound and wide-ranging psychological and spiritual transformation.

- *Integral Life Practices:* Recently, even more ambitious programs have emerged that seek to enhance all major dimensions of health: physical, mental, emotional, and spiritual (Leonard and Murphy 2005; Wilbur et al. 2008). Integral life practice (ILP) is based on Ken Wilber's integral theory, which offers a comprehensive conceptual framework for integrating diverse perspectives and practices. ILP is unique in recognizing not only all major *dimensions* of health, but also all *levels* of possible psychological and spiritual development.

What is missing from all these programs? The answer is no surprise: entheogens. And this raises the obvious question: Why are they overlooked? Four possible answers deserve consideration:

- *Research Evidence:* Are entheogens overlooked because there is no research evidence for their benefits? Absolutely not! Over a thousand studies were done in the brief twenty-year period before the early 1970s when research was halted by government red tape and dwindling funding. Fortunately, new research has now begun (Griffiths and Grob 2010; Grob 2002; Walsh and Grob 2005; Winkelman and Roberts 2008).

- *Risks:* Have entheogens been overlooked because of their risks? In part, yes. When used unskillfully, they can result in extremely difficult acute states of mind and produce long-term psychological disruption in unstable individuals.

However, used skillfully, they are surprisingly safe. A comprehensive review of side effects concluded that "in well-screened, prepared, supervised, and followed-up psychiatric patients, taking pure psychedelic drugs, the incidence of severe adverse reactions is less than 1 percent. It is even lower in 'normal' volunteers" (Strassman 1997). In addition, the recent rebirth of research has already demonstrated, for example, therapeutic benefits for the dying as well as psychological and spiritual benefits for healthy people (Griffiths et al. 2011; Grob et al. 2011).

- *Cultural Misunderstanding:* So sensationalized were psychedelics by sensationalistic media madness that, for the most part, politicians and the public are aware only of their dangers and not at all of their therapeutic or entheogenic potentials. Nor is any distinction made between destructive, addictive chemicals such as cocaine on the one hand, and problematic but potentially beneficial substances such as psychedelics on the other.

- *Transient Benefits:* A final reason that psychedelics or entheogens are missing from mind-enhancing programs is that these drugs seem better at inducing transient altered states rather than enduring transformed traits. In fact, one of the central themes of Huston Smith's chapter in this book is that while it is clear that entheogens can produce religious experiences, it is less clear that they can induce religious lives. This fits very well with the more general principle stated in Brother David Steindl-Rast's Introduction that "A primary religious experience is no more (though also no less) than a seed for a spiritual life. A genuine encounter with the Ultimate does not guarantee a genuine spirituality."

So entheogenic experiences may not produce religious lives. However, they may still catalyze long lasting psychological and spiritual benefits as multiple personal reports and intriguing recent research clearly demonstrate (Winkelman and Roberts 2008; Grinspoon and Bakalar 1983; MacLean, Johnson, and Griffiths 2011; Vaughan 1983).

If we put all this information about entheogens together with the information on programs to enhance mental health, what do we get? Two principles stand out:

- First, a full life, let alone an enlightened life, requires a long-term multifaceted discipline of psychological, spiritual, and physical practices.
- Second, one element of such a discipline could be, for appropriate people under appropriate circumstances, an entheogenic experience. The rationale is that considerable research shows that entheogens can occasion genuine mystical experiences and long-lasting benefits in a large percentage of suitably selected and prepared people (Griffiths et al. 2011; MacLean et al. 2011).

In a sane society, with objective information about the benefits, risks, and skillful use of entheogens, these chemicals could be considered as one possible component of a well-rounded life and mind-optimizing program. Obviously they are not for everyone and must be used carefully and skillfully. Also, by themselves they do not constitute a full program for psychological or spiritual maturation (Walsh and Grob 2005). However, they may sometimes be valuable as one element of such a program, and they are also powerful and important research tools.

The authors in this book are pioneers in researching entheogens. The topics they cover are broad, and include multiple aspects: theoretical and practical, chemical and cultural, clinical and counseling, psychological and spiritual, and more. Their research and writings make a valuable contribution to a more balanced assessment of these curious substances with their remarkable mind-manifesting (psychedelic) and God-revealing (entheogenic) potentials.

Roger Walsh, M.D., Ph.D., is professor of psychiatry, anthropology, and philosophy at the University of California, Irvine. His publications include the books *Essential Spirituality: The Seven Practices Common to World Religions* and (with Frances Vaughan) *Paths Beyond Ego: The Transpersonal Perspective.* A native of Australia, he has been a student of contemplative practices for over twenty years. His writings and research have received over twenty national and international awards.

REFERENCES

Griffiths, R., and C. Grob. 2010. "Hallucinogens as medicine." *Scientific American* 303, 76–79. DOI: 10.1038/scientificamerican1210-76.

Griffiths, R., M. Johnson, W. Richards, B. Richards, U. McCann, and R. Jesse. 2011. "Psilocybin occasioned mystical-type experiences: Immediate and persisting dose-related effects." *Psychopharmacology*. DOI: 10.1007/s00213-011-2358-5.

Grinspoon, L., and J. Bakalar, eds. 1983. *Psychedelic Reflections*. New York: Human Sciences Press.

Grob, C., ed. 2002. *Hallucinogens: A Reader*. New York: Tarcher/Putnam.

Grob, C., A. Danforth, M. Gurpreet, S. Chopra, M. Hagerty, C. McKay, A. Halberstadt, and G. Greer. 2011. "Pilot study of psilocybin treatment for anxiety in patients with advanced stage cancer." *Archives of General Psychiatry* 68 (1), 71–78. DOI: 10.1001/archgenpsychiatry.2010.116.

Leonard, A., and M. Murphy. 2005. *The Life We Are Given*. New York: Tarcher/Penguin.

MacLean, K., J. Johnson, and R. Griffiths. 2011. "Mystical experiences occasioned by the hallucinogen psilocybin lead to increases in the personality domain of openness." *Journal of Psychopharmacology*. DOI: 10.1177/0269881111420188.

Strassman, R. 1997. "Biomedical research with psychedelics: Current models, future prospects." In R. Forte, ed. *Entheogens and the Future of Religion*. San Francisco, Calif.: Council on Spiritual Practices, 152–62.

Vaughan, F. 1983. "Perception and knowledge: Reflections on psychological and spiritual learning in the psychedelic experience." In C. Grinspoon and J. Bakalar, eds. *Psychedelic Reflections*. New York: Human Sciences Press, 108–14.

Walsh, R. 1999. *Essential Spirituality: The Seven Central Practices*. New York: Wiley & Sons.

———. 2011. "Lifestyle and mental health." *American Psychologist* 66(7): 579–92.

Walsh, R., and C. Grob, eds. 2005. *Higher Wisdom: Eminent Elders Explore the Continuing Impact of Psychedelics*. New York: SUNY.

Wilber, K., T. Patton, A. Leonard, and M. Morelli. 2008. *Integral Life Practice*. Boston: Shambhala.

Winkelman, M. and T. Roberts, eds. 2008. *Psychedelic Medicine: New Evidence for Hallucinogenic Substances as Treatments,* vols. 1 & 2. Westport, Conn.: Praeger.

For the Beauty of the Earth

For the beauty of the earth,
For the glory of the skies,
For the love which from our birth
Over and around us lies,
Lord of all to thee we raise
This our hymn of grateful praise.

For the wonder of each hour
Of the day and of the night,
Hill and vale and tree and flow'r,
Sun and moon and stars of light,
Lord of all to thee we raise
This our hymn of grateful praise.

For the joy of ear and eye,
For the heart and mind's delight,
For the mystic harmony
Linking sense to sound and light,
Lord of all to thee we raise
This our hymn of grateful praise.

For the joy of human love,
Brother, sister, parent, child,
Friends on earth and friends above,
For all gentle thoughts and mild,
Lord of all to thee we raise,
This our hymn of grateful praise.

FOLLIOTT S. PIERPOINT

Psychoactive Sacramentals

Brother David Steindl-Rast

Brother David Steindl-Rast, Ph.D., O.S.B., was born in Vienna where he studied art, anthropology, and psychology. After receiving a Ph.D. from the University of Vienna, he joined the Benedictine Monastery of Mount Saviour. After twelve years of monastic training and studies in philosophy and theology, Brother David received Vatican approval in 1967 to participate in a Christian Buddhist dialogue with Zen teachers Hakuun Yasutani Roshi, Shunryu Suzuki Roshi, Soen Nakagawa Roshi, and Eido Shimano Roshi. Together with Thomas Merton, Brother David contributed to the renewal of religious life, especially through the House of Prayer Movement of the 1970s. His books have been translated into many languages. *Gratefulness, The Heart of Prayer,* and *A Listening Heart* have been reprinted and anthologized for well over a decade. Brother David has co-authored *Belonging to the Universe,* a dialogue on new-paradigm thinking in science and theology with physicist Fritjof Capra and *The Ground We Share* on Buddhist and Christian practice with Robert Aitken Roshi. For decades, Brother David has divided his time between periods of a hermit's life and extensive lecture tours. At present, his efforts are concentrated on serving a worldwide community for grateful life and action by means of an ambitious, interactive website: gratefulness.org.

◈

This book is apt to stretch a reader's consciousness a few notches. All the more so because it is not pushy. There is strength in gentleness. But no matter how gentle the process of stretching, the unknown toward which we stretch will make us uneasy. This book will stir up fears. Three are likely to arise: fear of inauthentic spirituality, fear of drugs, and fear of an ill-prepared encounter with the holy. All three are reasonable fears; all three can be overcome by open-minded reasoning plus a modicum of courage. This is not a book for the timid, but it will reward the courageous.

In my own Catholic Christian tradition, sacramentality is not something to be toyed with. It has the feel of a high-security area. The very term "sacramental" (used in the book's title with theological precision as a noun) has the ring of a warning sign: Danger! High voltage! It points toward nothing less than encounter with God. Sacramentals are natural things—spring water, ashes, herbs—through which faith encounters God's power. I take this seriously. But precisely because I take it so seriously, I must allow God to choose the means and circumstances of this encounter. Because I have faith in the Church's traditional sacramentals, I ought to be able to stretch that faith to include the possibility of encountering God through all available sacramentals.

Whatever we receive with the trusting courage of faith can become a means for encountering God. Food shared and eaten in gratefulness becomes an encounter with God's life-sustaining love. The waters at Lourdes and other sacred places bring health of mind and body to countless pilgrims who encounter in faith God's power to heal. The Creator of life-giving bread and health-giving water created also psychoactive sacramentals. Can we then forbid God to work through them as well, for our good?

Water, fire, wind that blows where it will—these biblical images want to remind us that no one can put divine aliveness in a box. Communion with that source of life demands that our consciousness must stay ever ready to be stretched. In our society few people have close enough contact with nature to be conscious of a higher power at work in it and through it. This was different, I remember, during my childhood in the Austrian Alps. On Easter morning we would run down to wash in the mountain stream, never doubting that God's blessing touched us through the ice cold water on our skin. And in a nearby shrine we could drink from a healing spring that flowed out from under the altar. Faith simply accepted with gratefulness that God works through all created things. All?

If we can encounter God through a sunrise seen from a mountaintop, why not through a mushroom prayerfully ingested? But precisely because an overpowering encounter with God through an entheogen can happen to one who is quite unprepared for it, we must ask: Can this be genuine? Especially those who have spent years and decades in ascetical effort are apt to sneer at "instant enlightenment" or "effortless beatific vision." "How could one get it so cheaply?" they ask. "Can this be genuine spirituality?" My answer is this: A primary religious experience is no more (though also no less) than a seed for a spiritual life. A genuine encounter with the Ultimate does not guarantee a genuine spirituality. The experience may be authentic, but how authentic their spirituality will be depends on what those who had the experience do with it. Will they allow it to transform their lives? Will they have determination and patience enough to let the light, which they glimpsed for a moment, gradually penetrate every small detail of their days? Not a few men and women who have risen to this task bear witness that entheogens first helped them open their eyes to that light. Honesty demands that we acknowledge this.

Yet, can you blame someone who is so deeply aware of the devastation caused by drug abuse that the mere mention of psychoactive substances triggers panic? There is good reason to be wary of mind-affecting drugs. They can cause chemical damage to the brain and body, create addiction, or engender dangerous behavior. But not all drugs are alike. The classic entheogens, unlike drugs such as cocaine and alcohol, have virtually no organic toxicity. Their addictive risk is small: too small to measure when used in ceremonial settings. Entheogenic traditions from Eleusis to the Native American Church have succeeded in creating ritual contexts in which hazardous acting-out is virtually unknown.

The wise will feel a fear far greater than fear of inauthentic spirituality or fear of drugs, namely the fear of an ill-prepared encounter with the holy. Psychoactive sacramentals may open us for an experience of transcendent reality, but who is ready to meet this *mysterium tremendum*? The holy can destroy those who stumble into its awful presence unprepared. Should we avoid it, then? If we do, how can we survive, cut off from the primary religious experience of ultimate communion?

What is most distinctive about the spiritual awakening in our time is a looking beyond secondary religious phenomena—doctrine, ethics, ritual—to their primary source. Not as if doctrine, ethics, and ritual were unimportant. They are important, and precisely for this reason we must cultivate the experience on which their survival depends. After all, what is doctrine, if not an attempt to put into words the heart's communion with the ineffable? What is ethics, if not willing commitment to the demands this communion makes on us? What is ritual, if not the celebration of the primary religious experience of communion? Secondary religious phenomena give us fresh access to that primary experience from which they well up, as from their source. They provide channels in which the energy of primary religious experience can flow: irrigation channels for the world's wastelands. Even churches can become wastelands, if they close themselves off from the living waters of the Spirit, if they think that secondary religious experiences can replace the primary one.

Yes, in whatever form we dare to approach the holy, we must always do so with fear and trembling. We must do everything we can to prepare ourselves. There is reason to fear overconfident blundering into the presence of a power that takes us beyond ourselves. Yet there is still greater reason to fear a timidity that shrinks from the experience of ultimate communion. Christian tradition has long known this timidity and called it "sloth," a refusal to rise to grace-filled opportunities. This fear produces isolation, alienation, and violence; it keeps the world divided and at war. The primary religious experience stretches our awareness just far enough to catch at least a glimpse of universal belonging; this makes us ready to share, to trust, to love. The future of our planet will depend on whether or not we translate this vision into reality. This takes courage.

At this moment in history, nothing could be more dangerous for the future entrusted to us than a closed mind. If we don't dare to live with our minds wide open, they close up and shrink. The authors of this book discuss the entheogens as powerful tools for opening our minds. Various spiritual traditions offer other tools for the same end. Immersion in silence can dissolve the walls of the mind. The practice of gratefulness can open the mind's eye to see each detail of daily life bathed in "light invisible." Selfless service, too, can open heart and mind until we see God's face in the faces of all who suffer. The entheogens, with their own particular properties, are spiritual tools among many. We are free to choose. But while the means are optional; the end is not. The future depends on stretching our consciousness far enough soon enough. In view of this supreme challenge, *Psychoactive Sacramentals* [*Spiritual Growth with Entheogens*] is truly a timely book.

DAVID STEINDL-RAST, PH.D., O.S.B.
MOUNT SAVIOUR MONASTERY
FEBRUARY 2, 2000

1

If I Could Change Your Mind

Sermon by Rev. Mike Young

Mike Young is the only original subject in the 1962 Good Friday Marsh Chapel Experiment willing to speak publicly about it. He is currently minister of the First Unitarian Church of Honolulu. He previously served UU churches in Tampa, Florida; West Los Angeles and Palo Alto, California; and was Campus Minister at Stanford University from 1965 to 1969.

The vision was not "pantheistic." The morning star was not the object of my veneration. It was, to use very traditional language, "an outward and visible sign of an inward and invisible grace," the standard definition of a sacrament. Was it a "mystical experience"? I don't think so. I did not lose myself or merge with the star. I did not return as a drop of water to the great ocean or soar out of my body. I knew where I was and who I was at all times. What I felt was an Other moving toward me with a power of affirmation beyond anything I had ever imagined

could exist. I was glad and grateful. No theory that what happened to me was "artificially induced" or psychotic or hallucinatory can erase its mark. "The bright morning stars are rising," as the old hymn puts it, "in my soul."

HARVEY COX, *TURNING EAST*, 1977

Given November 5, 1995, at The First Unitarian Church of Honolulu and combined here with his 1995 article "An Invitation to Entheological Dialogue."

If, on some Sunday morning, I would step up here into the pulpit and announce to you that I had an experience available to you, that you could come to the church on a given Saturday afternoon and spend with me between six and eight hours and I guarantee—virtually guarantee; at least almost guarantee; well, pretty certainly guarantee; oh, a good chance—that you would experience a total transformation of your own mind, the way you saw yourself, the way you experience the world out there and your relationship to it. How many would be interested? (About a dozen hands went up!)

There are a few adventurers left.

On Good Friday, April 20, 1962, I was a subject in one of the last legal experiments with psilocybin done in this country. Walter Pahnke, a young minister and physician, was working on his Ph.D. in the psychology of religion. His mentors were Richard Alpert, whom you know now as Ram Dass, and Timothy Leary, whom you know now as . . . well, Timothy Leary. During studies when psilocybin was given to prisoners at Walpole State Prison in Massachusetts, they observed that these almost entirely uneducated prisoners described their experiences under the drug in language that sounded like they had flipped open almost at random the literature of the great mystics of the East and West—a vocabulary that no one had ever dreamed was inside their heads.

Walter said, "We've got to test this." He developed a rather complex and interesting series of questionnaires and then trained housewives to administer them. The questionnaires were to be used in analyzing written and taped material to determine whether or not the experience could be categorized as a religious experience. He then collected his subjects. He figured that the group of people most likely to have a religious experience would be a bunch of theological students. Well, if he'd asked my opinion on that I would have told him that's probably the last group of people that is likely to have any kind of first-hand religious experience. We'd all been inoculated against it. We gathered at Boston University's Marsh Chapel. Howard Thurman, the Dean of Chapel at Boston University, was doing a Good Friday meditation service upstairs in the main sanctuary of the chapel. We were downstairs in a small chapel in the basement. There were twenty of us. Half of us got the placebo and half of us got the real thing.

More than twenty-five years later, a young graduate student named Rick Doblin decided to attempt to do what Walter Pahnke intended to do, which was a twenty-five-year follow-up. Unfortunately, Walter Pahnke was killed in an accident and never had a chance to finish all of the follow-ups to this particular experiment. Rick was having difficulty finding all of the participants. Walter Pahnke had been too effective in protecting our identities so that we would not be embarrassed if, one day, as sadly it turned out, it became a bad thing to have ever been involved in such an experiment. I was one of those who had not been particularly quiet about having been involved in that experiment, so I helped Rick locate others. Some of them were still friends of mine. All but one were contacted, and that one was not contacted because he is dead. There are limits.

Of the nineteen who were contacted, nine were placebo receivers and ten were the actual drug receivers. Of the placebo receivers, only five are still in the ministry. Of the ten who received the drug, eight are still in the ministry. The difference isn't statistically significant but it's interesting. All except one of us who got the drug said afterwards, "Yes, this definitely was a religious experience." And that one has significantly changed his mind over the years about whether or not it was a religious experience. I know, because that one is me.

For the first time since the mid-1960s, the FDA is approving research into the therapeutic use of hallucinogens with specific groups of people, beginning with patients facing life-threatening diagnoses. I guess the theory is "you can't hurt them any more." One of the things that has come out of the preliminary research with terminal patients and these substances is that a very large percentage of the patients describe as a result of the drug experience the loss of the fear of death. The second population is comprised of those who experience acute pain, intractable pain, pain that simply doesn't respond to our usual methods of dealing with pain. These folks find that, after a single experience with the drug, dramatically fewer painkillers are needed. And finally, those afflicted with alcohol and drug addiction are beginning to be used as subjects in these experiments. This is happening not in irresponsible places. It is happening in some of the best research institutions. It is happening in VA hospitals. For example, at the VA hospital in Tampa, where I used to be minister, Dr. Kolb is involved in research with addicts. I was disappointed in leaving because I looked forward to helping with the set and setting for the drug experience in the research.

The preliminary conclusions from the research are really very fascinating. If the research is permitted to continue as it is now; if the results of the research are as preliminary indications suggest (a big *if,* because in the middle of the research we might very well find, "Hey, this is a bad idea. Let's stop doing it."); if as a result, terminal patients, intractable pain patients, and addicts begin to be treated with these substances across the country, then several major upheavals are going to occur in this culture. The first one has to do with our attitudes toward drugs.

We simply are virtually unable to make the distinction between differing kinds of drugs. Doctors complain frequently that they prescribe a drug for someone, and the person says dumb things like, "No, I don't want to take the antibiotic. It's a drug." We have succeeded with the "Just say 'no'" rhetoric in some of the queerest places.

What is going to happen when the families and friends and fellow researchers and nurses and treatment teams who have been involved in the therapeutic use of these substances, who, when they have witnessed the patients' experiences, heard their stories, seen their life transformations, say, "Me, too."? This will not be irresponsible kids throwing a fistful of pills on the carpet in a room somewhere and saying, "Grab one and see what it does." This will be responsible adults who say, "Something about that experience was overwhelmingly life-transforming for my loved one. I want that experience, too."

Institutionalized religion has been all but completely co-opted in the "War on Drugs." We have labeled all drug use outside the strict medical model as naughty. It is a curious logic: if you want to use drugs and you're not sick, you are naughty. If you persist, you are sick, and we'll give you some other drugs. Many physicians won't prescribe addictive painkillers even for terminal patients in acute pain for fear they'll become addicted. The fear here is that the doctor will be perceived as "naughty." Prescribing a non-addictive "bad" drug that obviates the need for addictive drugs is "naughty" for the same reason—namely, our moralistic response to the problems created by a drug-saturated and drug-obsessed culture.

The religious establishment has overwhelmingly bought all of this and painted itself into an especially awkward corner. It used to be that you were naughty if you did something that harmed another. Now it has come to be that you are naughty if you appear not to disapprove sufficiently of naughtiness. That appearance of approval has us tied up in knots. We are faced now with the possibility of some drugs that do very positive things to otherwise normal—not sick—people. This is not a context that is promising for useful public policy decision-making. Here are some drugs that reshape and reframe our meaning-making in ways that we religious leaders have always said were good. How could that be naughty?

We pastors of every denomination across the country are unprepared for our congregations telling us, "Knock off your stupid, narrow, provincial divisions about whose creed is right. It is the transformation of human life that religion is about, not about beliefs." And when that happens, my colleagues who have virtually completely bought into the "Just say 'no'" mentality for drugs are going to be in an awful situation.

At the same time, precisely because the very nature of the experience, for a great many of those who experience it, is inherently a religious experience, the researchers desperately need our input on how to create the set and setting, the expectations, and the context that are such a powerful part of determining what the outcome of the experience will be. At the moment, any standard brand minister who dares to work with a researcher in doing just that, in shaping the set and setting for people who are going to be involved in the experiments, risks losing his or her job. There is not a single denomination—mine included—that does not have very strong, very problematic, ambiguous feelings about this whole issue.

I have insisted that this is a religious experience, and that this is one of the things that is going to be problematic. When I use the phrase "religious experience," I mean the following kinds of things. I mean an experience, however *Pow!* or ordinary and mundane, that has the result of reordering your valuing; that turns the world that you have taken for granted in a new direction, opening possibilities for you; an experience that gooses you into transcending your small self. It is this opening up of blocked areas of growth that makes an experience religious. It may and often does involve resultant changes in beliefs, but is not about a certain set of beliefs. In fact, it is more often about shedding beliefs.

The standard model for the experience is that one is having some real and acute conflicts. Somewhere inside of you are two things that say, "yes, yes, yes" and "no, no, no." You cannot say both, be both, and live both at the same time. The conflict is about something that is real enough to put you in significant turmoil. In the process of letting yourself really experience those contradictory desires, you are driven into what is referred to in literature as "the dark night of the soul." At some point in that dark night there is a twist, a change, a movement, a light comes on, or something slips. What once was a conflict has opened at another level and the impasse is gone. The result is experienced as ecstasy.

The heroine of Tom Robbins' *Another Roadside Attraction* says, "I'm only interested in three states of consciousness. I'm interested in amnesia, euphoria, and ecstasy. Amnesia is when you don't know who you are and desperately want to know. Euphoria is when you don't know who you are and don't care. Ecstasy is when you know exactly who you are and still don't care."

Psilocybin and similar substances appear to have the potential to facilitate this experience of ecstasy. The religious experience, drug related or not, is not the end. It is pathless. It is a "goose." It is a grabbing and shaking, but you still have to do something with what happens there, with the vista that was opened, with the possibility that became available. The proof of the experience is in the fruits, not in the size of the *Pow!* that goes with it.

What a wonderful irony to all of this: at the moment it is completely illegal for a religious leader to administer a religious experience to you in this way. But it is quite legal for a scientist to administer a religious experience to you in this way. The irony of it has many, many levels. The first piece of the irony, for me, is that we have indeed made the scientists the high priests of our technological society. Those same high priests are now finding that they are in fact going to have to learn how to be priests for real. Many of them are acutely aware of their own inadequacies. They are aware that they are not liturgists, that they are not poets of the human spirit. That sensitivity will be needed to provide the tools—the language and imagery—that will enable people to utilize the full potential of the sacramental drug experience.

The drug experience can evoke a reordering, a reframing, of the experiencer's meanings and meaning-making. The ego-loss experienced with LSD, the sense of reconnectedness with MDMA, the standing-naked-before-the-infinite, out-of-the-body experience with ketamine: these provide the occasion for the reframing of existential questions (such as "Who am I?" and "What is, therefore, important?") that the experiencer realizes they have gotten so wrong. This reframing and reconnecting, this remembering of ourselves, is what pushes and pulls us to be more than we are. Spoken of in different ways and sought by different means, it is at the heart of our various spiritual disciplines. But when it is short-circuited into obsessive ideology, it merely multiplies dogmatism.

There are a couple of real drawbacks to the religious experience afforded by a drug. One is that people come back from the experience with a new language (that they found themselves using during the experience), and this new language has cosmic authenticity. The language is experienced as the truth because of the power of the experience. The self-transcendence and self-transformation associated with these drugs do not occur in a particular theological language. Here is an experience that has all of the outcomes we have said we seek but consistently confirms none of our particularistic theological languages. We know that the experience occurs in symbols, images, and language partly determined by set and setting. But similar experiences of self-transcendence and self-transformation occur for Catholics and Baptists, Jews and Buddhists, Unitarians and Two-Seed-in-the-Spirit Evangelicals, and Reformed Expiationists. Some occur in language more or less familiar to the experiencer, and some do not. But clearly the same experiences lie behind our diversity of theological language. Ecumenically oriented clergy are prepared to be tolerant of one another. But we are not prepared for our entire historical universe of discourse to be called into question, nor have we prepared our parishioners for this.

The diversity of theological language will challenge the particularities of our religious heritages in unprecedented ways. Religious people and clergy alike tend to regard various religious languages as competing claims of truth. That the experience behind our language is the same human experience is going to produce some serious cognitive dissonance. So far the dissonance has been confined to small pockets within faith traditions. For example, Benedictine contemplatives have more in common with Buddhist monks than they do with the Pope. I experienced this first-hand at the Buddhist/Christian Dialogues in Berkeley in 1987. Even the most liberal within our constituencies must suspect us of heresy.

Back in the 1960s, I had occasion to "trip-sit" some bad LSD trips. Several of us noted at the time that a common feature of the bad trip was that the tripper had no language for what was happening. On the other hand, in the minds of those who had some familiarity with mystical traditions, virtually identical imagery was integrated much less threateningly. Those who expected oneness with the universe without the dark night of the soul were terrified and fled ego-less into the demonic ether. When a Westerner says, "I am God," we lock him up in the funny farm. When a Hindu says it, his fellow Hindus say, "Ah, you finally got it!"

We also found that the experience tended to give cosmic validity to whatever language mediated it. We often had to remind our trippers that the experience was happening inside their own heads: that the images were the furniture of their own minds. Some came back believing in spirits and demons with a literalness that might embarrass even a fundamentalist.

How do we prepare people for the fact that the experience is REAL and at the same time linguistically mediated; that the language by which the experience is represented is metaphorical? How can we teach ourselves and our fledgling mystics to be "multi-lingual" in preparation for an experience that promises to totally reshape that most basic human tool, the language of meaning? We have to learn in a hurry or miss an incredible opportunity.

In the old days, the bad acid trips were frequently as much from the lack of religious preparation as anything else. When users found themselves with their egos dying, they panicked. Nobody had ever told them that the dark night of the soul is a normal experience for those who stand naked before the universe and themselves. Nobody had told them that they were going to experience being one with the universe. Not just think they were, or come to believe it, kind of. Rather, they were going to experience, in the corpuscles of their beings, that there is no boundary between where "I" stops and the universe begins. That can scare you to death! How do we prepare people for those kinds of experiences?

How do we learn to most usefully and effectively evoke the set and create the setting for non-particularistic religious experience? Traditional liturgy isn't the answer, if for no other reason than that it casts the participant as a spectator. "Generic" religious language is not promising; what I've seen so far has the power to evoke nothing but boredom. If we can't even agree on how to conduct public prayer in the civic religion, how can we hope to shape the drug experience set and setting for people of infinitely diverse interior mythic dialogue?

My working hypothesis is that we must start the experience with some understanding of the diversity of theological language, before the experiencers embark on the drug experience. I would prepare them with a conceptual model to demonstrate that the experience is primary and that the language they find themselves using to apprehend and integrate it is decidedly secondary. I would illustrate it with the best of art, poetry, and imagery from all of our heritages, from secular humanism to contemplative mysticism. Somewhere in all that metaphor, they may be given permission to find their own interpretation of the experience.

The religious use of psychoactive drugs presents fascinating challenges. Over the next ten years, religion as you and I know it is going to be shaken. Our cultural notions of how to respond appropriately to the very real dangers of drugs (with emphasis on "appropriately") is going to be shaken as hard or harder.

If research in the therapeutic use of these substances moves along as we expect it to, and if it produces fruits of spiritual import as expected; then those of us in the existing religious communities are going to have to respond. The continued negative response to these substances in the face of their spiritual transformative power (with the dying, for example) simply isn't going to fly. Those of us with expertise in creating positive and transformative liturgical experiences need to learn how to do so with these substances as well, otherwise we abandon the field to those with an orientation that is problematic at best and potentially destructive at worst.

Yet I am painfully aware of the fragility of social institutions and the difficulty of creating them out of whole cloth. If I am right about the virtually inevitable situation mentioned above, we will desperately need poet-liturgists and pastor-spiritual directors who are trained and experienced in creating the appropriate set and setting as well as follow-up support and guidance. We need this for the people afflicted with alcohol and drug addiction, suffering acute pain, and facing life-threatening diagnosis—to say nothing of the normal people for whom this will open the way. As someone said, "You can't unring the bell." To which I add, then we'd better become skilled bell ringers.

2

Do Drugs Have Religious Import?

A THIRTY-FIVE-YEAR RETROSPECT

Huston Smith

Huston Smith, Ph.D., has taught religion and philosophy at Washington University, MIT, Syracuse University, and the University of California at Berkeley. His dozen books include *Why Religion Matters: The Fate of the Human Spirit in an Age of Disbelief; Cleansing the Doors of Perception: The Religious Significance of Entheogenic Plants and Chemicals; Beyond the Post-Modern Mind; Forgotten Truth: The Common Vision of the World's Religions;* and *The World's Religions,* which has sold more than two and a half million copies. He has produced award-winning films on Hinduism, Tibetan Buddhism, and Sufism. In 1996, Bill Moyers devoted a five-part PBS special to Smith's life and work.

Among the predictable characteristics of mystical experience are a sense of the sacredness of all life and a desire to establish a new, more harmonious

*relation with nature and with other human beings. There
is a corresponding renunciation of the various expressions
of self-seeking, including the ethos of manipulation and
control. Mystical experience is manifest in a great many
forms, some of which are of rather doubtful value. But only
an empathic, self-forgetting mystical outlook, it could be
argued, can restore to humankind the attitude toward life
that will make possible its long-term survival.*

DAVID M. WULFF, *PSYCHOLOGY OF RELIGION:
CLASSIC AND CONTEMPORARY VIEWS,* 1991

Few pleasures are greater than the chance to think together with kindred spirits about matters of importance, so I thank you for the opportunity to set the agenda for this evening. That's basically what I will be doing. Aldous Huxley is such a significant figure in our area of interest that I will use a remark of his as my epigraph for what I shall say. During a seminar at M.I.T. in the early 1960s, he said that nothing was more curious, and to his way of thinking more important, than the role that mind-altering plants and chemicals have played in human history. Huxley's signature is written all over that statement—the way he mixed the sublime with the wry, the curious with the significant. I see it as charting our course for this evening.

When I am asked to speak, I always glance at the program to see what it says I'm supposed to do, for I regard it as something like a contract between speaker and audience. And what it says here—I'm reading from the program—is that I'm to give a keynote address. We can forget all about that. There are few things I would less like to pontificate about than the entheogens, and I'm also familiar with the Taoist adage, "The ax falls first on the tallest tree." So let's scrap that keynote address hype. My entry will be simply the first in our conference-long succession of ruminations on our common theme. I have been asked to lead off because I may be the one here who first wrote about the entheogens, despite the fact that two of our number—Frank Barron and Ralph Metzner—actually predate me in their involvement with entheogens. What the program asks me to do is enter a thirty-five-year retrospect on our subject.

To organize that retrospect, I propose to move successively through the essays I have written on the entheogens, summarizing briefly the thesis I set forth in each. The first piece was titled "Do Drugs Have Religious Import?" and it appeared in *The Journal of Philosophy* in 1964. I subdivided this relationship into four parts. Historically we can trace the interface between drugs and religion back to the twilight zone of prehistory. *Phenomenologically*, which is to say descriptively, no clear distinction is perceptible between mystical experiences that are chemically occasioned and ones that are not. On that point, I referred to an experiment I conducted when I was asked to speak on the subject at Princeton University. I distributed to the audience first-person reports of two mystical experiences, one written by one of the greatest known mystics in history, and the other by a subject in Leary's early Harvard experiments. I then asked the audience to guess which was which. Slightly more than half guessed wrong.

When we turn from phenomenology to *philosophy*—the third category—the issue moves beyond descriptions of experiences to the truth of their deliverances. There I argued that the truth of such revelations is objectively indeterminable. This is but one instance of the fact that life and the world are religiously ambiguous. We all have opinions, if not convictions, on the subject, but it is impossible to prove whether the skeptic, the believer, or the agnostic is right.

I linger on that point for a moment, because I find that many people are disappointed to hear it. They would like to have proofs that provide answer books for what to believe. Or rather, they think that's what they would like. What they overlook is that proofs would turn people into automata, for all they would have to do is look up the answers to life's problems and snap them into place. This would simplify life, but it would also strip us of our dignity, the opportunity to make up our own minds. Kierkegaard is good on that point.

The final section of that first-mentioned article dealt with the staying power of drug-induced experiences. Whereas phenomenologically they are indistinguishable from their opposites, they seem to have less effect on subsequent life. I'm speaking of averages.

Before I leave that initial article: Those of you who know me know that I have had a lifelong, professional love-hate relationship with contemporary philosophy. I'm a *jnana yogi* for sure, but that doesn't map well onto the analytic philosophy that has dominated philosophy in this second half of the twentieth century. As a consequence of my disaffection, my standing in the American Philosophical Association is, as the Spanish or our Mexican neighbors would say, *muy malo.* It gave me enormous satisfaction, therefore, when the editor of the association's official publication, *The Journal of Philosophy,* informed me recently that the essay I have been summarizing here has been anthologized twenty times (mostly in introductory philosophy textbooks), which is more than any other article published in the journal. That includes Dewey, Whitehead, and Willard Quine.

On to my second piece . . . When the "psychedelic sixties" began to deteriorate, I wrote an article for *Christianity and Crisis* that I titled "Psychedelic Theophanies and the Religious Life," which expanded on the argument that the positive carryovers from drug-induced mystical experiences appear to be less than the carryover from experiences that occur au naturel, so to speak. I proposed some explanatory reasons for that fact, if fact it be. I will not list those reasons here. I shall proceed directly to my third essay, which was prompted by Gordon Wasson's work.

Wasson's claim that India's god Soma was the *Amanita muscaria*—commonly known at the fly agaric mushroom—bore directly on my work in comparative religion, for the identity of the soma plant had baffled the Indologists since the inception of their discipline. Sanskrit scholars acknowledge that the tenth book of the Rig-Veda, which is devoted entirely to hymns to the god Soma, surpasses the other books in the awe of its tone, yet the identity of the plant that hosted Soma had been lost. Over two hundred plants were proposed as candidates in the nineteenth century, but none carried the day. If a retired banker, albeit a world-class mycologist, had solved the mystery, this was news.

I spent a summer shuttling from Cambridge to Connecticut, often staying overnight in Wasson's home, as we worked through his evidence and discussed the eighteen reviews of his book that had then appeared: seventeen of which validated his conclusion. The result was my overview of the dramatic story titled "Wasson's SOMA," which appeared as a lengthy feature review in *The Journal of the American Academy of Religion*.

Left to my own devices, my entries on the subject would have ended with those three pieces, but when *ReVision* asked if I would like to contribute to the special issue it was mounting on the entheogens, I realized that I did have two further thoughts on the subject that I had not put into print. I entered them in a short piece.

The more important of the two points picked up on a suggestion by Raymond Prince, a medical anthropologist at McGill University. Noting that certain infectious diseases, and also severe ordeals such as long marches and near starvation, affect brain chemistry in ways that parallel the entheogens, Prince hypothesized that in the course of human history; probably more chemically traceable mystical experiences have been occasioned by those traumas than by the ingestion of psychotropic plants. That seemed plausible to me, and a dramatic example jumped out at me when I came upon a book titled *Newman's Mediterranean Voyage*.

John Newman was one of the towering intellects of the eighteenth century, with a mind so magisterial that (a) his *Idea of the University* is still considered one of the best books on higher education ever written, (b) every Catholic university in the English-speaking world boasts a Newman Center named after him (he was a convert to Catholicism), and (c) his hymn, "Lead Kindly Light," continues to be a favorite of both Catholics and Protestants. That much I had known. What I had not known, and what *Newman's Mediterranean Voyage* added to the picture, was that in his early twenties Newman was totally demoralized. He was discouraged to the point of despair, and not only without any idea as to what he might make of his life, but without confidence that he could make anything of it. In an effort to extricate him from his depression his parents arranged a Mediterranean holiday for him, but on it he contracted typhoid fever. For several days he was delirious, and in the course of his delirium he had an experience that transformed his life. Not only did it pull him out of his depression by convincing him that God had a great purpose for his life; it directed the course of his life from that time forth, and infused him with almost superhuman energy. The relevance of this story to the topic of our conference need hardly be spelled out. Typhoid fever is one of the diseases that alter brain chemistry in much the same way as entheogens.

In a separate category from the articles I have mentioned, I place the appendix to my *Forgotten Truth*. Folded as it is into the argument of the book, it has probably had a wider audience than all my journal articles put together, discounting the fact that "Do Drugs Have Religious Import?" has been widely anthologized. That appendix summarizes the work of one of our company, Stanislav Grof, and offers his work as support for The Great Chain of Being, the conceptual spine that underlies all the great wisdom traditions of history described in *Forgotten Truth*. I recount how Grof's work with over two thousand patients who received LSD in the course of clinical treatment shows those patients experiencing, successively, the four levels of reality that the great Chain delineates, rising from the lowest level of ordinary reality to the ineffable *ens perfectissimum* at the top.

That's the retrospective I was asked to deliver. I have traced the story through my own writings about the entheogens, these being where my thoughts on the subject have unfolded. Before closing, however, I would like to speak more personally for a paragraph, and then conclude with two questions.

The personal word is this: I was initiated to the entheogens through Timothy Leary and psilocybin in his home in Newton on New Year's Day, 1961. The day didn't change my worldview, for the Great Chain of Being had already moved to the center of my convictions through thirty years of *jnanic* work with the great religions. What the day accomplished, you will not be surprised to hear, was to enable me for the first time to *experience* the respective levels of the Chain, all the way to its top. The dominant effects of the experience were two: awe (which I had known conceptually as the distinctive religious emotion, but had never before experienced so intensely) and certainty. There was no doubting that the Reality I experienced was ultimate. That conviction has remained.

As for my two questions:

First, what do we think of the following assertion by Stephen Jay Gould? I cite it—as Theodore Anderson did as the epigraph to his chapter on the pharmacology of peyote (and the issue of its abuse) in the book I edited with Reuben Snake, *One Nation Under God: The Triumph of the Native American Church*—because it says more about the legal situation respecting entheogens than any other brief statement I know.

> Our current drug crisis is a tragedy born of a phony system of classification. For reasons that are little more than accidents of history, we have divided a group of nonfood substances into two categories: items purchasable for supposed pleasure (such as alcohol), and illicit drugs. The categories were once reversed. Opiates were legal in America before the Harrison Narcotics Act of 1914, and members of the Women's Christian Temperance Union, who campaigned against alcohol during the day, drank their valued "women's tonics" at night, products laced with laudanum (tincture of opium).
>
> I could abide—though I would still oppose—our current intransigence if we applied the principle of total interdiction to all harmful drugs. But how can we possibly defend our current policy based on a dichotomy that encourages us to view one class of substances as a preeminent scourge while the two most dangerous and life-destroying substances by far, alcohol and tobacco, form a second class advertised in neon on every street corner of urban America?

The question that quotation raises is: What, if anything, do we do about the bizarre, chaotic legal situation that now governs the use of entheogenic substances? What are the political dynamics that move into place crazy laws like the ones now saddling us, and what can—should—we do to change them?

My other question is the presiding theoretical one for persons with our interests. What, practically speaking, should be the interface between entheogens and religion? It is encouraging that a respected theological seminary is co-sponsoring this conference, but what might the next step be?

My personal, very tentative suggestion is to see if the drug authorities would be willing to approve of a duly monitored experiment on the issue. Find a church or synagogue, presumably small, that is sincerely open to the possibility that God might, in certain circumstances, work through selected plants or chemicals (as I personally believe he did through Soma and Newman's typhoid fever and continues to work through the peyote of the Native American Church). Permit this church to legally include a psychoactive as sacramental, perhaps once a month in its Eucharist. And finally, commission professional social scientists to observe what happens to the congregation in respect to religious traits—notably compassion, fervor, and service. A variant on this proposal would be to obtain legal permission for seminary students to have at least one entheogen experience in a religious setting if they so wanted.

I was fortunate in being introduced to the entheogens as part of Harvard University's 1960–63 research program when they were not only legal, but respectable. I support the efforts of the Council on Spiritual Practices to afford others the same opportunity.

Holy Names

Mother Goddess of the earth,
Father Ruler of the sky,
What name shall we call the God
That lives in mind, beyond the I?

THOMAS B. ROBERTS, 2001

3
From State to Trait

THE CHALLENGE OF TRANSFORMING TRANSIENT INSIGHTS INTO ENDURING CHANGE

Roger Walsh

Roger Walsh, M.D., Ph.D., is professor of psychiatry, anthropology, and philosophy at the University of California, Irvine. His publications include the books *Essential Spirituality: The Seven Practices Common to World Religions* and (with Frances Vaughan) *Paths Beyond Ego: The Transpersonal Perspective.* A native of Australia, he has been a student of contemplative practices for over twenty years. His writings and research have received over twenty national and international awards.

In this panel I'd like to take up a theme that has been implicit in earlier talks and echoed throughout the conference: the difficulty of stabilizing insights and breakthroughs. This focus echoes the concern with which Huston Smith concluded his classic paper in *The Journal of Philosophy,* "Do Drugs Have Religious Import?" over thirty years ago (Smith 1964). There he said that it's clear that drugs can induce religious experiences, but it's less clear that they can induce religious lives.

The basic question here is: how can these powerful, profound, and potentially transformative experiences be used as catalysts for real transformation? It's important to remember that this is not a problem unique to entheogens. It is a problem common to psychotherapy and spiritual disciplines in general. In psychotherapy it is sometimes called "the problem of generalization": how do you get a person's insights to generalize outside the consulting room? So it's not a unique problem, but it's a very important one. I assume that most people who have researched this issue carefully conclude that entheogens can occasionally induce long-lasting benefits.

For many people, one of the major areas of growth that arises as a result of entheogenic experiences is an interest in religion, spirituality, and mysticism. There has been much debate over whether entheogens can induce genuine mystical experiences (Grof 1998). By "genuine" I mean experientially indistinct from classic experiences. The weight of evidence seems to suggest that they can. In addition, the philosopher Stace's argument of so-called "causal indifference" implies that in some ways it doesn't matter what causes the experience (Stace 1960). If the experience is indistinguishable from others, then it's the real thing; although, that does not say that the after-effects are necessarily the same. So, given this capacity for entheogens to induce genuine spiritual and mystical experiences, what then are their advantages and disadvantages compared to formal spiritual practices, and what can we do to increase the chances that such experiences will result in long-term beneficial transformation?

CHEMICAL VERSUS CONTEMPLATIVE EXPERIENCES

Although these days it is not politically correct to acknowledge, there are some (not unproblematic) advantages to entheogens. These include the relative ease, speed, intensity, and depth of the experience, and the fact that it can be controlled to some extent as regards timing. You sit down to meditate, and you hope that sometime in the next twenty years you'll have a breakthrough, which is a little different from being able to schedule it for Saturday afternoon. Of course, there are no guarantees even when you schedule it for Saturday afternoon, but still there is that hope.

But clearly there are disadvantages, and I intend to categorize them in four ways. There are the issues of uncontrollability, integration, misuse, and the limited capacity for stabilizing the gains.

Uncontrollability: Chemically induced experiences can be unpredictable, overwhelming, and uncontrollable. I think of a metaphor of strapping a rocket—an unguided missile—on one's back as opposed to learning to fly a plane.

Integration: I find a useful map here is Piaget's. Piaget speaks of assimilation and accommodation. During development a child's experiences are either assimilated into the existing cognitive structure or they bust that cognitive structure and force the child to accommodate to the new experience. With assimilation the child takes an experience and just fits it into his or her box. With accommodation the child has to construct a bigger box.

This distinction is crucial because entheogens may induce experiences that are powerfully challenging to individual as well as social systems. They challenge beliefs, values, behavior, and lifestyles, both in the social groups we are part of and in society at large. These experiences seem to demand that we accommodate, that is enlarge our cognitive maps, if we are to understand and research adequately.

Contemplatives may have a distinct advantage here because, as Louis Pasteur said, "chance favors the prepared mind." Ideally the contemplative will already have in place a belief system and worldview large enough to contain the mystical experience when it finally occurs, a tradition and social group to support it, an ethic to guide its expression, and a discipline to repeat, cultivate, deepen, and stabilize it (Walsh 1990). It is likely that the contemplative's mind is somewhat prepared, but there's no guarantee that this will be the case for an entheogen user.

Of course, one of the hallmarks of good therapy is the preparation, but there is a limit to what one can do in a few sessions of preparation compared to years of contemplative practice.

Misuse: There's a recurrent mistake that we tend to make in our thinking about profound experiences: we adopt implicitly a mechanistic model in which we assume that experiences do things to us instead of remembering that we use experiences. That's a key factor in why different people have such different outcomes. What's clear is that any experience—particularly a powerful, potentially transformative experience—has the potential both for transforming and for being co-opted by the ego structure. It's important to remember that some people get worse in psychotherapy. There has been significant realization that some people can actually use the psychotherapeutic experience to make themselves worse. So, again, the problem of difficult reactions, and so forth, is not unique to the entheogens. In the spiritual arena this is known as spiritual materialism, the tendency to co-opt experiences for things like ego inflation. These are problems of misuse.

Limited Capacity for Stabalizing the Gains: This challenge concerns the limited capacity we seem to have to catalyze ongoing development as a result of a single experience. What are the issues here? I think we need to distinguish two distinct dimensions in thinking about this problem of stabilizing any insights or breakthroughs obtained in drug-assisted therapy. We need to think of both the developmental stages and the psychological processes that are involved in transpersonal growth.

There are many different models of transpersonal stages. For simplicity's sake, I want to refer to a Tibetan Buddhist model. This has four distinct stages: first is intellectual comprehension, second is direct experience, third is stabilization of the experiences, and fourth is liberation.

Stabilization itself involves two phases. The first is being able to re-introduce the experience voluntarily, and the second is a penetration or extension of the characteristics of the experience state into the usual waking state. So this stabilization of altered states is a general process of moving from state to trait, from peak to plateau experience (Maslow 1971), or from trait to stage (Wilber, Engles, and Brown 1986). As

Huston Smith so beautifully put it: "It's the challenge of transforming flashes of illumination into abiding light" (Smith 1976).

There are specific examples of this transition in various traditions. For the Transcendental Meditation practitioner, it's the challenge of transforming transcendental consciousness into cosmic consciousness; for Sufis it is the movement from remembrance of the heart to remembrance of the soul; in Buddhism it is the transformation of prompted states of consciousness to unprompted or automatic states; in Christianity it is the progression, which St. Teresa spoke of, from the spiritual betrothal to spiritual marriage.

Using the four-stage model of the Tibetan Buddhists, I would suggest that the entheogens usually only move people from stage one to stage two. That is, they may move some people from intellectual understanding to some direct experience. Experiences can occur spontaneously, or they can occur as a result of practice or by the use of entheogens; but stabilization and liberation, as far as I can see, almost always demand prolonged contemplative discipline, and attempts to "stay high" by repetitive heroic doses of entheogens have been notoriously unsuccessful.

The reason becomes apparent when we examine the psychological processes that are involved in this kind of stabilization or development. There are at least seven common elements involved in authentic spiritual practice. These are the development of ethics, stabilization of attention, emotional transformation, motivational shifts, refinement of awareness, the cultivation of wisdom, and service (Walsh 1999). My working hypothesis is that profound experiences are most likely to induce enduring transformations by offering glimpses of deeper, more accurate views of the mind, of cosmos, and of reality. Even very brief glimpses can induce long-lasting changes in understanding and cognitive maps. For example, imagine that you're going through an unknown territory at night; there's a single flash of lightning for an instant, and suddenly you have a glimpse of the way things really are. Likewise, accounts suggest that even brief experiences of the Buddhist nirvana, or momentary near-death experiences, can forever change a person's life in some ways—not all people, but at least some people (Ring 1986). Likewise, in Tibetan Buddhism the teacher introduces the view, a glimpse of reality, at the beginning of practice.

My sense is that these brief insights can sometimes result in shifts in motivation. A new, deeper understanding of mind, self, and reality can result in a reorientation of values, motives, and behaviors. This may not necessarily occur, but observations from psychotherapy, contemplative practices, and drug-assisted therapy suggest that it can. Out of such deeper understanding can flow an ethic; transpersonal ecology and deep ecology are based in large part on the idea that a glimpse or experience of unity of ourselves with all life will induce a spontaneous, compassionate outflow of behavior (Fox 1990). This is by no means guaranteed, but it is a possibility.

On the other hand, I suspect that emotions accompanying a single experience will fade with time. Likewise attentional stabilization (concentration) will not be much enhanced by a single or even a few experiences. Concentration seems to require prolonged meditative practice.

SUMMARY

What this suggests is that entheogenic experiences may facilitate transpersonal development in some individuals. However, entheogens are most likely to be effective for stabilization of altered traits and for continued development if they are used in conjunction with a contemplative discipline. That, in fact, was the conclusion of a number of self-transcenders, people who'd had profound entheogenic experiences and had also been involved in deep contemplative practices (Walsh 1982). So, as Huston Smith wrote presciently in 1964, it seems clear that entheogens can produce religious experiences, but less clear that they can produce religious lives. I think that now, several decades later, we can see the accuracy of that statement. But we can also now better understand why it's accurate. Last, we can say that by themselves, entheogens may not produce religious lives, but they may initiate and deepen the religious lives of those who commit themselves to some form of spiritual practice.

REFERENCES

Fox, W. 1990. *Transpersonal Ecology.* Boston: Shambala.

Grof, S. 1998. *The Cosmic Game.* Albany, N.Y.: SUNY Press.

Maslow, A. 1971. *The Farther Reaches of Human Nature.* New York: Viking.

Ring, K. 1986. "Near-death experiences: Implications for human evolution and planetary transformation." *ReVision* 8 (2): 75–86.

Smith, H. 1964. "Do drugs have religious import?" *The Journal of Philosophy,* 61: 517–30.

———. 1976. *Forgotten Truth: The Primordial Tradition.* New York: Harper & Row.

Stace, W. T. 1960. *Mysticism and Philosophy.* Philadelphia: Lippincott.

Walsh, R. 1982. "Psychedelics and psychological well-being." *Journal of Humanistic Psychology* 22: 22–32.

———. 1990. *The Spirit of Shamanism.* Los Angeles, Calif.: J. P. Tarcher.

———. 1999. *Essential Spirituality. The Seven Practices Common to World Religions.* New York: John Wiley & Sons.

Wilber, K., J. Engler, and D. Brown, eds. 1986. *Transformation of Consciousness: Conventional and Contemplative Perspectives on Development.* Boston: New Science Library/Shambhala.

4

The Potential of Entheogens as Catalysts of Spiritual Development

Stanislav Grof

Stanislav Grof, M.D., is a psychiatrist with more than forty-five years of experience in research of non-ordinary states of consciousness. In the past, he was Principal Investigator in an LSD research program at the Psychiatric Research Institute in Prague, Czechoslovakia, and Chief of Psychiatric Research at the Maryland Psychiatric Research Center in Baltimore. Currently, he is Professor of Psychology at the California Institute of Integral Studies (CIIS), conducts professional training programs in holotropic breathwork and transpersonal psychology, and gives lectures and seminars worldwide. He is one of the founders and chief theoreticians of transpersonal psychology and the founding president of the International Transpersonal Association (ITA). Among his publications are over one hundred papers in professional journals and the books *Realms of the Human Unconscious; LSD Psychotherapy; The Adventure of Self-Discovery; Beyond the Brain; The Holotropic Mind; The Cosmic Game; The Consciousness Revolution* (with E. Laszlo and P. Russell); and *Psychology of the Future.*

◈

[W]hich, after all, was more likely to happen first: the spontaneously generated idea of an afterlife in which the disembodied soul, liberated from the restrictions of time and space, experiences eternal bliss, or the accidental discovery of hallucinogenic plants that give a sense of euphoria, dislocate the center of consciousness, and distort time and space, making them balloon outward in greatly expanded vistas? . . . We have to remember that the drug plants were there, waiting to give men a new idea based on a new experience. The experience might have had, I should think, an almost explosive effect on the largely dormant minds of men, causing them to think of things they had never thought of before.

MARY BARNARD, *THE MYTHMAKERS*, 1966

It seems that many people started their presentations by sharing some of their personal history and talking about their relationship with the topic of their presentation, and I will do the same. My personal history is noteworthy in this regard, since I had a completely atheistic background when I encountered entheogens. For me it was not so that my first entheogenic experience confirmed or deepened something that I already believed in; it was a 180-degree turn.

The reason for my atheistic background was a dramatic event in my parents' history. They met and fell in love in a small Czech town, and when they wanted to get married, there was a serious problem. My mother came from a very strict Catholic family and my father's family had no church affiliation. My grandparents insisted that the only decent joining was one that happened in the church. But my father was a pagan by the Church's definition and they refused to conduct the marriage ceremony.

This created a tremendous turmoil and, for a while, it seemed that the marriage would not happen at all. Then my grandparents found a brilliant solution, which was a major financial donation to the church. This helped to loosen the church's standards, and the priest agreed to marry a pagan. As a result, old dreams of my grandparents came true. They lived on Main Street, right across the street from the church, so that they could roll the carpets from the house to the altar and provide a direct route for the guests from the wedding ceremony to the banquet inside their house.

All traffic on Main Street was stopped, and it was a big event that the whole town talked about for some time. But my parents got so angry about this whole thing that they decided not to commit me or my brother to any religion and to let us make our own choice when we would come of age. Consequently, I had no formal exposure to religion in my childhood. Our classes in religion meant a welcome leisure for me. I went for a walk, read a book, or played soccer.

And with this background I enrolled in the medical school of Charles University in Prague. And medical study certainly is not something that particularly cultivates mystical awareness under any circumstances. But I studied medicine in Prague at a time when Czechoslovakia was controlled by the Soviet Union and had a Marxist regime. We really received the purest materialistic indoctrination there is. Everything that even remotely smacked of philosophical idealism or mysticism was either censored out or ridiculed.

So I am a somewhat rare example of a person who was brought to spirituality and mysticism through clinical and laboratory work. Usually, it is the other way round. People come to science from a religious background and when they get exposure to materialistic science, they tend to reject indiscriminately anything religious and spiritual, because they consider it irrational, absurd, and childish. In addition to my medical training, I also had an orthodox Freudian training and personal analysis.

To become a medical doctor, a psychiatrist, and a psychoanalyst was a late decision in my life. In my childhood and adolescence, I spent much time drawing and painting and my dream was to embark on a career in animated movies. At that time, Walt Disney was my hero and my personal idol. After finishing the "real gymnasium," an equivalent of the American high school, I applied to the Barrandov Film Studios in Prague and was accepted. Everything seemed to suggest that I had found my life career.

However, all that was turned around when a friend of mine introduced me to Sigmund Freud's *Introductory Lectures to Psychoanalysis*. I read the book in one sitting and, within two days, I decided to apply to medical school with the explicit goal of becoming a psychoanalyst. And an important part of my attraction to psychoanalysis was Freud's rational explanation of religion. I loved to read books about mythology and about the great religions of the world, but my interest in these matters was purely intellectual and artistic. Not having had a religious background, I could not understand how it was possible that millions of people would actually take seriously something as blatantly irrational and ridiculous as mysticism, spirituality, and religion.

And Freud seemed to have the answer: religion was an obsessive-compulsive neurosis of mankind, and obsessive-compulsive neurosis was a private religion. Ritual behavior that we see in both these situations can be explained by suppression of anal impulses from childhood. It seemed to make sense! At the time, I was also impressed by Freud's explanation of totemism, based on Ferenczi's case of a little boy who developed a complex neurosis involving chickens after having been pecked on his penis by a mother hen in a pigsty. It was not until much later that I realized that Freud completely missed the point. He did not recognize that the key to understanding religion is a direct experience of the spiritual dimensions of reality.

As I was learning more about psychoanalysis, I developed a deep inner conflict. I continued to be enthusiastic about its theoretical aspects, but became increasingly disappointed with its potential as a therapeutic tool. I realized that psychoanalysis had a narrow indication range, required enormous investment of time, money, and energy and, even after a long time, it showed generally meager clinical results. I reached a point where I started to regret that I had chosen to study medicine and psychiatry. I kept nostalgically returning in my mind to the animated movies and felt that my career choice was a serious error.

Just as this conflict was reaching critical proportions, something unexpected happened that radically changed the course of my life. This was the period in psychiatric history that saw the advent of psychopharmacology and its early triumphs. It was the time of the first tranquilizers—reserpine, chlorpromazine, and a few others. We conducted a large study of Melleril, a tranquilizer that came from the Swiss pharmaceutical company Sandoz. As a result, we had a good working relationship with Sandoz and, as part of our cooperation with this company, we received one day a large box full of ampoules. With it came a letter describing the substance involved, its chemistry, pharmacology, and also its history. It was LSD-25, a powerful psychoactive drug, whose effects on consciousness were discovered by Albert Hofmann when he accidentally intoxicated himself during its synthesis. Albert would probably prefer to call it serendipity.

The accompanying letter suggested that this substance, administered in absolutely minuscule dosages of millionths of a gram, was capable of inducing an "experimental psychosis," a state similar to naturally occurring psychoses. Clinical and laboratory research of LSD thus could provide insights into the enigma of psychosis, particularly schizophrenia. One could study various parameters before, during, and after the LSD experience and determine what biochemical and physiological changes in the body are correlated with psychological abnormalities during the time the drug took effect. And the Sandoz people were asking us if we would work with this substance and give them some feedback on whether there was legitimate use for LSD in psychiatry.

But the Sandoz letter also suggested another fascinating possibility—that LSD might be useful as a tool for very unconventional training of psychiatrists, psychologists, students of medicine and psychology, and psychiatric nurses. It could give mental health professionals the opportunity to spend a few hours in the world of their patients. As a result, they would be able to understand their patients better, be able to communicate with them more effectively, and hopefully have better therapeutic results. Naturally, I got very excited, and I would not have missed such an opportunity for anything in the world. And I became one of the early volunteers in this research.

My preceptor, Docent Roubícek was very interested in electroencephalography. So, I had to agree to have an EEG record taken before, during, and after the experiment. And at that time Doctor Roubícek was particularly fascinated by what is called "driving the brain waves," that is trying to entrain the frequencies of the brain waves by some external input, either acoustic or visual. So, I had to agree not only to have my EEG taken but also to have my brain waves driven in the middle of this experiment.

What actually happened was that approximately two and a half hours into the session, a research assistant appeared and took me to a small cabin. She carefully pasted the electrodes all over my scalp and asked me to lie down and close my eyes. Then she placed a giant stroboscopic light above my head and turned it on. At this time, the effects of the drug were culminating and that immensely enhanced the impact of the strobe. I was hit by a radiance that seemed comparable to what it must have been like at the epicenter of the atomic explosion in Hiroshima. Today I think a more appropriate comparison would be to the Primary Clear Light, the light of supernatural brilliance that, according to *The Tibetan Book of the Dead,* Bardo Thödol, appears to us at the moment of death.

I felt that a divine thunderbolt catapulted my conscious self out of my body. I lost my awareness of the research assistant, the laboratory, the psychiatric clinic, Prague, and then the planet. My consciousness expanded at an inconceivable speed and reached cosmic dimensions. There was no more difference between me and the universe. The research assistant carefully followed the protocol: she shifted the frequency of the strobe gradually from two to sixty cycles per second and back again and then put it for a short time in the middle of the alpha band, the theta band, and finally the delta band.

While this was happening, I found myself at the center of a cosmic drama of unimaginable dimensions. In the astronomical literature that I later collected and read over the years, I found possible names for some of the fantastic experiences that I had experienced during those amazing ten minutes of clock time. I would say today that I possibly experienced the big bang, passage through black and white holes, identification with exploding super novas and collapsing stars, and witnessed many other strange phenomena.

Although I had no adequate words for what had happened to me, there was no doubt in my mind that my experience was very close to what I knew from the great mystical scriptures of the world as Cosmic Consciousness. Even though my psyche was deeply affected by the drug, I was able to see the irony and paradox of the situation. The Divine manifested and took me over in a modern laboratory in a Communist country, in the middle of a serious scientific experiment conducted with a substance produced in the test tube of a twentieth-century chemist.

When the strobe was turned off, my consciousness began to shrink very rapidly. I found the planet, Prague, the clinic, and finally my body and was extremely impressed by what had just happened. I had played with the strobe before and experienced some pretty colors and patterns, but nothing like what happened in combination with LSD. So I knew that the drug was somehow the key to my experience. This event generated in me a profound intellectual interest in nonordinary states of consciousness. I felt strongly that this was by far the most fascinating area that as a psychiatrist I could research.

I joined a group of researchers led by Dr. Milos Vojtechovsky, who at the time had access to several entheogens, and was heading a team conducting a multidimensional comparative study of these substances. We had a group of experimental subjects, mostly young professionals (including ourselves), who were interested in participating in this research. They would come for a day at a time to the research institute and have a session with one of the substances we were working with.

These experimental days had a very rigid and busy schedule. We collected samples of blood and urine every hour on the hour, measured pulse and blood pressure, and administered a battery of psychological tests. And this was all done on a double-blind basis. Each time, the experimental subject would have a session with a different entheogen under the same circumstances. And then one day was a session with a placebo.

We had at the time at our disposal psilocybin, psilocin, mescaline, and of course, LSD. It was also the time when Stephen Szara and his coworkers in Budapest, Hungary, did research with the tryptamine derivatives, and we received from them dimethyltryptamine (DMT), diethyltryptamine (DET), and dipropyltryptamine (DPT). We also were corresponding with Humphry Osmond and Abe Hoffer, and they sent us some adrenolutine and adrenochrome.

We conducted these laboratory experiments for about a year and a half. This research followed very much the "experimental psychosis" model. We conducted drug sessions with our "normal volunteers" as I described it. And we also found psychotic patients, whom we matched with the experimental subjects by age, sex, IQ, and by some other parameters. And we brought these patients to the research institute for a day, and they were subjected to the same testing procedure as the drug subjects.

We were comparing the results, looking for similarities and differences. We were interested if various entheogens had drug-specific effects or if they induced, by and large, the same type of experience. And we were, of course, curious if the changes in the tests after the administration of these substances to "normal volunteers" would converge with the findings in psychotic patients. My initial understanding was that the drug experience was a "toxic psychosis," that somehow the experiences following the administration of the substances were artificially produced by the interaction between the drug and the brain. And then I started noticing some very interesting things that were incompatible with this concept.

The entheogens showed incredible interindividual variability. When we gave LSD, or some similar substance, in the same dosage under the same circumstances to a number of people, everybody would have a totally different experience. For example, one person's experience looked like a very productive and intensive session of Freudian psychoanalysis. He or she would relive various traumatic experiences from infancy and childhood and have all kinds of remarkable psychological insights.

Somebody else's experience would be primarily somatic. He or she would get very sick and spend much of the session with a terrible headache and throwing up. For many subjects, the session was primarily an esthetic experience. A few people got very anxious and paranoid, others angry, manic, and so on. And some people, in spite of the questionable set and setting, managed to have profound mystical experiences with feelings of cosmic unity, total bliss, and profound inner peace.

And then we found out that, when we repeated the sessions in the same person, there was also an equally astonishing intra-individual variability. Each of the consecutive sessions in a series was different and there seemed to be a certain progression from session to session. This was a very important moment in my personal and professional life. I realized that LSD did not induce a "toxic psychosis," but was a nonspecific catalyst. The LSD experiences were not toxic artifacts, but authentic contents from deep recesses of the psyche. It became clear to me that the LSD did not produce them, but released them from the repositories in the unconscious.

At that point, I started seeing LSD as a tool for exploration of the deep dynamics in the psyche that are normally not available for direct observation and study, a tool that could play a similar role in psychiatry that the microscope plays in biology and the telescope in astronomy. Because of my Freudian background, I knew that the possibility of getting to unconscious contents faster and reaching deeper into the psyche should have important therapeutic implications. I felt that LSD might be a tool that could deepen, intensify, and accelerate psychotherapy. I lost interest in the laboratory experiments and took this experimentation into the clinical setting. LSD seemed to be the way to heal the gap between the power of psychoanalysis as an explanatory system and its ineffectiveness as a therapeutic method.

This was the beginning of a fantastic personal and professional adventure that has now lasted over forty years. And this brings me now to the topic of my talk. It turned out that the experiences did not stay in the realm of postnatal biography and the individual unconscious, which, according to Freud and the handbooks of academic psychiatry, is the extent of the human psyche and the reach of human consciousness. In serial LSD sessions, practically all my patients moved very quickly beyond these narrow boundaries and into the domains described in the mystical literature of the world.

In most of them, the entry into these new domains began with a deep encounter with birth and death. They found themselves involved in a life and death struggle, trying to free themselves from the clutches of what felt like a birth canal. This was accompanied by powerful physiological responses—choking, intense pains in various parts of the body, nausea and vomiting, and circulatory changes. These experiences were typically accompanied by numinous archetypal visions of demonic and divine figures. Initially, I had no idea what was happening and where all this was taking us. It was actually quite uncomfortable and scary. After all, here was clearly a powerful and very mysterious process that I did not understand, and yet I was in a position where I was responsible for the results.

And then I had several LSD sessions myself with high dosages, which were pretty terrifying and taxing; they all took me to what I call today the perinatal area. But I made it through and had extraordinary experiences of psychospiritual death and rebirth. These sessions were very healing and, as a result, I became increasingly comfortable with similar states in other people. I lost the fear of these experiences and was able to be genuinely supportive for my clients who were going through similar ordeals, to give them encouragement, and to convey a sense of trust in the process.

As we continued this work, with the increasing number of serial sessions we saw more and more spiritual experiences that were now coming without the admixture of perinatal elements. These were encounters with archetypal figures, visits to mythological realms, past life experiences, experiential identification with other people, animals, and plants, episodes of cosmic union, and so on. It became clear that all the phenomena emerging in sessions with entheogens—biographical, perinatal, and transpersonal—formed an integral experiential continuum. I could not accept any more the position of academic psychiatrists, who see the biographical elements as normal constituents of the psyche and refer to perinatal and transpersonal experiences as psychotic.

It became particularly difficult for me to see these experiences as products of some yet unknown pathological process afflicting the brain, when it became clear that they had extraordinary healing and transformative potential. What was manifesting in LSD sessions had to be normal constituents of the human psyche, but of a psyche whose dimensions were infinitely larger than we could have ever imagined. In view of these observations, the individual psyche was commensurate with all of existence, like Jung's "anima mundi," or the Hindu Atman-Brahman.

My research started as a search for more effective therapy for depression, phobias of different kinds, asthma, migraine headaches, and other clinical problems. It was initially an attempt to deepen and accelerate psychoanalysis and make it more effective. But it turned out that it was not possible to draw a clear line between therapy that goes to the core of the problems and the spiritual journey. What began as a therapeutic quest for the roots of emotional and psychosomatic problems changed spontaneously into a spiritual and philosophical quest. Healing now became a side effect of the mystical quest.

Non-ordinary states of consciousness that occur in shamanic rituals, in entheogenic states, powerful experiential psychotherapy, or in systematic spiritual practice represent an important subgroup of "non-ordinary" or "altered states of consciousness." They are states that have an extraordinary healing and heuristic potential. I coined for them a special name—"holotropic"—because I am convinced that they deserve to be distinguished from the rest of non-ordinary or "altered" states. Holotropic states clearly do not deserve to be called psychotic and attributed to mental illness of unknown origin. I believe that systematic study of these states would cause a revolution in psychiatry and psychology that would be as radical and far-reaching as the quantum-relativistic revolution in the first decades of this century was for physics.

It is interesting in this regard to compare the worldview of the Western industrial civilization with that of the ancient and preindustrial cultures. Over the centuries, scientists have systematically explored various aspects of the material world and have accumulated an impressive amount of information that had not been available in the past. They have replaced, corrected, and complemented earlier concepts about nature and the universe. However, the most striking difference between the two worldviews is not in the amount and accuracy of data about material reality; that is a natural and expected result of scientific progress. The most profound and striking disagreement revolves around the question of whether or not existence has a sacred or spiritual dimension.

The answers that these two human groups give in this regard are diametrically opposite. All the human groups of the preindustrial era were in agreement that the material world, which we perceive and in which we operate in our everyday life, is not the only reality. Their worldview included the existence of hidden dimensions of reality inhabited by various deities, demons, discarnate entities, ancestral spirits, and power animals. Preindustrial cultures had a rich ritual and spiritual life that revolved around the possibility of achieving direct experiential contact with these ordinarily hidden domains and beings and to receive from them important information or assistance. They believed that it was an important and useful way to influence the course of material events.

According to Western science, the history of the universe is the history of developing matter. Life, consciousness, and intelligence are accidental by-products, epiphenomena of material processes. Neuroscience tells us that consciousness emerges out of the complexity of the physiological processes in the brain, and is thus critically dependent on the body. In this worldview, there is no place for spirituality of any kind. Nothing but matter really exists.

From the materialistic perspective, there also cannot be any doubt that death of the body, particularly of the brain, is the absolute end of any form of conscious activity. When we accept the basic premise about the primacy of matter, this conclusion is logical, obvious, and unquestionable. Belief in any form of consciousness after death, posthumous journey of the soul, or reincarnation seems naive and ridiculous. It is dismissed as a product of wishful thinking of people who are unable to accept the obvious biological imperative of death.

To take spirituality seriously indicates a lack of education, superstition, primitive and magical beliefs, or primary process thinking. In intelligent people, belief in God is interpreted as projection of primitive infantile images of parental figures in the sky. And direct experiences of the spiritual dimensions of reality—holotropic experiences—are diagnosed without discrimination as symptomatic of mental disease. Western psychiatry makes no distinction between a mystical or spiritual experience and psychosis.

This attitude pathologizes the entire spiritual history of humanity. All great religions of the world were inspired by powerful visionary experiences of their founders and sustained by divine epiphanies of their prophets, mystics, and saints. These experiences, revealing the existence of sacred dimensions of reality, served as a vital source of all religious movements.

Gautama Buddha, meditating in Bodh Gaya under the Bo tree, had a dramatic visionary experience of Kama Mara, the master of the world illusion, who tried to detract him from his spiritual quest. He first used his three seductive daughters in an effort to divert Buddha's interest from spirituality to sex. When this attempt had failed, he brought in his menacing army to instigate in Buddha the fear of death, intimidate him, and prevent him from reaching enlightenment. Buddha successfully overcame these obstacles and experienced illumination and spiritual awakening. On other occasions, Buddha also envisioned a long chain of his previous incarnations and experienced a profound liberation from karmic bonds.

The Islamic text Miraj Nameh gives a description of the "miraculous journey of Mohammed," a powerful visionary state during which archangel Gabriel escorted Mohammed through the seven Moslem heavens, Paradise, and Hell (Gehenna). During this visionary journey, Mohammed experienced in the seventh heaven an "audience" with Allah. In a state that was described as "ecstasy approaching annihilation" he received from him a direct communication. This experience and additional mystical states that Mohammed had over a period of twenty-five years became the basis for the suras of the Qur'an and for the Moslem faith.

In the Judeo-Christian tradition, the Old Testament offers a colorful account of Moses's experience of Yahwe in the burning bush, a description of Abraham's interaction with the angel, and other visionary experiences. The New Testament describes Jesus's experience of the temptation by the devil during his stay in the desert. Similarly, Saul's blinding vision of Christ on the way to Damascus, St. John's apocalyptic revelation in his cave on the island Patmos, Ezekiel's observation of the flaming chariot, and many other episodes clearly are transpersonal experiences in holotropic states of consciousness. The Bible provides many other examples of direct communication with God and with the angels. In addition, the descriptions of the temptations of St. Anthony and of the visionary experiences of other saints and Desert Fathers are well-documented parts of Christian history.

Mainstream psychiatrists interpret such visionary experiences as manifestations of serious mental diseases, although they lack adequate medical explanation and the laboratory data to support this position. Psychiatric literature contains numerous articles and books that discuss what would be the most appropriate clinical diagnoses for many of the great figures of spiritual history. St. John of the Cross was called a "hereditary degenerate," St. Teresa of Avila was dismissed as a severe hysterical psychotic, and Mohammed's mystical experiences were attributed to epilepsy.

Many other religious and spiritual personages, such as the Buddha, Jesus, Ramakrishna, and Sri Ramana Maharshi have been seen as suffering from psychoses, because of their visionary experiences and "delusions." Similarly, some traditionally trained anthropologists have argued whether shamans should be diagnosed as schizophrenics, ambulant psychotics, epileptics, or hysterics. The famous psychoanalyst Franz Alexander, known as one of the founders of psychosomatic medicine, wrote a paper in which even Buddhist meditation is described in psychopathological terms and referred to as "artificial catatonia."

Western industrial civilization thus has no use for holotropic states; it has rejected or even outlawed the means and contexts for inducing them and puts pathological labels on those people who have them spontaneously. This is in sharp contrast with all the ancient and preindustrial cultures that have held holotropic states in great esteem and spent much time and effort developing safe and effective ways of inducing them. They used them as a principal vehicle in their ritual and spiritual life and for several other important purposes.

In the context of sacred ceremonies, holotropic states mediated for the natives direct experiential contact with the archetypal dimensions of reality—deities, mythological realms, and numinous forces of nature. Another area where these states played a crucial role was diagnosing and healing of various disorders. Although aboriginal cultures often possessed impressive knowledge of naturalistic remedies, they put primary emphasis on metaphysical healing. This typically involved induction of holotropic states of consciousness—for the client, for the healer, or both of them at the same time. In many instances, a large group or even an entire tribe entered a healing trance together, as it is, for example, until this day among the !Kung bushmen in the African Kalahari Desert.

Holotropic states have also been used to cultivate intuition and extrasensory perception for a variety of practical purposes, such as finding lost persons and objects, obtaining information about people in remote locations, and for following the movement of game. In addition, they served as a source of artistic inspiration, providing ideas for rituals, paintings, sculptures, and songs. The impact that the experiences encountered in these states had on the cultural life of preindustrial societies and the spiritual history of humanity has been enormous.

The differences of opinion between the industrial societies and native cultures concerning spirituality are usually explained in terms of superiority of Western materialistic science over primitive superstition. During more than four decades of my involvement in consciousness research, I have come to a very different conclusion. The difference in the two worldviews reflects primarily the ignorance and naiveté of modern society concerning holotropic states.

Unlike an average Westerner, people in native cultures have regularly experienced holotropic states in their ritual and spiritual life. Their worldview includes their insights from these experiences, which unambiguously reveal the existence of the spiritual dimension in the human psyche and in the universal scheme of things. I have yet to meet a single Westerner who has had powerful transpersonal experiences and continues to subscribe to the monistic materialism characterizing modern science.

Michael Harner, an anthropologist in good academic standing, who also underwent a shamanic initiation during his fieldwork in the Amazonian jungle and practices shamanism, suggests that Western psychiatry is seriously biased in at least two significant ways. It is ethnocentric and also "cognicentric" (a more accurate word might be "pragmacentric").

The *ethnocentric bias* reflects the fact that Western psychiatry has a certain idiosyncratic understanding of the human psyche in health and disease and considers this perspective to be the only correct one and superior to that of any other group. What does not make sense to a behaviorist or psychoanalyst is seen as psychotic or at least primitive and superstitious. When a Western psychiatrist comes to India and sees what the sadhus or yogis are doing, he or she would consider them schizophrenics, ambulant psychotics, or at least borderline cases. The same would happen in relation to Siberian, Mexican, or Native American shamans.

But because we are talking about ethnocentrism, the same is true also the other way around. If we brought a Mexican shaman to a place like Los Angeles—and I am not talking about the time when the people living there were burning their own houses, but an average ordinary day in that city—he or she would think that we have all gone crazy. They would not be able to understand what we have done to the earth that we come from and that nourishes us, covering every square yard of the ground with asphalt and cement or poisoning the soil with toxic chemicals. They would see us pursuing more power, more status, more money, more fame in a situation where we cannot breathe the air anymore, and they would question the quality of the food we eat and the water we drink.

According to some estimates, in the Middle Eastern war of 1991 as many as 200,000 people were killed in a way that resembled a game in a computer parlor, pushing buttons and things going up in flames, with several dozens of casualties on our side, most of them by friendly fire. Deliberate oil spills seriously damaged life in the Persian Gulf for the next twenty years, and six hundred oil wells were deliberately ignited, as if we did not have enough pollution. We all watched it on the television screen, and it is just another day in Western civilization. And when somebody has a past life experience, he or she is labeled psychotic, hospitalized, and put on tranquilizers. Under these circumstances the question, "What is sanity and what is mental disease?" becomes somewhat arbitrary. This is what Michael Harner means when he talks about the ethnocentric bias of our psychiatry.

Harner also says that psychology and psychiatry have a *cognicentric bias*. What he means by this is that theoretical speculations in these disciplines are based exclusively on observations and experiences made in the ordinary state of consciousness. All evidence from any form of research involving nonordinary states has been ignored, whether it comes from history, comparative religion, anthropology, or from various areas of modern consciousness research—parapsychology, thanatology, entheogenic research, or experiential psychotherapies.

None of this evidence has been admitted and taken into consideration, in spite of the fact that much of it has been amassed by respectable scientists with good credentials and published in professional journals and books. I will mention just one salient example: It has been repeatedly observed that the consciousness of people in a state of clinical death can detach from the body and move to various close or remote locations while maintaining the capacity to perceive the environment.

Ken Ring is now studying people who are congenitally blind because of organic reasons and have never seen anything in their entire life. In near-death experiences when their consciousness leaves the body, they can see without the mediation of the optical system. This is a very critical challenge for monistic materialism of contemporary science! Physicists needed much less discrepancy with the Newtonian world-view to recognize the need for a radical paradigm shift to quantum-relativistic physics. Consciousness research accumulated a large number of similar challenging observations and it did not make a dent in the ivory tower of materialistic science.

All this evidence forces us to reevaluate our position toward genuine spirituality, which is based on direct personal experience. However, a necessary prerequisite is to differentiate clearly between spirituality and religion. Western religious life is to a great extent based on faith and belief, rather than direct experience. If we are "believers," we go to church, and we listen to a sermon by an appointed representative of the church who might or might not have had any direct experiences. This person reads or talks about experiences that happened to some people two thousand years ago.

But if somebody had a really full-blown mystical experience in today's church, the average minister would very likely call the ambulance and send the afflicted person to a psychiatrist, convinced that that kind of thing should not happen in the church. Imagine, for example, St. Francis of Assisi, in the scene from the movie *Brother Sun, Sister Moon* that portrays his ecstatic rapture. If something like this would happen in today's church, the individual involved would definitely end up on tranquilizers and with a diagnosis. There thus is a fundamental difference between direct spiritual experience and religious activity in the way it is practiced in most mainstream religions.

When C. G. Jung was over eighty years old, he gave a wonderful interview to a BBC reporter that was later released as a film called *Face to Face*. At one point, the reporter asked him: "Dr. Jung, do you believe in God?" A wonderful smile appeared on Jung's face, and he responded something like: "I don't believe, I know. I have had the experience of being grabbed by something that was far bigger and more powerful than myself." What he was saying was that if we have to use the term belief, we do not know what we are talking about. That means that we do not have anything to go by.

Somebody simply did a good job of convincing us about certain realities, or we read a persuasive argument, but as long as we call it "belief," whatever we say really has very little relevance. Jung also said in one of his books that one of the main functions of mainstream religion is to protect people against direct experience of God. Walter Houston Clark, who had taught psychology of religion for about twenty-five years and then had a personal mystical experience, said that he suddenly understood what he was teaching all those years.

His favorite saying following this experience was that much of mainstream religion reminded him of a vaccination. You go to church and get a little something that then protects you against the real thing. You think that you have already arrived because you go to church on Sunday. That belief then becomes a serious obstacle in any kind of spiritual quest that would have to involve some personal practice leading to direct experiences.

In 1973, I was invited to a very fascinating conference called "Ritual: Reconciliation and Change," which was organized by Margaret Mead, Cathy Bateson, and the Wenner-Gren Foundation, which is a very unusual anthropological society in New York City. After WWII, they bought a castle in Austria and had it beautifully renovated. They regularly held two to three conferences a year at the castle. Our conference did not involve reading papers; we all had to prepare pre-prints and know each other's material. We then met in one of the halls of the castle at a large round table, about eighteen of us, brainstorming the problem of ritual for about a week.

Margaret believed that the fact that the technological societies have lost meaningful rituals contributes to social psychopathology. We do not have socially sanctioned situations where people, particularly the adolescents, can work through deep destructive and self-destructive impulses and emotions. When such contexts are not provided, those impulses are acted out in our everyday life. Instead of seeing certain manifestations as part of a controlled situation in a ritual, we see them in the evening news.

For me, the most interesting experience at this conference was observing and hearing an Irish Catholic priest, Father O'Dougherty. He was a member of a Vatican committee that was scrutinizing the lives of saints using psychiatric criteria. Based on their psychiatric assessment, when they found indications of pathology, they eliminated the saint in question from the Christian calendar. By the time of our meeting, they had eliminated about sixteen of them, including St. Christopher. We had a very interesting situation—I was a psychiatrist trying to suggest that some of the experiences that appear to be psychotic are really difficult experiences of a mystical nature, crises of spiritual opening. Father O'Dougherty was a representative of the church, advocating that we should use psychiatric perspectives and sanitize religious history.

I would like to turn briefly to research with entheogens and its relation to spirituality. Scientific research with these substances started relatively late, at the turn of the nineteenth century, and the clinical work that was done in the first decades of this century involved primarily mescaline. There was also some study of bulbocapnine and a few other substances, but the main focus was on mescaline. This chapter was closed in 1927 by a book called *Der Meska-linrausch* (Mescaline Intoxication) by Kurt Beringer. It is interesting that in this early stage of research, the researchers did not consider any therapeutic use and did not discover the spiritual potential of entheogens. The states induced by them were seen as toxic psychoses that might provide interesting inspiration for artists, but these other two dimensions went unnoticed.

This makes it very different from the history of LSD, where we find very early, already in Stoll's first clinical paper, the notion that we should explore the therapeutic potential of this substance. The observations concerning the mystical and spiritual experiences in entheogen sessions appeared also early in the literature about the effects of LSD. This started a heated academic discussion about the nature and meaning of this phenomenon; it raised some questions that have not been resolved to this day.

The opinions in these debates crystallized into four groups. The first position was that of ultramaterialistic scientists who were very excited because they believed that this meant the end of any ontological claims of mysticism and religion. What spiritual literature describes as deep insights into the nature of reality are not legitimate dimensions of existence but artifacts of some metabolic aberrations in the brain. Religious and mystical phenomena can be reduced to brain physiology and biochemistry.

The second attitude was, in a sense, a polar opposite of the first one. It asserted that the entheogens are substances that can induce genuine mystical experiences. These experiences provide insight into real, but ordinarily invisible, numinous dimensions of reality. This means that entheogens are not just ordinary chemicals; they represent a very special category. They are sacred substances, sacramentals. The professionals and laypersons who saw it this way took basically the position of shamans from the aboriginal cultures who talk about sacred plants, "flesh of the gods."

The third opinion was quite interesting: mystical experiences occasioned by entheogens are phenomenologically indistinguishable from other mystical experiences, as was shown, for example, in Walter Pahnke's famous Good Friday Experiment. But they are not really authentic and equally valuable as the experiences that come as a result of rigorous spiritual discipline, like prayer, meditation, and various ascetic practices, or that come as divine grace. The experiences induced by entheogens appear to be mystical, but they are really pseudo-mystical.

In this situation, the final decision about these experiences is left to theologians and spiritual teachers. Unfortunately, there has been no agreement among them on this issue. There were people like the Oxford religious scholar R. C. Zaehner, the author of a book on drugs and mysticism, or Meher Baba with his pamphlet entitled *God in a Pill?* who were adamant in their assertions that entheogen experiences are not authentic spiritual phenomena.

On the other hand, I had long discussions with several Tibetan lamas, including Lama Govinda, who had had the opportunity to experience LSD. They all agreed that this substance, used responsibly and with the proper attitude, was a valuable tool for spiritual practice and an "accelerator of karma." Many years ago, I also personally gave LSD to Solon Wang, a prominent Buddhist scholar from Chiang Kai-Shek's inner circle in Taiwan. After a lifetime study of Buddhism and rigorous practice that had failed to bring him the expected results, he had in his first entheogen session what he considered to be an absolutely authentic experience of nirvana. He wrote about it later in his book.

And then there is the fourth opinion, which has best been expressed by Huston Smith. He suggested that the mystical experiences induced by the entheogens are authentic but that, in and of themselves, they do not necessarily result in a spiritual way of being. In other words, unless they happen in the right context and are followed by systematic spiritual practice, they are not in the same category as those experiences that we read about in the spiritual literature. This is also my position on this subject.

In the light of the observations from the study of holotropic states, the current contemptuous dismissal and pathologization of spirituality that is characteristic of monistic materialism appears untenable. In holotropic states, the spiritual dimensions of reality can be directly experienced in a way that is as convincing as our daily experience of the material world. It is also possible to describe step-by-step procedures that facilitate access to these experiences. Careful study of transpersonal experiences shows that they are ontologically real and inform us about important aspects of existence that are ordinarily hidden.

In general, the study of holotropic states confirms C. G. Jung's insight that the experiences originating on deeper levels of the psyche (in my terminology: "perinatal" and "transpersonal" experiences) have a certain quality that he called (after Rudolph Otto) "numinosity." The term *numinous* is relatively neutral and thus preferable to other similar names, such as religious, spiritual, mystical, magical, holy, or sacred, which often have been used in problematic contexts and are easily misleading. The sense of numinosity is based on direct apprehension of the fact that we are encountering a domain that belongs to a superior order of reality, one that is sacred and radically different from the material world.

To prevent misunderstanding and confusion, which in the past compromised many similar discussions, it is critical to make a clear distinction between spirituality and religion. Spirituality is based on direct experiences of nonordinary aspects and dimensions of reality. It does not require a special place or an officially appointed person mediating contact with the divine. The mystics do not need churches or temples. The context in which they experience the sacred dimensions of reality, including their own divinity, are their bodies and nature. And instead of officiating priests, they need a supportive group of fellow seekers or the guidance of a teacher who is more advanced on the inner journey than they are themselves.

Direct spiritual experiences appear in two different forms. The first of these, the experience of the *immanent divine,* involves subtly, but profoundly transformed perception of the everyday reality. A person having this form of spiritual experience sees people, animals, and inanimate objects in the environment as radiant manifestations of a unified field of cosmic creative energy and realizes that the boundaries between them are illusory and unreal. This is a direct experience of nature as god, Spinoza's *deus sive natura.* Using the analogy with television, this experience could be likened to a situation where a black and white picture would suddenly change into one in vivid color. In both cases, much of the old perception of the world remains in place, but is radically redefined by the addition of a new dimension.

The second form of spiritual experience, that of the *transcendental divine,* involves manifestation of archetypal beings and realms of reality that are ordinarily transphenomenal, meaning unavailable to perception in the everyday state of consciousness. In this type of spiritual experience, entirely new elements seem to unfold or explicate—to borrow a term from physicist David Bohm—from another level or order of reality. When we return to the analogy with television, this would be like discovering that there exist other channels than the one we have been previously watching.

For many people, the first encounter with the sacred dimensions of existence often occurs in the context of the death-rebirth process, when the experiences of different stages of birth are accompanied by visions and scenes from the archetypal domain of the collective unconscious. However, the full connection with the spiritual realm is made when the process moves to the transpersonal level of the psyche. When that happens, various spiritual experiences appear in their pure form, independently of the fetal elements. In some instances, the holotropic process bypasses the biographical and perinatal levels altogether and provides direct access to the transpersonal realm.

Spirituality involves a special kind of relationship between the individual and the cosmos and is, in its essence, a personal and private affair. By comparison, organized religion is institutionalized group activity that takes place in a designated location—a temple or a church—and involves a system of appointed officials who might or might not have had personal experiences of spiritual realities. Once a religion becomes organized, it often completely loses the connection with its spiritual source and becomes a secular institution that exploits human spiritual needs without satisfying them.

Organized religions tend to create hierarchical systems focusing on the pursuit of power, control, politics, money, possessions, and other secular concerns. Under these circumstances, religious hierarchy, as a rule, dislikes and discourages direct spiritual experiences in its members, because they foster independence and cannot be effectively controlled. When this is the case, genuine spiritual life continues only in the mystical branches, monastic orders, and ecstatic sects of the religions involved.

Brother David Steindl-Rast, a Benedictine monk and Christian philosopher, uses a beautiful metaphor to illustrate this situation. He compares the original mystical experience to the glowing magma of an exploding volcano, which is exciting, dynamic, and alive. After we have this experience, we feel the need to put it into a conceptual framework and formulate a doctrine. The mystical state represents a precious memory, and we might create a ritual that will remind us of this momentous event. The experience connects us with the cosmic order, and this has profound direct impact on our ethics—our system of values, moral standards, and behavior.

For a variety of reasons, in the course of its existence, organized religion tends to lose connection with its original spiritual source. When it gets disconnected from its experiential matrix, its doctrines harden into dogmas, its rituals into empty ritualism, and its cosmic ethics into moralism. In Brother David's simile, the remains of what once was a vital spiritual system now resemble much more the encrusted lava than the electrifying magma of the mystical experience that created it.

People who have experiences of the immanent or transcendent divine open up to spirituality found in the mystical branches of the great religions of the world or in their monastic orders, not necessarily in their mainstream organizations. If these experiences take a Christian form, the individual would feel resonance with St. Teresa of Avila, St. John of the Cross, Meister Eckhart, or St. Hildegarde von Bingen. Such experiences would not result in appreciation for the Vatican hierarchy and the edicts of the popes, nor would they convey sympathy for the position of the Catholic Church on contraception or of its ban on women in the clergy.

A spiritual experience of the Islamic variety would bring the person close to the teachings of various Sufi orders and instigate interest in their practices. It would not generate enthusiasm for the religiously motivated politics of some Moslem groups or passion for jihad, the Holy War against infidels. Similarly, a Judaic form of this experience would connect the individual to the Jewish mystical tradition, as expressed in the Kabbalah or the Hassidic movement, and not to fundamentalist Judaism or Zionism. A deep mystical experience tends to dissolve the boundaries between religions, while the dogmatism of organized religions tends to emphasize differences and engender antagonism and hostility.

True spirituality is universal and all-embracing and is based on personal mystical experience rather than on dogma or religious scriptures. Mainstream religions might unite people within their own radius, but tend to be divisive on a larger scale, because they set their group against all the others and attempt to either convert them or eradicate them. The epithets "pagans," "goyim," or "infidels" and the conflicts between the Christians and Jews, Moslems and Jews, Christians and Moslems, or Hindus and Sikhs, are just a few salient examples. In today's troubled world, religions in their present form are part of the problem rather than part of the solution. Ironically, even differences between various factions of the same religion can become a sufficient reason for serious conflict and bloodshed, as exemplified by the history of the Christian Church and the ongoing violence in Ireland.

There is no doubt that the dogmas of organized religions are generally in fundamental conflict with science, whether this science uses the mechanistic-materialistic model or is anchored in the emerging paradigm. However, the situation is very different in regard to authentic mysticism based on spiritual experiences. The great mystical traditions have amassed extensive knowledge about human consciousness and about the spiritual realms in a way that is similar to the method that scientists use in acquiring knowledge about the material world. It involved methodology for inducing transpersonal experiences, systematic collection of data, and intersubjective validation.

I would like to close with Ken Wilber's statement concerning the authenticity and ontological status of spiritual experiences: "If there appears to be a conflict between religion and science, it is very likely bogus religion and bogus science." The people who get involved in this kind of an argument probably do not really understand what characterizes good science and do not know what is genuine religion based on and grounded in deep personal experience. I believe that used responsibly and in a mature way, the entheogens mediate access to the numinous dimensions of existence, have a great healing and transformative potential, and represent a very important tool for spiritual development.

5

Psychoactive Sacramentals

WHAT MUST BE SAID

Charles T. Tart

Charles T. Tart, Ph.D., is credited with founding the psychological specialty of altered states of consciousness in 1969 with his pioneering anthology *Altered States of Consciousness*. He is recognized internationally for research on altered states, transpersonal psychology, and parapsychology. His thirteen books include *Transpersonal Psychologies; Open Mind, Discriminating Mind;* and *Waking Up: Overcoming the Obstacles to Human Potential*. They synthesize Buddhist, Sufi, and Gurdjieffian mindfulness training ideas. He is currently Professor Emeritus of Psychology at the University of California at Davis, a Core Faculty member at the Institute of Transpersonal Psychology, and Senior Research Fellow of the Institute of Noetic Sciences.

Those familiar with Eliade's Shamanism may recall that this distinguished historian of religion once had a very different notion about the historical place of hallucinogens in shamanism . . . "Narcotics," he wrote, "are only a vulgar substitute for 'pure' trance." When Siberian shamans do use

the fly-agaric mushroom, Amanita muscaria, *and other chemical means of attaining the ecstatic state, it is "a recent innovation and points to a decadence of shamanic technique."*

. . . [I] should note that in the last years of his productive life, although unable to amend his views in a new, revised edition of Shamanism, he had discarded his view of the use of hallucinogenic plants as "degeneration" of the shamanic techniques of ecstasy. The work done by ethnobotanists and ethnographers on the vast complex of shamanic uses of sacred plants in the Americas, the emerging philological evidence for widespread and very ancient use of the fly-agaric mushroom in Europe, and, finally, the new radiocarbon dates from the American Southwest, he told me not long before his death, had convinced him that we were indeed dealing with an archaic phenomenon and that there was no phenomenological difference between the techniques of ecstasy, whether "spontaneous" or triggered by the chemistry of sacred plants.

PETER T. FURST, "AN OVERVIEW OF SHAMANISM,"
IN *ANCIENT TRADITIONS: SHAMANISM IN
CENTRAL ASIA AND THE AMERICAS,* 1994

I have had a very hard time deciding what to talk about here, and the more I've heard various people speak, the harder this has become. This is particularly true when I hear people speaking from their heart about experiences that are deep and real and vital to them. And I think, "What do I have to say that is appropriate to this level of heart?" My head says, "Well, there's a simple intellectual explanation for that. You're in the wrong state of consciousness to speak about matters of the heart, or perhaps the wrong state of being." I've already thought about an answer for that in proposing state specific sciences many years ago: an idea still, unfortunately, too far ahead of its time in most fields (Tart 1972a, 1972b, 1975a).

I've also had a hard time figuring out what to speak on simply because some of the things talked about here are too profound for me. I don't understand them that well. But my salvation in figuring out what to say was the realization that we are supposed to take a long-term view of psychoactive sacramentals and their implications, so I'm going to reflect on a synthesis of some ideas I have about this area—"Things That Ought To Be Said"—to use that wonderful title I got from Tom Roberts. I will try to speak from both my heart and my head and try to synthesize these things.

I'm going to introduce two main themes. The first one I will begin by saying something about my background with the entheogens.

THEME ONE: THE VALUE OF ENTHEOGENS

As Huston Smith said in his talk, I can say that my encounter with the entheogens has not fundamentally changed my worldview. I was already thinking, believing in that direction. Of course it made me realize how incredibly shallow my worldview was.

When I was an undergraduate student I came across Aldous Huxley's *Doors of Perception* shortly after it was published, and I thought it was a fabulous book. It made perfect sense to me. So I read Huxley's book, intellectually agreed with it, thought it was very interesting, and put it aside. It was like science fiction, one of those strange things that happens somewhere else. Then, in 1960, I met Ivo Kohler, an Austrian psychologist who was spending his sabbatical leave at Duke University, and who had done experiments with mescaline in Europe in the 1930s. As we got to talking, he stated that he had never heard of any experiments in which Americans had taken mescaline. He wondered if their reactions would be different from Europeans. So, being a patriotic, red-blooded American boy, I volunteered to represent my country!

On the morning of May 14, 1960, I made the sacrifice of not eating breakfast (which was quite a sacrifice at that time!) and showed up in the laboratory, and he gave me some mescaline sulfate in warm water. It was like drinking vomit, but I figured it was for science, and it was a noble cause, so "okay." In retrospect, I realized that he gave me a pretty hefty dose, viz. four hundred milligrams.

We sat around and waited for the drug to take effect. A couple of hours later he said, "Do you want to go home, or should I give you some more?" because, basically, nothing had happened. If I pressed on my eyeballs, I could say, "Well the phosphenes are maybe ten percent brighter than normal." I didn't see why people would write a book about this. It wasn't at all interesting. Fortunately, I chose to take some more, and I learned a great deal from that, because about half an hour later I went from being perfectly "normal" to the peak of the experience within a minute or so. The experience is more fully described elsewhere (Tart 1983).

One of the things I learned was that for all my intellectual openness, I was a "control freak," and my psychological processes were more than sufficient to wipe out the biochemical effects of the drug until I was absolutely overwhelmed by it. That was a very important thing to learn.

This initial experience was profound. My worldview wasn't fundamentally changed, but it became alive. I realized, for instance that I had used the word "beauty" all my life, yet I had never known before what "beauty" meant. I hadn't had the slightest idea! Over the following years I had quite a few other experiences in experimental settings with psilocybin and LSD. I later found out that this research was sponsored by one of the front foundations set up by the CIA. So I want to thank the CIA for giving me these powerful drugs when I was young and impressionable. I'm not sure the experiment turned out quite the way they would have liked, but I'm very grateful to them!

What did I learn from these early experiences? Well, of course, I learned a great deal about the nature of the human mind, things that had been just odd bits of intellectual knowledge before. For example, I realized that a psychoactive drug could destabilize some processes, but that psychological stabilization mechanisms might still be more than sufficient at stabilizing the overall pattern of conscious functioning, such that there is no change in state of consciousness. Much of this has been reflected in my more systematic work on understanding altered states (see Tart, works from 1969–94). In particular, my systems approach (see *States of Consciousness,* Tart 1975c) recounts a lot of my early experiences in a more professional and scientific framework.

The entheogens were also important for me because my orientation has always been spiritual, even though I am very heavily involved in the scientific side of things. I'm not going to say too much about what I have learned in the entheogenic sense, though, partially because I'm still digesting it. I really can't figure out a lot of what I've learned yet. Also, some of it was, frankly, too sacred to let my ordinary mind even think about it much. It's in there for when it's necessary.

I also realized that I needed entheogens badly. There are some people who get five minutes of meditation instruction, and five minutes later they have a profound metaphysical experience. And there are some people, like me, who have very stubborn minds, who need, as it were, to be kicked very hard in the head in order to notice anything different. The entheogenic "kick in the head" has been extremely valuable to me. What I didn't get from entheogens is what the more neurotic and immature parts of my mind wanted, and I'm glad I never got it. I basically wanted God to show up, in a gentle way that wouldn't startle me, and hand me a certificate of guaranteed safety and surety forever, probably one I could show to my friends! Fortunately, that hasn't happened. Instead, I've been challenged, which I think is what's really important.

I eventually stopped personal involvement with the substances. I think stopping was right for me, although that may change someday; I don't know. After Huston's talk, where he mentioned stopping, I wondered why I stopped. One of the first reasons I thought of was "Well, I'm getting old, and I'm not very curious anymore." Then I looked at the elder statesmen at this conference, people like Huston and Myron and Sasha, and thought, "That excuse is not going to fly. It doesn't cut any ice with me, because I'm kind of a kid like they are, really."

Partly, I stopped because I already had plenty to work with. I didn't need new insights and new information. There's a wonderful old Sufi teaching story in one of Idries Shah's books about a man walking along the road who sees a flat rock. Painted on it are the words, "Turn me over and read." He turns it over, and it says, "Why do you seek more knowledge when you make so little use of what you already have?" That story gets to me. Partly, I stopped out of fear. The experiences with the entheogens were overwhelming in some cases. Partly, I stopped out of other interests and also out of satisfaction in a sense. The work that I do in life turns out to be helpful to some people, and I'm very glad to be in such a position. But the main reason I stopped was a realization of how much work I needed to do on my ordinary self.

We've talked a little bit about the need to integrate the insight from entheogen sessions with ordinary life. If I can grossly overgeneralize for a minute, I would say that after having watched the "psychedelic scene" for thirty-five years, there are two kinds of people who have gone through it. One of these types is a person who took the drugs, had some wonderful insights, and then took them again—and again and again and again. Most of these people basically remained the same neurotic people they ever were, but instead of talking about office politics, they talked about bad vibes in the cosmos. That is, I saw the example that lots of experience doesn't necessarily make anyone more mature. As to the second type: I saw some people who used the substances infrequently, but who worked a great deal on integrating the experiences into their lives, usually found some spiritual path within life as part of a daily practice, and became very mature.

Now, this is a gross overgeneralization and particularly inapplicable to a third category of people represented at this meeting, people I have not known before, such as those involved in the União do Vegetal or the Santo Daime, who have a consistent social framework for working with the substances as sacramentals, as entheogens. But I personally needed to work on everyday life. It was clear to me that entheogenic experience was not enough. I could have a profound experience, and in a short time my intellect took it over and made it "clever"—and shallow. I can get drunk on ideas. That's very easy for me, and the idea replaces the reality. The result is that I've always been a nice guy, but shallow. You wouldn't come to me if you were really in trouble and needed a friend who could help you on a deep level. So, I needed to work on life practices. I needed to work on what you might call "emotional purification and growth," and more specifically, what I want to emphasize today because it's relevant to integrating these experiences into life, I needed to work on mindfulness.

This is what my focus has been for the last two decades. Mindfulness of each little moment in life, to penetrate below the surface, because it is quite clear to me that ordinary consciousness is an ongoing soap opera. It's a daydream that takes us away from contact with the moment-to-moment realities of life, both the mundane and the spiritual realities. So I've worked on trying to develop some degree of mindfulness. The ways I did this may not necessarily be the ways for people in general, but I did things like formal mindfulness meditation, Buddhist *vipassana*. At first I was not very good at it, but eventually, I learned to sit and develop some degree of mindfulness. I did it in terms of Aikido, a body discipline that emphasizes constantly paying attention to what is really happening. It was always wonderful discipline for me to find that I'd been out on the mat having a daydream about, "Hey, I'm a martial artist. I'm really with it! Oops, how did this fist get in my face all of a sudden?" whereas if I actually paid attention to mundane reality, there was time to be loving and blending with my partner as well as effective in self-defense.

But the mindfulness work that most affected me was discovering the works of G. I. Gurdjieff and his emphasis on developing mindfulness as part of everyday life (see Ouspensky 1949, or my two books about Gurdjieff, *Waking Up* (Tart 1986a) and *Living the Mindful Life* (Tart 1994d). This is not necessarily mindfulness about grand ideas and visions and insights. These heady concepts are the things that are dangerous for me. As I say, I can get intellectually drunk on ideas. It's the moment-by-moment things like, "Gee, feel my body sensations, I must be afraid, or I must be sad to notice things like that," or noticing enough about the moment to realize "Yes this person's saying something interesting, but listen to their tone of voice. They are asking for help. There is something there deeper to pay attention to." So, I have been focusing on mindfulness as a way of trying to take what vision I've had from the entheogenic experiences and bring it back into life. And, mindfulness also goes hand in hand with developing a little bit of compassion. I'm not very good at it, but I'm not the emotional cripple that I once was.

This is the first theme: that the entheogens have been very important in my life, and there has been a need to be mindful. Now let me introduce a second theme that came to me as I was sitting here listening to these wonderful stories and ideas.

THEME TWO:
THE NEGATIVE SIDE OF ENTHEOGENS

Some years ago, approximately two hundred feet to the left of the room we are sitting in at this conference, when the Institute of Transpersonal Psychology was located on this campus, I heard another story from a friend and colleague who got it from the man who played the central role in the story, who I'll call Dr. M. It's supposedly a true story.

Dr. M was a psychotherapist. Before the Second World War, he had been, among other things, a diver, back in the days of the big brass helmets and inflated suits. He was doing some rescue diving in a flooded valley and somehow got trapped underwater. For what seemed hours he couldn't move and couldn't see because the water was so muddy. It was a time of great terror for him. He'd been trapped when the current entangled him in the branches of a downed tree. He was actually there for only five minutes before being freed, but he learned something about the effects of sensory deprivation and disorientation when you are under stress!

Dr. M. became a member of the O.S.S. during the Second World War and, according to him, the O.S.S. knew about LSD and used it as a key ingredient in an interrogation technique. The technique they used was as follows:

They would take a German prisoner who was likely to know things that were valuable, be friendly with him, but with a little hidden edge and at one point slip him a big dose of LSD and a fast-acting barbiturate in his coffee, such that it would knock him out before the LSD really came on. With little grins of triumph, I suppose, "We've poisoned you, you bastard!" While the prisoner was unconscious, they would put him in a diving suit filled with padding so that he couldn't move, but without any obvious restraints that would give a body sense. The interrogators would put the diving suit on a rack in a tank, then fill the tank with ink so that the prisoner was in total blackness and silence. The barbiturate would wear off. The prisoner, who had almost certainly never heard of a hallucinogenic drug, much less had any experience with it, regained consciousness at the peak of a hallucinogenic experience.

Torture is an old-fashioned term for this. But it got more sophisticated than that. The air supply coming in had a smell of sulfur with it, and two voices were piped in. One was an evil-sounding voice, that of an actor playing the role of the Devil, saying, "This man's soul is mine!" The second actor, with a wonderfully sweet voice, played the role of Jesus, arguing to give the prisoner a chance. If only he would cooperate, there was a chance for the prisoner to redeem himself. It was supposedly a very effective interrogation technique.

I don't know that this story is factually true, that it really happened, but from all we know about set and setting, quite clearly this could work as an interrogation technique. It would not work well on anybody in this conference because we would recognize, "Oh, somebody slipped me a drug, and there is something funny going on here." But for somebody who didn't even know what hallucinogens were, whose only previous belief system to account for strange experiences was that they had gone insane or died, who thought they had been poisoned, who smelled the fires of hell . . . very, very powerful. I'll leave it to the philosophers as to whether this is more or less humane than thumb screws and hot irons and that kind of thing.

But this story illustrates a point—that entheogens don't automatically guarantee an entheogenic experience. They don't automatically guarantee growth or love or light or revelation. They can be used in the service of other belief systems and used in a very nasty kind of way. So, this is the thing that ought to be said, the thing that is really one of the main things on my mind after thirty-five or so years of thinking about this: simply because you are involved with entheogens, just because you are using them in a spiritual context, does not guarantee truth and growth and compassion's light. Entheogens are powerful helpers, but they don't guarantee these outcomes. Our dignity, our humanity in a sense, is that we are challenged to use these entheogens properly and to grow with them. The growth is not simply given to us. We have to use our heads as well as our hearts to really make the best use of entheogens.

I mentioned that the mindfulness work of G. I. Gurdjieff has always been very helpful to me. He made a wonderful, apparently paradoxical little saying once that I think summarizes my feelings on the need to use both heart and head here. "Work as if everything depends on work, and pray as if everything depends on prayer." Work as if everything depends on work: nobody's going to give you anything. If you don't make the effort, if you don't get things straight, if you don't get your house in order, you are going to get nothing. You must give it all you can and do your very best. Pray as if everything depends on prayer: understand that we are such tiny creatures in a vast universe, and yet there is Grace. There are gifts that can be given. Both these things are true simultaneously, and in the paradox of these—of being open, receptive, and humble, yet doing the best we can at all times, using our gifts—something can be found.

I have tremendous respect for the revelations, visions, whatever you want to call them, that can occur with the use of the entheogens. I also feel it's essential to practice humility about them. Revelation may come from the highest possible source, but I'm the one hearing it, I'm the one putting it into my memory, I'm the one unknowingly working it over with my belief system. Particularly, my feeling after years of working in this and related areas is that we have to develop mindfulness about the way we live our everyday life. Even if we have had a transcendent experience, our ordinary mind, our ordinary personality ("false personality" as Gurdjieff so nicely called it) is going to work that stuff over. It's going to take living processes and concretize them, turn them into fixed truths somehow, instead of allowing us to incorporate knowledge and grace into our daily lives. Our ordinary mind is going to develop emotional attachment of some sort to what we've learned, and once we've developed the emotional attachment, we are going to start defending that attachment.

I'm pretty good at defending my attachments while appearing open, and appearing open makes for a much more offensive kind of defense—ah, I meant to say "effective," not "offensive,"—but that's an excellent and revealing slip of the tongue! Effective also. And when we become defensive, of course, we begin to attack subtly, or not so subtly, things that we don't agree with, and we develop a certain kind of arrogance. Mindfulness—learning to tune in on a moment-by-moment basis to what am I thinking, what am I feeling, what am I sensing, what's the state of the world around me, what's my state and so forth—helps to point out how these things occur. This is usually quite disgusting when you see how your mind works, but eventually, you start to develop a little space to catch these things before they manifest. I've talked about this mindfulness in my two recent books, *Waking Up* (Tart 1986a) and *Living the Mindful Life* (Tart 1994d). This pursuit and investigation of mindfulness will probably continue to be the main focus of my personal and professional efforts for some time to come. I'm a long way from being good at it!

We should always try to learn from each other about the entheogens; about the way we are using them in our life, because that's part of practicing humility and mindfulness. In this room, for instance, we have a tremendous amount of accumulated wisdom and experience to share. So, my advice to your heads: Work as if everything depends on work. Let's do those scientific experiments, let's use our intellectual knowledge, and let's examine things. How do our findings connect? Are there contradictions? Are there illogicalities? How can we make more effective efforts? And so forth.

We should pray as if everything depends on prayer—use science and intellect in the service of the heart. And we should also use our intellect to purify the heart. Just because I feel something deeply doesn't mean I am correct. Just because I feel certain of something doesn't mean I am right. A constant openness, coupled with the discipline of being mindful about what we are actually doing, can make a difference as to whether the substances are used as entheogens or as ways of manipulating belief, emotions, and behavior. Drugs can be very effective brainwashing tools. It's quite frightening to think about that.

I pray that what I've said may be helpful to people. I will now try to take my own advice and be quiet and listen and learn from what other people have to say.

REFERENCES

Note: Many of these articles are available online at www.paradigm-sys.com /cttart.

Ouspensky, P. D. 1949. *In Search of the Miraculous.* New York: Harcourt, Brace & World.

Tart, C., ed. 1969. *Altered States of Consciousness: A Book of Readings.* New York: John Wiley & Sons.

———. 1970. "Marijuana intoxication: Common experiences." *Nature* 226: 701–4.

———. 1972a. "Scientific foundations for the study of altered states of consciousness." *Journal of Transpersonal Psychology* 3: 93–124.

———. 1972b. "States of consciousness and state-specific sciences." *Science* 176: 1203–10.

———. 1974. "On the nature of altered states of consciousness, with special reference to parapsychological phenomena." In W. Roll, R. Morris, and J. Morris, eds., *Research in Parapsychology.* Metuchen, N.J.: Scarecrow Press, 163–218.

———. (1975a). "Science, states of consciousness, and spiritual experiences: The need for state-specific sciences." In C. Tart, ed. *Transpersonal Psychologies.* New York: Harper & Row, 11–58.

———., ed. *Transpersonal Psychologies.* New York: Harper & Row, 61–111.

———. 1975c. *States of Consciousness.* New York: E. P. Dutton.

———. 1977. "Drug-induced states of consciousness." In B. Wolman et al., eds., *Handbook of Parapsychology.* New York: Van Nostrand Reinhold, 500–525.

———. 1978a. "Altered states of consciousness: Putting the pieces together." In A. Sugerman and R. Tarter, eds. *Expanding Dimensions of Consciousness.* New York: Springer/Verlag, 58–78.

———. 1978b. "Psi functioning and altered states of consciousness: A perspective." In B. Shapin and L. Coly, eds., *Psi and States of Awareness*. New York: Parapsychology Foundation, 180–210.

———. 1979. "Science and the sources of value." *Phoenix: New Directions in the Study of Man* 3: 25–29.

———. 1980. "A systems approach to altered states of consciousness." In J. Davidson, and R. Davidson, eds., *The Psychobiology of Consciousness*. New York: Plenum, 243–69.

———. 1981. "Transpersonal realities or neurophysiological illusions? Toward a dualistic theory of consciousness." In R. Valle and R. von Eckartsberg, eds., *The Metaphors of Consciousness*. New York: Plenum, 199–222.

———. 1983. "Initial integrations of some psychedelic understandings into everyday life." In L. Grinspoon and J. Bakalar, eds., *Psychedelic Reflections*. New York: Human Sciences Press, 223–33.

———. 1986a. *Waking Up: Overcoming the Obstacles to Human Potential*. Boston: New Science Library.

———. 1986b. "Consciousness, altered states, and worlds of experience." *Journal of Transpersonal Psychology* 18: 159–70.

———. 1987a. "The world simulation process in waking and dreaming: A systems analysis of structure." *Journal of Mental Imagery* 11: 145–58.

———. 1987b. "Altered states of consciousness and the possibility of survival of death." In J. Spong, ed., *Consciousness and Survival: An Interdisciplinary Inquiry into the Possibility of Life Beyond Biological Death*. Sausalito, Calif.: Institute of Noetic Sciences, 27–56.

———. 1988. "From spontaneous event to lucidity: A review of attempts to consciously control nocturnal dreaming." In Gackenbach, J., and S. LaBerge, eds. *Conscious Mind, Sleeping Brain: Perspectives on Lucid Dreaming*. New York: Plenum, 67–103.

———. 1989a. *Open Mind, Discriminating Mind: Reflections on Human Possibilities*. San Francisco: Harper & Row.

———. 1989b. "Enlightenment, altered states of consciousness and parapsychology." In B. Shapin and L. Coly, eds., *Parapsychology and Human Nature*. New York: Parapsychology Foundation, 150–69.

———. 1989c. "Extending mindfulness to everyday life." *Journal of Humanistic Psychology* 30: 81–106.

———. 1990a. "Psi-mediated emergent interactionism and the nature of consciousness." In R. Kunzendorf and A. Sheikh, eds. *The Psychophysiology of Mental Imagery: Theory, Research and Application.* Amityville, N.Y.: Baywood, 37–63.

———. 1990b. "Mindlessness and mindfulness in daytime and nighttime dreaming." *Lucidity Letter* 9 (1): 49–81.

———. 1991a. "Multiple personality, altered states and virtual reality: The world simulation process approach." *Dissociation* 3: 222–33.

———. 1991b. "Influence of previous psychedelic drug experiences on students of Tibetan Buddhism: A preliminary exploration." *Journal of Transpersonal Psychology* 23 (2): 139–73.

———. 1993a. "Marijuana intoxication, psi, and spiritual experiences." *Journal of the American Society for Psychical Research* 87: 149–70.

———. 1993b. "Drugs and the path." *Gnosis* 26 (Winter 1993): 23.

———. 1993c. "Mind embodied: Computer-generated virtual reality as a new dualistic-interactive model for transpersonal psychology." In K. Rao, ed., *Cultivating Consciousness: Enhancing Human Potential, Wellness and Healing.* Westport, Conn.: Praeger, 123–37.

———. 1994a. "The human mind: Survival after death." In L. Bessette, ed., *Le Processes de Guerison: Par de la Souffrance ou la Mort (Healing: Beyond Suffering or Death).* Montreal, Quebec: Publications MNH, 305–16.

———. 1994b. "The structure and dynamics of waking sleep." *Journal of Transpersonal Psychology* 25(2): 141–68.

———. 1994c. "Compassion, science and consciousness survival." *Noetic Sciences Review* 29 (Spring 1994): 9–15.

———. 1994d. *Living the Mindful Life.* Boston: Shambhala.

6

Unitive Consciousness and Pahnke's Good Friday Experiment

Paula Jo Hruby

Paula Jo Hruby, Ed.D., LCPC, received her doctorate in educational psychology from Northern Illinois University. She has taught and conducted research at the university level, consulted for educational and research organizations, and maintains a psychotherapy practice. Currently, she is the Associate Director at Mutual Ground, Inc., in Aurora, Illinois, where she counsels survivors of sexual assault and domestic violence. Her passion is investigating and facilitating the maximization of an individual's potential by using the mind/body/emotions/spirit connection to heal.

The principle of causal indifference is this: If X has an alleged mystical experience P1 and Y has an alleged mystical experience P2, and if the phenomenological characteristics of P1 entirely resemble the phenomenological characteristics of P2 so far as can be ascertained from the

descriptions given by X and Y, then the two experiences cannot be regarded as being of two different kinds—for example, it cannot be said that one is a "genuine" mystical experience while the other is not—merely because they arise from dissimilar causal conditions.

The principle seems logically self-evident. . . . [T]hose who have achieved mystical states as a result of long and arduous spiritual exercises, fasting, and prayer, or great moral efforts, possibly spread over many years, are inclined to deny that a drug can induce a "genuine" mystical experience, or at least look askance at such practices and such a claim. Our principle says that if the phenomenological descriptions of the two experiences are indistinguishable, so far as can be ascertained, then it cannot be denied that if one is a genuine mystical experience the other is also. This will follow notwithstanding the lowly antecedents of one of them, and in spite of the understandable annoyance of an ascetic, a saint, or a spiritual hero who is told that his careless and worldly neighbor, who never did anything to deserve it, has attained to mystical consciousness by swallowing a pill.

W. T. STACE, *MYSTICISM AND PHILOSOPHY*, 1960

INTRODUCTION

Perhaps the most controversial and intriguing effect of psychoactive sacramentals (entheogens) is their potential to produce states of unitive consciousness, also called mystical experiences. Much of our discussion at this conference has been about these intriguing experiences: what characterizes them, what short-term and long-term effects they have, and what the research teaches us. I will attempt to define unitive consciousness and then present Walter N. Pahnke's typology of mystical consciousness. A short summary of Pahnke's Good Friday Experiment, the best-known example of experimental mysticism, is also presented.

The rest of the panelists will enhance and expand on the discussion of Pahnke's extraordinary research project, conducted in 1962.

WHAT ARE MYSTICAL EXPERIENCES?

Unitive states of consciousness, or mystical experiences, are both intriguing and misunderstood phenomena within the repertoire of human experience. They are often referred to as intense phenomenological experiences of awe/wonder, unity, and expanded sense of self (Assagiola 1965; Lukoff and Lu 1988; Maslow 1964; Pahnke 1969; Stace 1960). Characteristics commonly used to describe such experiences are feelings of positive affect (awe, wonder, sacredness, profound peace, joy), a sense of immediacy and temporality, a sense of timelessness and spacelessness, a noetic quality (an intuitive, nonrational certainty), and a sense of oneness or unity. This last characteristic—a feeling of spiritual unity—seems to be the most essential aspect of mystical experiences. Such experiences are also referred to as ego-transcendent states, intense religious or spiritual experiences, peak experiences, or cosmic consciousness.

Mystical phenomena have been viewed nonpathologically by most Eastern psychologies, philosophies, and religious traditions and by Western psychologies and counseling theories that incorporate Eastern thinking. Examples of such theories include psychosynthesis (Assagioli 1965), analytical psychology (Jung 1958), gestalt therapy (Brown, Carter, and Vargui 1974; Elkin 1979), and transpersonal psychology (Grof 1975; Walsh and Vaughan 1993a). Still, much of Western culture has no place for mystical experiences (Herrick 1994). Psychological and medical practices—psychiatry in particular—often consider such experiences pathological (Grof and Bennett 1992; Noble 1987). The inexperience of medical and mental health professionals at dealing with transcendent experience is known to have a deleterious effect on some individuals who are struggling to understand and integrate such experiences (Noble 1987; Roberts 1983).

Maslow (1964) and others have found that unitive states of

consciousness are nonpathological, normal, beneficial, and more common than generally believed (Greeley 1974; Hood 1975; Noble 1987; Wuthnow 1978). According to Maslow, striving for mystical experience is a significant and healthy human motivation. Surveying the literature on mystical experiences, Lukoff and Lu (1988) report that most investigators find such experiences to be psychologically and socially beneficial. Indeed, researchers have noticed that almost all people remember some mystical experience, whether or not we interpreted it as such (Steindl-Rast 1988).

PAHNKE'S DEFINITION OF MYSTICAL CONSCIOUSNESS

Pahnke (1963) identified nine interrelated categories that describe the core experience of mystical consciousness. He arrived at this phenomenological typology of the mystical state through his examination of the empirical analytical research conducted by Stace (1960) and of historical literature on mysticism. Pahnke used these nine categories as a springboard to develop the questionnaires for his research, later referred to as the "Good Friday Experiment." His categories are named and described below (Pahnke 1963; Pahnke and Richards 1969).

1. **Unity**: The hallmark of mystical consciousness is undifferentiated unity. This unity can be one or both of the following:
   - *Internal Unity*: the merging of self and the "inner world." This is a state of pure awareness in which the ego is transcended.
   - *External Unity*: the merging of the ego (self) and an object so that they are no longer separate. Consciousness transcends both the ego and the object. "All is One." The physical senses are the avenue through which unity is achieved with the outside world.

2. **Transcendence of Time and Space**: Characterized by one or all of the following:
   - loss of the usual sense of time and space; loss of personal sense of past, present, and future

- disorientation to three-dimensional perception of the environment
- experience of "eternity" or "infinity."

3. **Deeply Felt Positive Mood**: The most universal feelings are joy, blessedness, and peace, in close relation to love. Such feelings may occur during the peak of the experience or during the "ecstatic afterglow" when the peak has passed. These intensely felt, positive feelings are highly valued by those who experience them.
   - *Joy* may be exuberant or quiet in nature and may include feelings such as exultation, rapture, ecstasy, bliss, delight, and happiness.
   - *Peace* is of the profound nature that "passeth understanding."
   - *Blessedness* is closely related to Peace and may include feelings of beatitude, satisfaction, and/or a sense of well-being.
   - *Love* varies in intensity, from tenderness or deep concern for others, to love of or union with God, or even to feelings of sexual ecstasy that are more spiritual than erotic.

4. **Sense of Sacredness**: The sacred is defined broadly here as that which a person feels to be of special value and capable of being profaned. It can be described as:
   - a nonrational, intuitive response in the presence of inspiring realities
   - a sense of reverence or a feeling that one's experience is holy or divine
   - a feeling of profound humility, awe, wonder, or fear in the presence of the Infinite.

5. **Objectivity and Reality**: There are two interrelated aspects of these:
   - the insightful knowledge or illumination felt at an intuitive, non-rational level and gained by direct experience
   - the authoritativeness of the experience or the certainty that such knowledge is real, in contrast to the feeling that the experience is a subjective delusion. William James calls this immediate feeling of objective truth the "noetic quality."

6. **Paradoxicality**: Significant aspects of mystical consciousness contain the paradox of being true despite violating the laws of rational logic. Opposites are felt to be equally true and are grasped on a non-rational level. Examples of this paradoxicality include:
   - feeling as though one has died, yet knowing that one still exists
   - experiencing the empty unity or void that contains all reality
   - feeling as though out of one's body while still in it.

7. **Alleged Ineffability**: The mystical state is most difficult to explain or communicate in words, particularly during the actual experience.
   - Language seems to be inadequate to express/reflect the experience accurately.
   - It is difficult to explain an experience to someone who has never had it. Later, with time given to integrate and absorb the experience, articulation may become possible to some degree. Thus, this ineffability is supposed.

8. **Transiency**: The duration of the mystical state of consciousness is finite and is realized by contrast when the experience is over. It may exist for a few seconds, minutes, or hours, then one returns to the usual state of consciousness. This is an important difference between mystical consciousness and psychosis.

9. **Persisting Positive Changes in Attitude and/or Behavior**: When a person goes through an experience characterized by the eight categories above, she/he often has simultaneous changes in attitudes or behaviors in one or more of the following areas:
   - *Toward Self:* increased integration of the personality; renewed sense of self-worth; relaxation of ego defenses; increased self-acceptance; increased faith in personal creativity; increased optimism
   - *Toward Others:* greater sensitivity; increased tolerance; more compassion and love. These changes reflect the meaning of Buber's "I-Thou" relationship.
   - *Toward Life:* changes in values, purpose in life, sense of meaning; increased vocational commitment; loss of fear of death; increased appreciation for the whole of creation

- *Toward the Mystical Experience Itself:* believing that the experience has value and that something useful was learned. If the experience is positive, it is usually considered a high point in the person's life, and she/he may try to repeat it. At best, one realizes that the experience is not an end itself or a means to an end but a balance of both. These changes extend over a longer period of time than the few minutes or hours of the primary experience.

Unlike the first eight categories, this last cannot be assessed immediately. Rather, it represents James' (1902) criterion of "the fruits of life." For James, the means by which one has a mystical experience does not matter. What counts is *how* the experience affects one's life.

Pahnke developed a self-report questionnaire based on the nine categories describing mystical consciousness. He used this questionnaire in his Good Friday Experiment.

THE GOOD FRIDAY EXPERIMENT: PAHNKE'S STUDY IN EXPERIMENTAL MYSTICISM

Purpose: On Good Friday, April 20, 1962, Pahnke conducted a randomized, controlled, matched-group, double-blind experiment in order to: (1) gather empirical data about the altered state of consciousness experienced with psilocybin in a religious setting and (2) compare these data with the nine categories of mystical consciousness (Pahnke 1963).

Subjects: The volunteer subjects were twenty middle-class male Christian theological students who were screened extensively regarding mental health issues, physical wellness, and history of religious or mystical experiences.

Method: Subjects were divided into five groups of four students each, with two leaders per group. The leaders were research assistants who were well informed regarding the potential positive and negative effects of psilocybin, and who had previous personal experience with psilocybin or similar drugs. Half of the subjects (experimentals) received 30 mg of psilocybin. The control half received 200 mg of nicotinic acid, a vitamin that causes feelings of warmth and tingling of the skin (a nonactive placebo was expected by the subjects). Half of the leaders (one per group) received 15 mg of psilocybin.

The subjects and leaders were located in a chapel that received, via loudspeaker from the main sanctuary, the Good Friday service consisting of prayers, organ music, solos, and personal meditation time. The minister was Rev. Howard Thurman, mentor of Martin Luther King, Jr. Pahnke designed the experiment around a service that would be spiritually meaningful and familiar to the participants. He had encouraged the students to prepare seriously for the experience through self-examination, meditation, and spiritual readings.

Results: Both shortly after the experiment and six months later, the subjects were asked to write a description of their experience, answer a questionnaire, and participate in an interview. Statistical analysis of these data indicated that the experimentals had a significantly more intense experience than did the controls in eight of the nine categories of mystical typology for each method of measurement. The only category that less clearly differentiated the two groups was sense of sacredness.

Conclusions: The phenomenological experiences of the experimental subjects were indistinguishable from, or even identical to, the characteristics of mysticism defined a priori. The completeness of the categorical experiences varied; however, each category was experienced to some degree. Both groups felt a *sense of sacredness* to some extent (most likely because the subjects were all divinity students and the experiment was conducted during a religious ceremony).

The drug, set, and setting were all very important in determining the outcome. Since Pahnke assumed the set (internal, psychological mind-set) and setting (external, physical environment) to be the same for both groups, the drug was concluded to be the differentiating factor between the experimentals and the controls. Eight of the ten experimentals described the experience as affecting them profoundly. They indicated that contemplation of the experience caused them to rethink their life philosophies and values and to integrate what they had learned into their spiritual and worldviews.

HOOD'S DEFINITION OF MYSTICISM: MYSTICISM SCALE

Currently, the *Mysticism Scale* is the most commonly used instrument for assessing mystical experience (Hood, Morris, and Watson 1993; Doblin 1990; Lukoff and Lu 1988). Ralph W. Hood, Jr. developed the scale (a self-report of past experiences of mystical phenomena) to assess eight of the nine characteristics delineated by Stace (Hood 1975). Many of Hood's categories are similar if not identical to Pahnke's categories. This is not surprising since they both built upon Stace's seminal work, *Mysticism and Philosophy* (1960). The following is Hood's description of the categories of mystical experience:

1. **Ego Quality**: the experience of expansion or transcendence of consciousness beyond the empirical ego. This egolessness can be experienced as absorption into something greater than the self.
2. **Unifying Quality**: the perception that everything is actually the same thing—all is One.
3. **Inner Subjective Quality**: the perception that everything, both animate and inanimate, is alive or aware and/or not dead.
4. **Temporal/Spatial Quality**: the experience that time and space have been modified, even to such an extreme that neither seems to exist.
5. **Noetic Quality**: the recognition that the experience is a source of valid, intuitive knowledge that is considered objectively true.
6. **Ineffability**: the difficulty in expressing the experience in words or conventional language.
7. **Positive Affect**: the positive feelings of joy, bliss, or wonder during the experience.

8. **Religious Quality**: the inherent feelings of sacredness, which may include a sense of mystery, awe, and/or reverence.*

A UNIVERSAL LIST OF
MYSTICAL CHARACTERISTICS

Although attempts have been made to define a core list of the characteristics of mystical experience, no such list has been universally accepted (Lukoff and Lu 1988). Indeed, there is some question regarding whether it is possible to define a universal core, particularly for an experience that is often described as ineffable (Walsh and Vaughan 1993a). Though ineffability is often alleged by those experiencing mystical states of consciousness, such experiences have also been described eloquently in prose by St. Teresa, St. John of the Cross, Meister Eckhart, and many others (James 1902; Stace 1960). The *Yoga-Sutra* of Pantanjali (Feuerstein 1989) and the classics of Indian spirituality are rich with such descriptions (Bhagavad Gita 1986; Dhammapada 1986; Upanishads 1975).

Besides the seemingly inherent difficulty of putting into language a mystical experience, there may be a cultural barrier to such communication. As McCready (1975) explains, the English language might not have the capability to adequately express such experiences. Also, Noble (1987), Wuthnow (1978), and others (Grof and Bennett 1992; Herrick 1994; Walsh 1995) have repeatedly noted the lack of acceptance of such experiences, particularly in Western society. This can be true to such an extent that the individual becomes hesitant to share an experience of mystical phenomena for fear of being labeled "crazy" or "weird." This may be especially true if an intense mystical state of consciousness is experienced while under the influence of a psychoactive substance (Maslow 1964). No matter how reticent individuals may be to share such experiences, there is something strangely familiar in the descrip-

---

*From "The Construction and Preliminary Validation of a Measure of Reported Mystical Experience," by R. W. Hood, Jr., 1975. *Journal of the Scientific Study of Religion.* Adapted with permission.

tions that touch us deeply. McCready (1975) speaks to this when he writes: "Mysticism seems strangely out of place in contemporary society. It seems as though it is a voice from our collective past. Yet we respond because there is some need within us to understand and to be a part of the force which binds life together" (McCready 1975, 69).

We have examined the characteristics and qualities of mystical experience as defined by Pahnke's Good Friday Experiment and Hood's *Mysticism Scale* as well as briefly explored Pahnke's research into experimental mysticism. The rest of the panel members will provide an in-depth and personal look at what happened during the Good Friday Experiment and bring us up to date on the effects of the experiment with the results of a twenty-five-year follow-up study.

REFERENCES

Assagioli, R. 1965. *Psychosynthesis: A Collection of Basic Writings*. New York: Viking Penguin.

Bhagavad-Gita. 1986. *The Bhagavad-Gita: Krishna's Counsel in Time of War*. Translated by B. S. Miller. New York: Bantam Books.

Bloomfield, H. H. 1991. "Transcendental meditation as an adjunct to therapy." In S. Boorstein, ed. *Transpersonal Psychotherapy*. Stanford, Calif.: JTP Books, 123–40. (Original work published 1980).

Brown, G., B. Carter, and S. Vargiu. 1974. "The farther reaches of gestalt therapy: A conversation with George Brown." *Synthesis* 1(1): 27–43.

Buber, M. 1970. *I and Thou*. Translated by W. Kaufmann. New York: Charles Scribner's Sons.

Bucke, R. M. 1901. *Cosmic Consciousness: A Study in the Evolution of the Human Mind*. Philadelphia: Innes & Sons.

Csikszentmihalyi, M. 1990. *Flow: The Psychology of Optimal Experience*. New York: HarperPerennial.

Dhammapada. 1986. *The Dhammapada*. Translated by E. Easwaran. Tomales, Calif.: Nilgiri Press.

Doblin, R. 1990. Pahnke's "Good Friday Experiment: A long-term follow-up and methodological critique." *The Journal of Transpersonal Psychology* 23(1): 1–28.

Elkin, E. 1979. "Towards a theory of transpersonal gestalt." *The Gestalt Journal* 2(1): 79–82.

Greeley, A. M. 1974. *Ecstasy: A Way of Knowing.* Englewood Cliffs, N.J.: Prentice-Hall, Inc.

Grof, S. 1975. *Realms of the Human Unconscious: Observations from LSD Research.* New York: Viking Press.

Grof, S., and H. Z. Bennett. 1992. *The Holotropic Mind: The Three Levels of Human Consciousness and How They Shape Our Lives.* San Francisco: HarperCollins.

Herrick, K. E. 1994. "Breakthrough in the DSM-IV: Can spirituality save psychiatry?" *Professional Counselor* 21(Feb.): 48.

Hood, R. W. Jr., 1975. "The construction and preliminary validation of a measure of reported mystical experience." *Journal for the Scientific Study of Religion* 14: 29–41.

Hood, R. W. Jr., R. J. Morris, and P. J. Watson. 1993. "Further factor analysis of Hood's Mysticism Scale." *Psychological Reports* 73(1): 1176–78.

James, W. 1902. *Varieties of Religious Experience.* New York: Random House.

Jung, C. G. 1958. "Psychology and Religion: West and East." In Read, H., M. Fordham, and G. Adler, eds., *The Collected Works of C. G. Jung.* Vol. 11. Translated by R. F. C. Hull. London: Routledge & Kegan Paul Ltd.

Lukoff, D., and F. G. Lu. 1988. "Transpersonal psychology research review: Topic: Mystical experiences." *The Journal of Transpersonal Psychology* 20(2): 161–84.

Maslow, A. H. 1964. *Religions, Values, and Peak-Experiences.* Columbus, Ohio: Ohio State University Press.

McCready, W. C. 1975. "A survey of mystical experiences: A research note." In Woods, R., ed. *Heterodoxy/Mystical Experience, Religious Dissent and the Occult.* River Forest, Ill.: Listening Press, 55–70.

Noble, K. 1987. "Psychological health and the experience of transcendence." *The Counseling Psychologist* 15(4): 601–14.

Pahnke, W. N. 1963. "An analysis of the relationship between psychedelic drugs and the mystical consciousness." Unpublished doctoral dissertation, Harvard University.

———. 1969. "Psychedelic drugs and mystical experience." In Pattison, E. M., ed., *International Psychiatry Clinics: Vol. 5. Clinical Psychiatry and Religion.* Boston: Little, Brown and Company, 149–63.

Pahnke, W. N., and W. A. Richards. 1969. "Implications of LSD and experimental mysticism." In Tart, C. T., ed. *Altered States of Consciousness.* Garden City, N.Y.: Anchor Books, 409–39.

Roberts, T. B. 1983. "New learning." In Grinspoon, L., and J. B. Bakalar, eds., *Psychedelic Reflections*. New York: Human Sciences Press, 234–52.

Stace, W. T. 1960. *Mysticism and Philosophy*. New York: Macmillan.

Steindl-Rast, D. 1988. "Thoughts on mysticism as frontier of consciousness evolution." In Grof, S., ed. *Human Survival and Consciousness Evolution*. Albany, N.Y.: State University of New York Press.

Upanishads. 1975. *The Upanishads: Breath of the Eternal*. Translated by Swami Prabhavananda and F. Manchester. New York: Mentor Books.

Walsh, R., and F. Vaughan, eds., 1993a. "Mapping and comparing states." *Paths Beyond Ego: The Transpersonal Vision*. Los Angeles: Jeremy P. Tarcher/Perigee, 38–46.

———. 1993b. *Paths Beyond Ego: The Transpersonal Vision*. Los Angeles: Jeremy P. Tarcher/Perigee.

———. 1995. "Phenomenological mapping: A method for describing and comparing states of consciousness." *The Journal of Transpersonal Psychology* 27(1): 25–56.

Wuthnow, R. 1978. "Peak experiences: Some empirical tests." *Journal of Humanistic Psychology* 18(3): 59–75.

7

Pahnke's Good Friday Experiment

A LONG-TERM FOLLOW-UP AND METHODOLOGICAL CRITIQUE

Rick Doblin

Rick Doblin, Ph.D., decided to become a psychedelic psychotherapist at age seventeen (in 1971) and promptly dropped out of New College (Sarasota, Florida) in 1972 in order to integrate overwhelming LSD experiences. Ten years later, he returned to New College to study transpersonal psychology and psychedelic research. In 1987, his undergraduate thesis was a twenty-five-year follow-up of Walter Pahnke's Good Friday Experiment. In 1986, he founded the Multidisciplinary Association for Psychedelic Studies (MAPS, www .maps.org) to support psychedelic research. MAPS now has about 1800 members. In 1990, he received a Masters in Public Policy from Harvard's Kennedy School of Government and also became a certified Grof Holotropic Breathwork practitioner. His doctoral dissertation, for a Ph.D. in Public Policy from the Kennedy School, was titled *The Regulation of the Medical Use of Psychedelic Drugs and*

Marijuana. He still wants to become a full-time psychedelic therapist one day.

Although a drug experience might seem "unearned," our evidence has suggested that preparation and expectation play an important part, not only in the type of experience attained, but in later fruits for life. Perhaps the hardest "work" comes after the experience which itself may only provide the motivation for future efforts to integrate and appreciate what has been learned.

WALTER N. PAHNKE, *DRUGS AND MYSTICISM*
(DISSERTATION), 1963

On Good Friday, 1962, before services commenced in Boston University's Marsh Chapel, Walter Pahnke administered small capsules to twenty Protestant divinity students. Thus began the most scientific of experiments investigating the potential of certain plants and chemicals to facilitate mystical experience (Pahnke 1963, 1966, 1967, 1970; Pahnke and Richards 1966). Half of the capsules contained thirty milligrams of psilocybin (an extract of psychoactive mushrooms) and the other half contained a placebo. According to Pahnke, the experiment determined that "the persons who received psilocybin experienced to a greater extent than did the controls the phenomena described by our typology of mysticism" (Pahnke 1963, 220).

This chapter is a brief methodological critique and long-term follow-up study to the Good Friday Experiment. Pahnke, who was both a physician and a minister, conducted the experiment in 1962 for his Ph.D. in Religion and Society at Harvard University, with Timothy Leary as his principal academic advisor (Leary et al. 1962, 1967, 1968). Describing the experiment, Walter Houston Clark (1961 recipient of the American Psychological Association's William James Memorial Award for contributions to the psychology of religion) writes, "There are no experiments known to me in the history of the scientific study of religion better designed or clearer in their conclusions than this one" (Clark 1969, 77).

A classic means of evaluating mystical experiences is by the fruits of such experiences. Thus, follow-up data is of fundamental importance in evaluating the original experiment. A six-month follow-up was part of the original experiment and a longer-term follow-up would probably have been conducted by Pahnke himself had it not been for his death in 1971. For over twenty-five years it has not been legally feasible to replicate or revise this experiment. Hence, this long-term follow-up study, conducted by the author, is offered as a way to advance scientific knowledge in the area of psychoactives and experimental mysticism. Lukoff, Zanger, and Lu's review (1990) of psychoactive substances and transpersonal states offers a recent overview of this topic.

Though all raw data from the original experiment (including the uncoded list of participants) is lost, extensive research over a period of four years and the enthusiastic cooperation of most of the original subjects have resulted in the identification and location of nineteen out of the original twenty subjects. From November 1986 to October 1989, this author tape-recorded personal interviews with sixteen of these subjects, meeting fifteen in their home cities and interviewing one subject over the telephone. All sixteen subjects participating in this long-term follow-up (nine from the control group and seven from the experimental group) were also re-administered the one-hundred-item, six-month follow-up questionnaire used in the original experiment.

Of the remaining three subjects from the experimental group, one is deceased. The identity of another is unknown. One subject declined to participate, citing concerns about privacy. One subject from the control group declined to be interviewed or to fill out the questionnaire because he interpreted Pahnke's pledge of confidentiality to mean that the subjects should not talk about the experiment to anyone. This author's discussion of the meaning of confidentiality and mention of the explicit support for the long-term follow-up by Pahnke's wife failed to enlist his participation.

Informal discussions were also conducted with seven out of the ten of Pahnke's original research assistants in order to gather background information about the experiment. At the time of the experiment, these people were professors or students of religion, psychology, and philosophy at universities, colleges, and seminaries in the Boston area.

DISCUSSION

The Good Friday Experiment is one of the preeminent experiments in the scientific literature on mystical experience. Despite the unavoidable failure of the double-blind due to methodological shortcomings and the use of several imprecise questions in the questionnaire used to quantify mystical experiences, the experiment's fascinating and provocative conclusions strongly support the hypothesis that psilocybin can help facilitate mystical experiences when used by religiously inclined people in a religious setting. The experiment also supports the hypothesis that those psilocybin subjects who experienced a full or a partial mystical experience would, after six months, report a substantial amount of positive, and virtually no negative, persisting changes in attitude and behavior.

This long-term follow-up, conducted twenty-four to twenty-seven years after the original experiment, provides further support to the findings of the original experiment. All seven psilocybin subjects participating in the long-term follow-up, but none of the controls, still considered their original experience to have had genuinely mystical elements and to have made a uniquely valuable contribution to their spiritual lives. The positive changes described by the psilocybin subjects at six months, which in some cases involved basic vocational and value choices and spiritual understandings, had persisted over time and had deepened in some cases. The overwhelmingly positive nature of the reports by the psilocybin subjects are even more remarkable because this long-term follow-up took place during a period of time when drug abuse in the United States was becoming the public's number one concern, with all the attendant social pressure denying the value of drug-induced experiences. The long-term follow-up interviews cast considerable doubt on the assertion that mystical experiences catalyzed by drugs are in any way inferior to nondrug mystical experiences in both their immediate content and long-term positive effects—a critique of the Good Friday Experiment advanced primarily by Zaehner (Bakalar 1985).

Unexpectedly, the long-term follow-up also uncovered data that should have been reported in the original thesis. Pahnke failed to report the administration of the tranquilizer Thorazine to one of the subjects who received psilocybin. There is no justification for this omission no matter how unfairly the critics of this research may have used the information or how minimal the negative persisting effects reported by the subject. In addition, Pahnke underemphasized the difficult psychological struggles experienced by most of the psilocybin subjects. These very serious omissions point to an important incompleteness in Pahnke's interpretation of the effects of psilocybin.

Some of the backlash that swept LSD and similar substances out of the research labs and the hands of physicians and therapists can be traced in part to the thousands of cases in which people who took the drugs in nonresearch settings were unprepared for the frightening aspects of the drug experience and ended up in hospital emergency rooms. These unfortunate instances of panic reaction have many causes, yet some of them stem from the way in which the cautionary elements of the Good Friday Experiment were inadequately discussed in Pahnke's thesis, subsequent scholarly reports, and the popular media. For example, *Time* magazine reported on the experiment in glowing, exaggerated terms, stating, "All students who had taken the drug [psilocybin] experienced a mystical consciousness that resembled those described by saints and ascetics" (*Time* September 23, 1966, 62).

The widespread use of drugs such as psilocybin and LSD, in both medical and nonmedical settings, began in the 1960s and is still taking place, apparently largely underground. Such use was partially founded upon an optimism regarding the inherent safety of the drug experiences that did not fully acknowledge the complexity and profundity of the psychological issues associated with them. With some proponents of the drugs exaggerating the benefits and minimizing the risks, a backlash was predictable. With the intriguing connection (reported by several psilocybin subjects) between mystical experiences and political action, the backlash may in retrospect have been inevitable (Baumeister and Placidi 1985).

Despite difficult moments experienced by several of the psilocybin subjects, the seven subjects who participated in the long-term follow-up reported a substantial amount of persisting positive effects and no significant long-term negative effects. Even the subject who was given Thorazine in the original experiment reported only "slightly harmful" negative persisting effects at the six-month follow-up. Secondhand information gathered during the course of the long-term follow-up suggests that his experience caused no persisting dysfunction and may even have had some beneficial effects.

The lack of long-term negative effects or dysfunction is not surprising. Strassman's review of all literature on controlled scientific experiments using drugs such as psilocybin and LSD in human volunteers found that panic reactions and other adverse reactions were extremely rare. He concluded that the potential benefits of future research outweighed the potential risks (Strassman 1984).

Even in light of the new data about the difficulties experienced by many of the subjects during the experiment, this long-term follow-up adds further support to the conclusion that additional studies are justified. Future experiments should be approached cautiously and carefully, with a multidisciplinary team of scientists involved in planning and implementation. Such a team should include psychiatrists, psychologists, and religious professionals from a variety of traditions, as well as authorities on drug abuse prevention, education, and treatment. Questions as fundamental as those raised by the Good Friday Experiment deserve to be addressed by the scientific community and pose special challenges to the regulatory agencies. Renewed research can be expected to require patience, courage, and wisdom from all concerned.

REFERENCES

Bakalar, J. 1985. "Social and intellectual attitudes toward drug induced religious experience." *Journal of Humanistic Psychology* 25(4): 45–66.

Barber, T. X. 1976. *Pitfalls in Human Research.* New York: Pergamon Press.

Baumeister, R., and K. Placidi. 1985. "A social history and analysis of the LSD controversy." *Journal of Humanistic Psychology,* 23(4): 25–60.

Beutler, L. E., and M. Crago. 1983. "Self-report measures in psychotherapy outcome." In Lambert, M., E. Christensen, and S. Dejulio, eds. *The Assessment of Psychotherapy Outcome.* New York: Wiley.

Clark, W. H. 1969. *Chemical Ecstasy: Psychedelic Drugs and Religion.* New York: Sheed and Ward, 77.

Di Leo, F. 1982. "Protocol: LSD-assisted psychotherapy correlation of peak experience profiles with behavior change." Appendix C: Peak experience profile. Unpublished.

Grof, S. 1975. *Realms of the Human Unconscious: Observations from LSD Research.* New York: Viking Press.

———. 1980. *LSD Psychotherapy.* Pomona, Calif.: Hunter House.

Harner, M., ed. 1973. *Hallucinogens and Shamanism.* New York: Oxford University Press.

Hoffman, A., C. Ruck, and R. G. Wasson. 1978. *The Road to Eleusis: Unveiling the Secret of the Mysteries.* New York: Harvest Books.

James, W. 1961, orig. 1902. *Varieties of Religious Experience.* New York: Collier Books.

Larson, D., et al. 1986. "Systematic analysis of research on religious variables in four major psychiatric journals, 1978–1982." *The American Journal of Psychiatry,* 143(3): 329–34.

Lasagna, L. 1985. *Clinical Trials in the Natural Environment.* Boston, Tufts University: Center for the Study of Drug Development, Reprint Series RS 8695: 45–49.

Leary, T. 1967. "The religious experience: Its production and interpretation." *Journal of Psychedelic Drugs,* 1(2): 3–23.

———. 1968. *High Priest.* New York: College Notes and Texts, Inc.

———. 1984. *Flashbacks.* Los Angeles: J. P. Tarcher.

Leary, T., et al. (1962). "Investigations into the religious implications of consciousness expanding experience." *Newsletter #1: Research Program on Consciousness-Altering Substances.* Cambridge, Mass.: Harvard University.

Lukoff, D., R. Zanger, and F. Lu. 1990. "Transpersonal psychology research review: Psychoactive substances and transpersonal states." *The Journal of Transpersonal Psychology,* 22(2): 107–48.

Pahnke, W. 1963. "Drugs and mysticism: An analysis of the relationship between psychedelic drugs and the mystical consciousness." Ph.D. dissertation. Harvard University, 220.

———. 1966. "The contribution of the psychology of religion to the therapeutic use of psychedelic substances." In Abramson, H., ed. *The Use of LSD in Psychotherapy and Alcoholism.* New York: Bobbs-Merrill, 629–49.

———. 1967. "LSD and religious experience." In DeBold, R., and R. Leaf, eds., *LSD, Man and Society.* Middletown, Conn.: Wesleyan University Press, 60–85.

———. 1969. "The psychedelic mystical experience and the human encounter with death." *Harvard Theological Review,* 62(1): 1–32.

———. 1970. "Drugs and mysticism." In Aaronson, B., and H. Osmond, eds. *Psychedelics: The Uses and Implications of Hallucinogenic Drugs.* Garden City, N.Y.: Anchor Books, 145–64.

Pahnke, W., and W. Richards. 1966. "Implications of LSD and experimental mysticism." *Journal of Religion and Health* 5 (3): 175–208.

———. 1969. Implications of LSD and experimental mysticism. *The Journal of Transpersonal Psychology* 1(2): 69–102.

Richards, W. 1975. *Counseling, peak experiences, and the human encounter with death.* Ph.D. dissertation, Washington, D.C.: Catholic University.

———. 1978. "Mystical and archetypal experiences of terminal patients in DPT-assisted psychotherapy." *Journal of Religion and Health* 17(2): 117–26.

Ring, K. 1982. *Life at Death: A Scientific Investigation of the Near Death Experience.* New York: Quill.

———. 1984. *Heading Toward Omega: In Search of the Meaning of the Near-Death Experience.* New York: Quill.

———. 1988. "Paradise is paradise: Reflections on psychedelic drugs, mystical experiences and the near-death experience." *Journal of Near-Death Experiences* 6(3): 138–48.

Rue, L. D. 1985. "Our most outrageous blind spot: The academic study of religion." *Chronicle of Higher Education* (29): 40.

Silverman, W. 1983. "Bibliography of measurement techniques used in the social scientific study of religion." *Psychological Documents* 13(7). Washington, D.C.: American Psychological Association.

Spilka, B., R. W. Hood Jr., and R. Gorsuch. 1985. *The Psychology of Religion: An Empirical Approach.* Englewood Cliffs, N.J.: Prentice Hall.

Stace, W. T. 1960. *Mysticism and Philosophy*. London: Macmillan.

Strassman, R. 1984. "Adverse reactions to psychedelic drugs: A review of the literature." *The Journal of Nervous and Mental Disease* 172(10): 577–95.

Time. 1966. "Mysticism in the Lab." September 23: 62.

Tooley and Pratt. 1964. Letter to the editor, *Behavioral Science* 9(3): 254–56.

Underhill, E. 1974, orig. 1910. *Mysticism*. New York: Meridian.

Wasson, R. G. 1968. *Soma: Divine Mushroom of Immortality*. Rome: Harcourt, Brace & Jovanovich, Inc.

Zaehner, R. C. 1972. *Zen, Drugs and Mysticism*. New York: Vintage Books.

Zinberg, N. 1984. *Drug, Set and Setting*. New Haven: Yale University Press.

LITERATURE RELATED TO
PAHNKE'S "GOOD FRIDAY EXPERIMENT"

Aaronson, B., and H. Osmond, eds. 1970. *Psychedelics: The Uses and Implications of Hallucinogenic Drugs*. Garden City, N.Y.: Anchor Books.

Abramson, H., ed. 1967. *The Use of LSD in Psychotherapy and Alcoholism*. New York: Bobbs-Merrill.

Bakalar, J. 1979–80. "Psychedelic drug therapy: Cultural conditions and obstacles." *Journal of Altered States of Consciousness* 5(4):297–307.

Bakalar, J., and L. Grinspoon. 1986. "Can drugs be used to enhance the psychotherapeutic process?" *American Journal of Psychotherapy* 40(3), July.

Clark, W. H. 1973. *Religious Experience: Its Nature and Function in the Human Psyche*. Springfield, Ill.: Charles C. Thomas.

D'Aquili, E. 1982. "Senses of reality in science and religion: A neuroepistimological perspective." *Zygon* 17(4): 361–84.

Dean, S., ed. 1975. *Psychiatry and Mysticism*. Chicago: Nelson Hall.

Deikman, A. 1982. *The Observing Self: Mysticism and Psychotherapy*. Boston: Beacon Press.

Dobkin De Rios, M. 1972. *Visionary Vine: Hallucinogenic Healing in the Peruvian Amazon*. Prospect Heights, Ill.: Waveland Press.

Efron, D., ed. 1967. *Ethnopharmacologic Search for Psychoactive Drugs*. Washington, D.C.: Public Health Service Publication No. 1645.

Grinspoon, L., and J. Bakalar. 1979. *Psychedelic Drugs Reconsidered*. New York: Basic Books.

———. eds. 1983. *Psychedelic Reflections*. New York: Human Sciences Press.

Huxley, A. 1954. *Doors of Perception*. New York: Harper.

Lee, M., and B. Schlain. 1986. *Acid Dreams: LSD, the CIA and the Sixties Rebellion.* New York: Grove Press.

Masters, R. E. L., and J. Houston. 1966. *The Varieties of Psychedelic Experience.* New York: Dell.

Maslow, A. 1964. *Religions, Values, and Peak Experiences.* New York: Viking Press.

Muller, R. 1982. *New Genesis: Shaping a Global Spirituality.* Garden City, N.Y.: Doubleday.

Myerhoff, B. 1974. *Peyote Hunt: The Sacred Journey of the Huichol Indians.* Ithaca, N.Y.: Cornell University Press.

O'Connell, S. 1983. "The placebo effect and psychotherapy." *Psychotherapy: Theory, Research and Practice* 20 (3): 335–57.

Pahnke, W. 1966. "Report on a pilot project investigating the pharmacological effects of psilocybin in normal volunteers." Massachusetts Mental Health Center. Unpublished Manuscript.

Persinger, M. 1987. *The Neurophysiological Basis for "God" Experiences.* New York: Praeger Press.

Prince, R. H., and D. H. Salman, eds. (1967). *Do psychedelics have religious implications? Proceedings of the third annual conference.* R. M. Bucke Memorial Society for the Study of Religious Experience. Quebec.

Ram Dass. 1974. *The Only Dance There Is.* New York: Doubleday.

Schmitz-Moorman, K. 1986. "Philosophical and theological reflections on recent neurobiological discoveries." *Zygon* 21(2): 249–57.

Shulgin, A., L. A. Shulgin, and P. Jacob III. 1986. "A protocol for the evaluation of new psychoactive drugs in man." *Methods and Findings in Experimental Clinical Pharmacology* 8 (5): 313–20.

Smith, D., ed. 1967–68. "Psychedelic drugs and religion." *Journal of Psychedelic Drugs* 1(2).

Smith, H. 1964. "Do drugs have religious import?" *The Journal of Philosophy* 61(18): 517–30.

Stafford, P. 1983. *Psychedelics Encyclopedia.* Los Angeles: J. P. Tarcher.

Weil, A. 1972. *The Natural Mind.* Boston: Houghton Mifflin.

Wilber, K., ed. 1984. *Quantum Questions: Mystical Writings of the Worlds Greatest Physicists.* Boulder, Colo.: Shambhala.

Wolman, B., and M. Ullman, eds. 1986. *Handbook of States of Consciousness.* New York: Van Nostrand Reinhold.

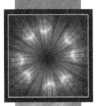

8

A Pilgrim's Visit to Marsh Chapel

Thomas Jenden Riedlinger

Thomas Jenden Riedlinger, M.T.S., F.L.S., is a writer and lecturer who lives with his wife Beverly Jenden Riedlinger in Olympia, Washington. A former Associate in Ethnomycology at Harvard Botanical Museum and a Fellow of the Linnean Society of London, he earned his bachelor's degree in psychology from Northwestern University and a master's degree in world religions from Harvard Divinity School. His published works include *The Sacred Mushroom Seeker,* a book of essays on ethnomycologist R. Gordon Wasson; *Mortal Refrains,* the complete collected poems, stories, and songs of Julia Moore, a nineteenth-century Michigan poet; articles in *Gnosis magazine, Journal of Humanistic Psychology, Journal of Psychoactive Drugs, Journal of Transpersonal Psychology, Medical Hypotheses, Psychedelic Monographs & Essays,* and *Shaman's Drum.*

Even in the universities of the Catholic ghetto in which I grew up, where metaphysical speculation was highly approved, the general assumption was that the noumenal order of things could not

be perceived. One got to it only by subtle argument, by "transcendental reductions" and other such inferential, speculative acrobatics. (The ordinary pious Catholic who prayed before the Blessed Sacrament may have known otherwise, but such pedestrian experience was typically ignored by professors of "natural theology" and theology.) But is metaphysics a matter of "immediate perceptions"? Without argument? The eyewitness of a hack reporter? If true, this would be first-order cultural news. Psychedelics provided the gate-opener for just this announcement.

DAVID TOOLAN, *FACING WEST FROM CALIFORNIA SHORES: A JESUIT'S JOURNEY INTO NEW AGE CONSCIOUSNESS,* 1987

This essay is adapted from the personal account of an anonymous fellow student at Harvard Divinity School. It describes what occurred when he took LSD on the morning of Good Friday 1994, and attended a three-hour church service starting at noon in Boston University's Marsh Chapel. According to the student: "I sat quietly during the service and experienced spiritual insights that transformed my understanding of the Christian faith. Though my use of LSD on that occasion was illegal I chose to take it as an exercise in freedom of religion, which did not intrude on other people's freedom. This account of my experience is offered in that spirit."

BACKGROUND

The original, so-called Good Friday Experiment held in 1962 was designed by Walter Pahnke, a doctoral student at Harvard Divinity School who already held an M.D. degree. He was assisted by Dr. Walter Houston Clark, a professor of the psychology of religion at Andover-Newton School of Theology, and by Dr. Timothy Leary, who then was teaching graduate student seminars in psychology at Harvard University.

The experiment was designed to test whether entheogens (in this case psilocybin) could induce a mystical experience if administered in the appropriate setting to people psychologically prepared for such an experience. Though subsequent critiques identified flaws in the experiment's design, it was among the best experiments using entheogens when these substances still were legal.

Pahnke and his colleagues assembled twenty divinity students (mostly from Andover-Newton) at Marsh Chapel on the Boston University campus on the morning of Good Friday 1962. Since the experiment was double-blind, neither the students nor the administrators knew which ten of the students got a pill containing 30 mg of psilocybin, and which ten got the placebo, niacin (chosen because it induces a physiological reaction—flushing—but no psychological effects). One problem with the experiment is that the effects of entheogens are so unmistakable that everyone present knew within about twenty minutes who got what.

The result was that more than half of the students who got psilocybin reported having a mystical experience compared with almost none of those who got niacin.

Pahnke wrote up the experiment for his doctoral thesis and went on to work with terminally ill cancer patients at Spring Grove Hospital in Baltimore. There he administered LSD and other entheogens to the patients (with their fully informed consent) in order to facilitate a psychological transition to a more cosmic perspective that in most cases eased their minds as they approached death. He himself died soon afterward, in 1971, while scuba diving in the ocean. His body was never recovered.

GOOD FRIDAY 1994

On the morning of Good Friday 1994, I and two fellow students—a man and a woman—from Harvard Divinity School met off-campus to share a religious experience inspired by Pahnke's experiment in 1962. I was then in the second semester of a master's degree program in world religions with an emphasis on mystical traditions. At 10:30 a.m. we ingested low doses of LSD. Each dose was equal, I would estimate, to 75 micrograms. A minimum optimal dose of LSD is normally 100 to 125 micrograms, but 75 is substantially above the basic threshold dose of 50.

After downing our experimental "sacramental" we walked from the vicinity of HDS to Boston University's Marsh Chapel, taking a path along the Charles River. As we entered the vestibule one of the first things I noticed was this statement emblazoned above the main doors leading into the nave:

LET THIS CHAPEL AT THE CENTER
OF THE UNIVERSITY CAMPUS
SIGNIFY FOREVER THE CENTRALITY
BOTH OF INTELLECTUAL AND EXPERIMENTAL RELIGION
IN EDUCATION AND ALSO OF DEVOTION TO GOD'S
RIGHTEOUS RULE IN HUMAN LIFE.

I assumed that these words had been written or spoken by Dr. Howard Thurman, an expert on religious mysticism who served as the Dean of Marsh Chapel from 1953 to 1965 and who conducted a Good Friday service there in 1962 during Pahnke's experiment. Later I learned that the source of the quote was former BU President Daniel L. Marsh, for whom the chapel is named, and whose ashes are interred in the communion rail.

Before entering the nave of the main chapel, my companions and I paid a visit to Robinson Chapel, a meditation sanctuary in the basement where the original experiment had taken place. The doors were open and the lights were on but it was empty. Someone had left a single red rose on an unadorned wood altar, which is located at the far end of the room just below three small stained glass windows, each measuring approximately three feet high by one foot wide. It reminded me of something I had read only two days earlier, in Walter Houston Clark's essay "Life Begins at Sixty" in *Psychedelic Reflections,* an anthology compiled by Lester Grinspoon and James Bakalar:

It began to dawn on me that the origins of some philosophical and religious ideas might be better understood by a scholar who had ingested and experienced the psychedelics. My basic view of the Bible changed when, under psilocybin, I witnessed the aura of a rose and realized that the burning bush of Moses was something very similar. Previously I had thought of the story as merely symbolic.

I also remembered these lines from Aldous Huxley's book *Heaven and Hell:*

"God first planted a garden." The statement expresses a deep psychological truth. Horticulture has its sources—or at any rate one of its sources—in the Other World of the mind's antipodes. When worshippers offer flowers at the altar, they are returning to the gods things, which they know, or (if they are not visionaries) obscurely feel, to be indigenous to heaven.

Had we been preceded that morning by another pilgrim? I promised myself that on future Good Fridays, if I should return to that chapel, I would leave a single red rose on the altar in gratitude—not homage—to the ones who went before us into the garden.

We then went upstairs and spent most of the next three hours attending the service from noon to 3:00 p.m., a series of ecumenical "meditations," with musical interludes, on the seven last statements of Jesus on the cross. (A similar service, including Howard Thurman's heartfelt reading of his "Prayer for Peace,"* was held on the day of the original experiment and piped downstairs into Robinson Chapel.) Each meditation began with a hymn, a Bible reading, and comments by a minister or theologian.

As I sat through the opening prayers and the first meditation, which included a moving, chromatic rendition of "Amazing Grace," I became introspective about my religious beliefs. From birth until late

---

*See page 104 for the text of the "Prayer for Peace."

adolescence I had been a Roman Catholic, but in high school my faith had succumbed to bitter cynicism. One thing in particular had made me disillusioned with the God of Christianity: a problem called "theodicy." According to Catholic teaching, God is infinitely powerful and infinitely good. As such, one would assume that God has both the power and the will to make a universe in which evil and suffering do not exist. And yet there is evil and suffering. This seems to indicate either that God is not all-powerful, that God is not all-good, or that there is no God. For most of the previous twenty-five years I had tended to embrace the latter option. But in truth I was only a "practical" atheist. Undecided as to whether God exists or not, I found the universe so basically unfair that in *effect* at least, it seemed to me, there is no God. What I regarded as especially unfair was the common belief that God creates all living things without letting them choose in advance if they want to be born into a world full of suffering where every living thing must eventually die. From this perspective I considered Christianity to be a kind of death cult, and its emblem—the crucified Jesus, who allegedly was God's own son—a fitting symbol of God's great injustice. "Christians testify that Jesus Christ was crucified, died, and was buried; on the third day he arose again from the dead," I used to tell my friends. "His resurrection is supposed to matter most. But then they symbolize their faith with little images of Jesus dead and nailed to the cross! That's pretty morbid, don't you think?"

Such had been my thoughts before Good Friday 1994. Now I found myself sitting at peace in Marsh Chapel, suffused with a spiritual glow of receptivity to God that I attribute to LSD's entheogenic effects. My eyes turned to a cross on the altar that did not include an effigy of Jesus. As I studied it, feeling myself on the verge of some new understanding, the Reverend Michael Thomas, a Lutheran Chaplain, read the following passage from Luke 23: 39–43 that was the focus of the second meditation.

One of the criminals who were hanged there [on crosses beside the cross Jesus was nailed to] kept deriding him and saying, "Are you not the Messiah? Save yourself and us!" But the other rebuked him, saying, "Do you not fear God, since you are under the same sentence of condemnation? And we indeed have been condemned justly, for we are getting what we deserve for our deeds, but this man has done nothing wrong." Then he said, "Jesus, remember me when you come into your kingdom." He replied, "Truly I tell you, today you will be with me in Paradise."

I had often heard this story growing up in the Catholic school system but never had I really taken notice of it. Now Rev. Thomas, in his comments that followed the reading, pointed out something that I had not known. Nowhere else in the New Testament does anyone call Jesus by his name when addressing him. In every other case he is called Lord or something similar. Only this criminal addressed him as a brother—without deference, with compassion—when they both were on the verge of death. He transcended his own suffering and mortal fear to ease another human being's pain. In doing so, it suddenly occurred to me, the criminal brought Jesus face to face with something Jesus had displayed to other people but which he himself, perhaps, had never seen before: the living Christ. That would have been a timely vindication of his mission, helping Jesus to transcend his own despair. He then rallied and offered the criminal words of encouragement.

In later months this insight helped resolve my animosity toward God and Christianity. Eventually I came to see the crucifix as representing something very different from what I thought before, both as a Christian and during my years as a practical atheist. What if Jesus really were the Son of God, not in the mortal sense of lineage but rather as God incarnated in one human being who, like any other human being, was denied the sure knowledge that each individual life is immortal. In the past I had imagined God as something like a schoolyard bully, willing to dish out a beating without knowing what it feels like to get one. Maybe God had come to see it that way, too, and decided to experience what we do in order to balance the scales of justice. The crucifixion then would be an act of perfect love by which God signaled that despite

God's silence we are not alone; that life has meaning; that our death is not the end. I do not know of any other god in any of the world's great religions throughout history who incarnated as a human being for that purpose. (Bodhisattvas come close but the Buddhist tradition does not represent them as gods.) This transformed my understanding of the crucifix from representing "Jesus dead and nailed to the cross" to a depiction of the *temporary* death of God by God's own choice.

A sea of change had occurred in my relationship to God. But I did not invest much time on that Good Friday working out the implications. Instead, at a point just before the meditation that began at 1:50, I experienced an urge to feel sunlight on my face, and I left the chapel. I had recently read a book by Llewelyn Powys (*Impassioned Clay*) in which he argues that the only true god for human beings is the sun, which induces and sustains all life directly or indirectly and illuminates what lies hidden in physical darkness. Yes, I thought, sitting outside on the steps of Marsh Chapel with spring in the air after Boston's worst winter in years, the sun is something like a god on days like this. It blessed me with a tactile glow that lasted well into the night.

Before returning to the service at 2:20, I revisited Robinson Chapel, this time alone. The lights had been turned off and the rose was gone. In the dark at the end of the room I saw the colors of the stained glass windows glowing like jewels on a black velvet cloth: cobalt blue and amethyst and garnet red and emerald and alabaster. For a while I watched from a distance, recalling the concept if not the particular words of Huxley's astute observation in *Heaven and Hell* about the evocative power of stained glass windows touching the unconscious. Then the central window caught my eye. I drew close and imagined my predecessors during the original experiment in 1962 doing likewise. Its theme was a biblical passage that the artist, Charles J. Connick, had worked into the design: "Ye shall know the truth, and the truth shall make you free." The words were inscribed on the pages of an open book held by a figure I took to be Jesus, who was rendered with unusual restraint: he seemed to me more human than exalted, yet divine in the sense that we all are emanations or mirrors of the ultimate ground of

Being. This puts a new spin on that famous New Testament passage in I Corinthians 13:12: "For now we see in a mirror, dimly, but then we will see face to face. Now I know only in part; then I will know fully, even as I have been fully known." No doubt the artist would have argued that I missed the point. But maybe not. Huxley in *Heaven and Hell* pointed out that the "best vision-inducing art is produced by men and women who have themselves had the visionary experience." In any case, it seemed to me while standing there that God indeed is light (John 1:5) and enlightenment therefore a sacrament.

When the service was over my two fellow students shared with me what they had experienced. The man, who is not a Christian, reported that the main chapel's architecture, heavily embellished with wood statues of Jesus, the gospel writers, and various saints, made him feel contemplative. "I felt repentant," he told me, "like it was a place for contemplation, where I could pursue my own line of thought undisturbed. The chapel was half-full and a short homily was being delivered. I looked at my program and read for a while, and when I had forgotten my self-consciousness started to better examine my thoughts without possibility of interruption. I knew I had three hours of peace, and that made me happy. I suddenly realized that I could begin serious meditation in this space. I was at home.

"It was a rather emotionless space, really," he continued. "My time was occupied with the incredible clarity of thought possible on LSD, so that I could follow any chain of ideas and associations as far as I liked. I began a one-pointed concentration meditation. I was rushing toward a tiny point at high speed, and leaving behind the physical presence of my surroundings. I was getting toward the ultimate samadhic state and, on the verge, I thought it wouldn't be the right place to experience bliss for an unpredictable length of time. So I stopped short of this breathtakingly successful exercise—breathtaking because it was so rapid and pure, with none of the normal distractions. And at that point I opened my eyes to the physical space I was in.

"It was all right. In retrospect, I must say that the rapidity of the near samadhi I had experienced could have been partly a function of the peacefulness and security of the chapel environment, both its physical silence as well as its temporal security; that it would be so for three hours, no matter what; and that I had no social obligations, such as 'touching base' with my companions."

The woman student later told me that her appreciation of entheogens "resides in the possibility to reaccess the soteriological drama and the divinity of Jesus, through a kind of liturgical theosis. I think I realized this at the Good Friday service." When I asked her to elaborate, she said:

"Entheogens take us beyond the boundaries of daily living, into a seldom-visited world, which we consider as *mysterium tremendum et fascinans,* a realm ascribed to God and/or to the recesses of our minds, of our psyches. However, they never take us into unknown lands. Entheogens, I believe, are revelatory media, channels unveiling what is hidden, not what is foreign. There is a difference. Entheogens do not "create" but they merely (I don't mean "merely" in a pejorative sense) unveil. Thus we ought not be surprised by what we encounter on an entheogenic journey, whether it be God or ourselves.

"What concerns me now," she said, "is the religious use of entheogens, hence the encounter of/with God. Entheogens taken at a high dose induce visions; taken at a lower dose—and this has been my experience so far—they are less vision-producing. However, something happens at whatever level of dosage. I have only read reports of visions. I will not comment on that since it is foreign to my experience. But what did I encounter? It was Good Friday; I encountered a crucified Christ. A vision? No—a revelation! A meeting that took place at the very core of my being, essence meeting essence.

"I guess the visceral problem between Christianity and entheogens resides in the theological approach. If these substances are used liturgically, we must be willing to construct a whole new theological paradigm that could sustain such a liturgical movement. And that," she concluded, "is the difficulty!"

On returning that night to my room in the HDS dormitory, I tried phoning Walter Clark to let him know that his good work is still appreciated. He had not answered an earlier letter and I had not followed up because I feared the worst and resisted confronting my fear. A woman answered: his new live-in housekeeper. No, Dr. Clark was unable to take phone calls; he's now ninety-one years old and pretty much out of it these days. His secretary has been discharged; he no longer has need of a secretary. But yes, she said, he does respond appreciatively to visitors even though he seldom recognizes anyone. I said that I would try to visit. Then I asked her to tell him that I and some friends had remembered him that day by making a pilgrimage to Marsh Chapel during the meditation service, and that we had found a red rose on the altar. "He'll know what that means," I said. She promised to convey the message.

Time ran out before I made that visit. Walter died on December 15, 1994, at the age of ninety-two. An obituary published in *The New York Times* noted: "He spoke out for people arrested for using LSD and other hallucinogenic substances for what they said were solely religious purposes." I have tried to do the same with equal honesty and courage in this essay describing my reasons for taking an illegal sacramental in the course of my personal faith journey.

"The Prayer for Peace" by Howard Thurman, recited by him at the service on Good Friday, 1962, in Boston University's Marsh Chapel:

Our Father, fresh from the world with the smell of life upon us, we make an act of prayer in the silence of this place. Our minds are troubled because the anxieties of our hearts are deep and searching. We are stifled by the odor of death, which envelopes the earth, because in so many places brother fights against brother. The panic of fear, the torture of insecurity, the ache of hunger, all have fed and rekindled ancient hatreds and long forgotten memories of old struggles when the world was young and Thy children were but dimly aware of Thy Presence in the midst. For all this we seek forgiveness. There is not one of us without guilt, and before Thee we confess our sins: we are proud and arrogant; we are selfish and greedy; we have harbored in our hearts and minds much that makes for bitterness, hatred, and revenge. While we wait in Thy Presence, search our spirits and grant to our minds the guidance and the wisdom that will teach us the way to take, without which there can be no peace and no confidence anywhere. Teach us how to put at the disposal of Thy Purposes of Peace the fruits of our industry, the products of our minds, the vast wealth of our land, and the resources of our spirit. Grant unto us the courage to follow the illumination of this hour to the end that we shall not lead death to any man's door but rather may we strengthen the hands of all in high places and in common tasks who seek to build a friendly world, of friendly men, beneath a friendly sky. This is the simple desire of our hearts, which we share with Thee in quiet confidence. Amen.

9

Las noches de los ayahuasqueros

Will Penna

Will Penna, retired now, has been a high school teacher of English and English as a Second Language both here and abroad for thirty-five years. His earliest entheogenic experiences date to almost forty years ago, influenced by Aldous Huxley's *The Doors of Perception,* Alan Watts' *The Joyous Cosmology,* and excerpts from Henri Michaux's journal of his mescaline experiments, *Miserable Miracle.* Prior to his ayahuasca journeys in the Amazon in 1994 chronicled here, he had gone through a powerful reintegrative experience during a California Men's Gathering. Much of his life experiences writing, traveling, reading, and reflecting can be glimpsed at his website www.BeatHippieRaver.com. He looks upon his spiritual journey to Nepal this fall, some seven years after the conference that was the genesis of this book, as the next classroom in his universal schoolhouse.

◆

One teacher suggested that the Adam [MDMA] experience facilitates the dissolving of barriers between body, mind, and spirit: one senses the aware presence of spirit infusing the structures of the body and the images and attitudes of the mind. Awareness expands to include all parts of the body, all aspects of mind, and the "higher" reaches of Spirit—thus permitting a kind of reconnecting, a remembering of the totality of our experience, an access to forgotten truths.

SOPHIA ADAMSON, *THROUGH THE GATEWAY OF THE HEART*, 1985

INTRODUCTION

In the fall of 1994, four companions and I made a spiritual journey from Northern California to several of the world's holiest places in Latin America: Lake Titicaca, Cuzco, Machu Picchu, the Chilean Andes for a total solar eclipse, the upper Amazon, Tikal, and Lake Atitlan. At each station of our journey we performed sacred rituals, usually with both fellow travelers and indigenous peoples. And as we five got deeper into our trek, the focus and direction of our pilgrimage became clearer to each of us.

For me, as a lifelong teacher of English and English as a Second Language, the call was the deep instruction that our Mother Earth and Father Sky were inexorably presenting to me at each turn. After thirty-four fulfilling years of teaching, an inner prompting had called me away from my classroom into other rooms of the universal schoolhouse. My therapist, one of the founders of the Spiritual Emergence Network, had used a term from transpersonal psychology to describe my state: a positive disintegration. Suddenly, my heart was no longer in the day-to-day practice of the schoolroom. With the connection between head and heart and body broken, I needed to surrender to that inner teacher, intuition, to take me where it would. And, quite unexpectedly, it took me to Pucallpa, Peru.

We five sojourners had done our homework months in advance. Some of us were fluent in Spanish and had traveled in Hispanic lands. All of us studied and shared with each other our learnings about the countries and cultures we would visit. We practiced and honed our backpacking skills and yeomanship. More importantly, we prepared ourselves through regular rituals to surrender to what would come to us. We clarified our intentions and invoked them to one another as we passed the pipe and shared our visions in our sacred circle beneath stars and moon, oak and redwood.

We knew we were on the edge of an "immense inevitability." We laughed at phrases like that, pretentious and portentous as they were, but they came to us at times. In our visions, mischievous machine elves showed up to both distract and lead us, and they became our totems: eagle, lion, turtle, and chameleon. The skies became lofty birds, the rivers became sinuous snakes, the forests became roaring beasts, the earth a sleeping soul. Yet only two of us had some slight idea, from our readings of the deep iconography, of what we were experiencing—and how it presaged what we would see in Pucallpa.

At this point, when we were planning our trip, Pucallpa was merely a point on a map, a place where a friend had said we could meet one Agustin Rivas, sculptor and leader for shamanic journeys. Although two of us had seen former shaman Pablo Amaringo's book of visionary art and stories, *Ayahuasca Visions,* none of us had planned to visit him or knew that he was in Pucallpa. Even I—the schoolteacher—did not know of his Usko-Ayar School of Amazonian Painting or its good works, both among those in the Peruvian Amazonas and its world-wide mission.

When we arrived in Pucallpa, only to find don Agustin busy elsewhere, a series of chance encounters led us to don Pablo, the school, and the three shamans, don Benito, don Guillermo, and don Francisco, who were to lead us on our first South American vision quests. The two visionary evenings recounted here were followed by further journeying with a don Leonardo when we stayed hundreds of miles north of Pucallpa in the Amazon, three hours by launch out of Iquitos on the border of Brazil and Colombia.

The sacred tea prepared by these ayahuasqueros consisted of *Banisteriopsis caapi,* the ayahuasca vine containing the beta-carbolines harmine, harmaline, and tetrahydroharmine, and *Psychotria viridis,* the chacruna vine containing N,N-dimethyltryptamine. The sacramental union of these two substances is regarded as creating a synergistic communion with their spiritual and earthly snake mothers. This connection is the basis for the sacrament's power in healing, guiding, and re-creating. The rest I have recounted in "Las noches de los ayahuasqueros."

I have attempted to capture, through use of Spanish and Quechua as well as English, my sense of the magic and the mystery of this healing, guiding, and re-creational experience for me. By interpreting them in context, I have endeavored to make foreign words and phrases transparent. I have tried, through not letting usual capitalization and punctuation break up the flow of language, to impart a sense of the spiritual channel I was in. If I have succeeded in some small measure to share this transformative experience with you, to that extent the Great Spirit has guided me.

Las noches de los ayahuasqueros

the journey begins

sangre de la selva
a fellow journeyer dreamed that phrase
out of my vision this first night with the shamans
blood of the jungle
pumps here now through each of us

es el tiempo del te con don benito
I approach him with my companions
seeking to have my ayahuasca vision quest
it is the time for you with don benito
now that evening brings us all here

cantos de los insectos y danzas de las plantas
around us in the palm thatch open bungalow
at least thirty other seekers wait as well
insects sing and plants dance
as we contemplate our own ceremony

ser listo es todo . . . estar listo es todo
don pablo shaman turned painter and teacher
has led me here in spirit and now the time has come
to be alert is all . . . to be ready is everything
for our vision and for our cure

sus sonrisas en la sombra
nervous children laugh and cry
a man coughs continually and a woman suckles as
their smiles in the darkness
begin to spread across all of us now

todo el mundo esta respirando
everyone becomes as one body
our breathing and our heartbeats
all the world is inhaling and exhaling
and we are parts of that whole

siempre estamos juntos siempre
the images inevitably arrive with
spanish subtitles and quechua sonorities
always we are together always
without our bidding or desire

la vida es sueno . . . un ilusion
the journey from everyday ego
carries us to amorphic anarchies
life is but a dream . . . an illusion
of the entity behind the dream

cielo hasta cielo hasta cielo
inside and outside . . . ceilings and heavens
boundaries are finally dissolved
heaven until heaven until heaven
dualisms are finally resolved

donde termina el mundo
our ancestors sing bittersweet songs

in the living vines we drink tonight
where the world ends
and we live on emboldened by their spirits

hueso de la noche
we are all part of one great animal
a body asleep to its parts
the bone of night
strong and sharp sweet and singing

gitana luna y tierra madre
just weeks before we journeyers saw
the lunar dancer eclipse the fiery sun
gypsy moon and mother earth
and our whole world stopped

¡alto, mas alto, joven de pelo de plata!
in my own crazy dancing journey I tell all
that I am fifty-seven going on seventeen
higher! ever higher, boy with the silver hair!
and my young companions are my teachers of life

estrellas Viejas . . . estrellas nuevas
we are all stars we are all starmatter
we are all lightbodies we are all light
old stars . . . new stars
it makes no difference where you are

estamos unidos . . . estamos como uno
we end where we began
with our identity encountered at last
we are united . . . we are as one
we come to know again as we once did before

vision one

sangre de la selva
red earth of pucallpa jungle palpitates in the night

sylvan alchemy transforms us to its will
backlighted clouds arch over us
es el tiempo del te con don benito
don guillermo y don francisco
the three dons sit before us
dogs bark at the nearly-full moon behind us
tuk-tuks putter and sputter on the road beyond
we visitors to the ceremony hover in, awe
canta de los insectos y danzas de las plantas
we find our place in the yellow light bulb night
the amazon abuzz and ashimmer before us

verde de verde de verde de verde
the green tea is passed and supped deeply
by gringos and other green participants
we wait . . . the readiness is all
ser listo es todo . . . estar listo es todo
the light shifts through the open thatch
shadows crawl across the pitched palm roof
silence becomes deafening
stillness becomes vertigo
I suddenly wonder . . . am I ready?
now that it is too late not to be ready
estan llamando . . . they are calling
estan corriendo . . . they are running

behind my eyelids another world unfolds
machine elves try to distract me
sus sonrisas en la sombra
diverting me with amusement park distractions
tempting me with fabulous rides to nowhere
but I push through their trompe l'oeil masque
smoke and mirrors: false doors and lascivious leers
to the realm of the angels
angelos arcangelos succubi y otros

silvery neon beings who usher me on
their beckoning arms outstretched to me
across an arc of ultraviolet sky

el primero arcoiris . . . the first rainbow to cross
reach out! reach out and join us! they urge
but the harder I jump the more daunting the task
then when I remember to breathe and relax
¡presto! todo el mundo esta respirando
and in that breath I am with them
we are one together in a timeless instant
but now they reach out to me across a watery gulf

el segundo arcoiris . . . the second rainbow to traverse
a wide fluid barrier heaves between us
here we are! here we are! come forward! they call
I try my best, set my mark, hunch forward
with all my might . . . but I know I cannot swim it
so I relax and breathe deeply again
and before I know it I am with them again
siempre estamos juntos siempre
indissolubly joined together forever as always
yet again we are apart and they are way above me

la vida es sueno . . . on ilusion
across still another rainbow . . . this time a stairway
el tercero arcoiris . . . escalera de la tierra invisible
as I strain to climb the massive stone steps
I realize I can never ascend them
but in a breath I am there with my guides
adonitas surrounding me . . . sheltering me
and yet one more time they fade before me

el cuatro arco . . . fiery films fan between us
I faint as fumes buffet my every move
but now I know I need only focus my energy

I inhale . . . exhale . . . inhale—and ¡presto!
before me all lies as long before
cielo hasta cielo hasta cielo
beyond the celestial blue beyond the nocturnal ceiling
beyond the waters beyond the land beyond the sky itself
solar others constantly urging me on and on
beyond the suns and stars whence we came
to the end of the world . . . donde termina el mundo
and so I know why I am here and where I have to go

vision two

hueso de la noche
this second night is seamless and sharp
the southern hemisphere sky static
don benito's jungly barrio rattles
children's firecrackers . . . boombox salsa
ailing autos . . . all compete tonight
in contrast with last night's ritual passage
this nocturnal dance is different for
gitana luna y tierra madre
etched in moonlight packs of dogs howl
counterpoint to the don's tea
one companion's vomit
spreads quicksilver across the earth
another jitters having lost his center and
a third has stayed at don pablo's school
rather than be here with us
but my angels are with me again

¡alto,mas alto, joven de pelo de plata!
they call ¡alto, mas alto!
and I roll my eyes higher and higher
behind the dome of my eyelids
until I see the iridescent night sky
filled with as many constellations as possible

but no more . . . until we arrive at
the fourth dimension

estrellas nuevas estrellas viejas
starlight starbright star I wish upon tonight
and below the stars they loom
circling the huge edifaces' pinnacles
countless golden zephyr star vehicles
each with a glowing chauffeur
urging me in . . . urging me on
but each time I approach
they disappear in a flash
space ship driver and all
¡presto! the cake falls in the oven
I relax I breathe and I rest my eyes
¡pero, mira! ¡templos de la ciencia!
and I see them all there again
or are they here and I there?

however it is I know that soon very soon
we will all be ready to drive
from their halls of science to
beyond the farthest galaxy
estamos unidos . . . estamos como uno
like we always were . . . always are
they call they fade away they call
I strain I breathe I strain I breathe
then it makes no difference
todo es igual

the spiritual eminence they call usko ayar
it is that one who reassures me
we are all part we are all whole
thus I also come to know once again
however the slowest among us moves
so too do we all move in the first dimension

the home from which we sprang
sacha-mama the forest
yaku-mama the waters
huaira-mama the air
usko ayar shows me
the three shamans
banco in the jungle bench
muraya in the watery realms
sumiruna in the skies above

usko ayar further shows me that
it is not yet time for my final trip
in the supay-lanchas to the land of the dead
the soul launches I have just seen
in the second dimension reveal to me
that I will come to know again
as I did as a child the abode of
sea and river spirits
earth and forest shades
air and wind ghosts
even the playful gnomes
who tried to distract me
during my first vision
finally usko ayar will guide me away
from fear that robber of souls
but now I am ready for the gifts
from the dons' third dimension
the realm of sacred songs and magic vapors

icaros sung with the visions

en-e-wah-yah en-e-wah-yah
ri-or-di-e ri-or-di-e
yeh-she-va-ro yeh-seh-va-ro

first one then another of the dons' voices rise
embroidering ethereal songs of the soul

their harmonies cross and crisscross
not unlike the shipibo needlework
following the warp and weave that
bind us all if we had eyes to see ears to hear
impossible registers from these old men
contralto castrato falsetto they suggest
sounds from the steppes of central asia
from tuva and tibet but also from titicaca
diaphanous like the andean quena
and my soul sings to their melodies
as I create sounds I never knew I knew

en-e-wah-yah en-e-wah-yah
ri-or-di-e ri-or-di-e
yeh-seh-va-ro yeh-seh-va-ro

in a language I never knew I knew
I join in the joyous and holy noise
the icaro choir moves from space to space
throughout this thatched roof temple
each one seeking to be cured approaches
and offers agua florida to the don
who opens it and anoints the seeker
with it as well as the rich tobacco smoke
con cuerpo preparado . . . el tabaquero fume
sacred fumes and blessed phlegm
the don chants smokes and lays on hands
singing and flinging each sacramental cure
until we are all bound for that night's glory

en-e-wah-yah en-e-wah-yah
ri-or-di-e ri-or-di-e
yeh-seh-va-ro yeh-seh-va-ro

the hovering sound shifts over and over
rising and falling throughout the congregation

first like the golden zephyr coming to take us away
then like a supay-lancha to return to the dead
or finally like a flying disk to carry us past the sun
we all feel it but they who kneel with their don
feel it most of all receiving their curing powers
oh! how pure and spare this unaccountable source
we have sung to the aliens . . . to those we dismiss
and we sing here now as if we've done this before
and from that other where and other when
vibrational healing resonates us up on its beam
gift of our blending of our nature and bonding of our
  soul

en-e-wah-yah en-e-wah-yah
ri-or-di-e ri-or-di-e
yeh-seh-va-ro yeh-seh-va-ro

10
Mysterious Tea

Annelise Schinzinger

Annelise Schinzinger is a hospice caregiver and practitioner of Chi Nei Tsang (Chinese Inner Organ Massage) in the San Francisco Bay Area. She holds a bachelor's degree from the University of California, Irvine, in Portuguese and Spanish and is certified in Human Resources Management. Ms. Schinzinger has worked as a translator and interpreter for ethnobotanists and environmentalists traveling to Brazil, feels passionately about the power of plants to expand consciousness and healing, and has worked with plant allies in Brazil since 1977. Her interests include the study and application of herbal preparations, the preservation of our sacred planet, and writing.

It is my firm conviction, based on more than fifteen years of specialized study of hallucinogens and culture, that these substances have played more than a minor role in structuring the lives, beliefs, hopes, and values of large numbers of people. Members of preindustrial societies in many cultures with varying epistemological perspectives have always incorporated mind-altering plants into facets of daily activity. The economic

behavior, the social organization, and the belief systems of
some societies, for example, have been affected by the use of
mind-altering plants. . . .

The contribution that anthropology can make to the
study of the use of mind-altering plants throughout the
world is to show how cultural variables such as belief
systems, values, attitudes, and expectations structure one
of the most subjective experiences available to humankind.

MARLENE DOBKIN DE RIOS, *HALLUCINOGENS:*
CROSS-CULTURAL PERSPECTIVES, 1990

I have had a close relationship with Hoasca (the Portuguese translit-
eration for Ayahuasca) since 1977, when I drank the tea for the first
time in Sao Paulo, Brazil, as a university student. A friend had told me
there was a tea that would be good for me. That's all he revealed, and
that's all I knew when I drank Hoasca for the first time. That experience at age twenty-one changed my life. The vivid memory of the
session remains with me to this day: symbols and images of spiritual
significance to me were engraved in my memory. My heart blossomed
with this first glass of Hoasca and with eagerness, innocence, and
some trepidation, I ventured forth into the new world that Hoasca
had opened in me.

Hoasca is the name given to a sacramental tea made from a vine
(*Banisteriopsis caapi*) and leaves from a bush (*Psychotria viridis*). Hoasca
facilitates unified consciousness and the clearing of mind and heart. In
1977, I became a member of the *Centro Espirito Beneficente União do
Vegetal* (Beneficent Spiritual Center Union of the Plants). Union of the
Plants refers to the union of the two plants Hoasca is made of: mariri
(*Banisteriopsis*) and chacrona (*Psycotria*). The connotation of union
extends further, to the union of masculine (*mariri*) and feminine (*chacrona*) and those principles within ourselves; the union of force (*mariri*)
with light (*chacrona*); and the alignment of human consciousness with
the spirit realm, and with all that is. Plant spirits are here to teach us
if we will only listen. I feel it is our responsibility, as part of conscious

creation, to embody the valuable insight gained in expanded states of consciousness and to manifest that insight in our lives.

Jose Gabriel da Costa (Mestre Gabriel) established the União do-Vegetal (UDV) in Porto Velho, Rondonia, on July 22, 1961. The UDV's teachings are based not only on the gifts Mestre Gabriel received in the enlightened state with Hoasca, but also on his years as a leader of *umbanda* (an African Brazilian sect), his Portuguese Catholic roots, exposure to *Mesa Branca* (Kardecist) spiritualism, and the influence of the shamanic practices of the Bolivian Indians with whom he tapped rubber and drank Ayahuasca. The result is a syncretic religion with a rich blend of traditions and beliefs molded into the cultural context of the environment of the times. The sixties in the Amazon were wild (reminiscent of the Wild West of the 1860s in the United States). Many immigranted to the forest, mostly rubber tappers, walked around armed, ready to pick a fight, and fight to the kill. In the Brazilian Amazon the União do Vegetal, with Mestre Gabriel as spiritual guide, represented order—a taming of the wild. Many of the men in Mestre Gabriel's time were rubber tappers and acted in violent or overtly aggressive ways. One mestre told us that before he began drinking the tea, he proclaimed in a drunken dare that he would bite off his thumb, and showed us the stubble that now remains. Through the expanding awareness Hoasca provides, the people learned to tame their tempers, respect themselves and others more, and consequently lead more peaceful lives. Members of the UDV were rebels in their day, in the sense that they defied authorities to practice their religion to the point of Mestre Gabriel being arrested and put in jail.

Hoasca is an entheogen and deserves to be regarded as a sacred substance and given that reverence. At a rock concert in Rio de Janeiro in 1991, Hoasca was sold in the parking lot by a vendor advertising it as an aphrodisiac. It is true that Hoasca can stimulate sexual energy through the expansive state of being it induces—a state of openness and receptivity in which defenses dissipate, heightening sensitivity, trust, and love. Misuse is subject to definition, which is often simply a judgment call, but it primarily has to do with whether a person is ready for Hoasca in the set and setting of his or her choice. Hoasca has a power to open one to all that is, and this power needs to be respected. Hoasca can stir up psychic compost as well as shoot one into the cosmos. I do not recommend casual or recreational use. When used with experienced people in sacred context a safety net is created. Following extensive investigation, the Brazilian Federal Narcotics Council (CONFEM) proclaimed in 1992 that they had found no evidence of Hoasca (or Daime) causing ill effects or abuse, and granted legal status for the use of Hoasca in religious contexts.

The UDV currently has seventy-six centers for distribution in Brazil, with over six thousand members. Regularly scheduled sessions are held on the first and third Saturdays of the month, from 8:00 p.m. to midnight, with participants often numbering in the hundreds. The environment of the sessions is harmonious, supportive, and orderly— necessary for such large numbers. In fact, obedience is key: obedience to the order and rhythm established in sessions, influenced by the flow of energy in Nature; and obedience to Spirit, as revealed to each individual. The UDV emphasizes the role of family and community, and people of all ages, walks of life, and religious backgrounds participate. Whether a maid or an engineer, an ex–Mother Superior or a doctor, members make a commitment to their spiritual growth. Entire families attend, from children to grandparents, although the official age to associate is eighteen—the age at which one is considered to have the ability to take responsibility for one's actions.

Hoasca is distributed by the mestre conducting the session, followed by the reading of the Statutes, which inform and connect participants with the purpose, history, and ideology of the União do Vegetal. The Statutes speak of *mariri* and *chacrona,* to awaken that which was sleeping and to open participants to the mysteries Hoasca reveals. *Chamadas* (calls/invocations) are made to ask Divine Nature for permission to penetrate the enchantments and to open the session. By accepting the invitation when the *burracheira* (pronounced bu-hah-shair-ra and meaning "strange force"/altered state of consciousness) presents itself, one is given the opportunity to enter an opened state of awareness. Music is played and *chamadas* are made to regulate the force and light of the session.

Communing with Hoasca is a journey of self-discovery. Hoasca incarnates Spirit in sentient experience, prompting some to refer to Hoasca as the religion of feeling. It is truly one of the best vehicles I know for openhearted sensitivity. Biochemically, neurotransmitters are stimulated when we drink the sacrament, but it is important to bear in mind that Hoasca is known as *cha misterioso* (mysterious tea). Sometimes we drink the tea and don't feel anything. I know of three men with a history of drug use who each drank the tea on six occasions thinking they were going to get high in the way they had with heroin, cocaine, or marijuana. It was not until they let go of the notion that Hoasca is a drug that they were able to experience the *burracheira*. There is more to the tea experience than the way the chemical components of *mariri* and *chacrona* interact with our bodies. The spirit of Hoasca plays a role, and this mystery I leave to Spirit.

I have noticed an often-remarkable change in people's attitudes and behavior prompted by the transformative power of the tea. When one drinks Hoasca and experiences an expanded state of consciousness, aspects of one's psyche that are not in alignment are brought to one's attention in a revelatory and often dramatic way. Once given the opportunity to see and experience the effects and repercussions of one's attitudes and actions, the next step depends upon the desire and will to follow the guidance and integrate the lesson into one's life. As an example, a boy I know was addicted to video games. That's all he wanted to do. One day he asked his father, a mestre, if he could participate in a session. In the enlightened state he was taken on a nightmarish ride through the video games, seen from the inside out. After the challenging ride, he decided he'd had enough of video games. Doing his schoolwork and playing outside became more meaningful.

Hoasca is a truth serum. On a personal level, Hoasca has been highly instrumental in helping me overcome a debilitating illness, by bringing into conscious awareness the root causes and effects of my attitudes, emotions, and behavior. Hoasca has enabled me to feel and perceive things on a deeper level, expanding my heart and inspiring compassion for all beings. I have seen people who have been addicted to nicotine, drugs, alcohol, and other vices drink Hoasca and quit immediately upon recognizing the extent of harm they were causing themselves and others. Hoasca has many ways of getting the message across, and it seems each way is tailor-made for the person and for that person's problem. I know that without Hoasca I would have grown spiritually, as is my nature, but the guidance and empowerment I received from this sacred tea over the years has helped me grow toward spiritual, psychological, and emotional well-being.

The União do Vegetal is a spiritual path that emphasizes taking good care of the physical: our natural environment, our bodies, relationships, home, work, community. The regularity of sessions allows for continuity of experience and relationship with Hoasca to be established. Drinking the tea twice a month facilitates "work" to be done on a step-by-step basis, with time in between to integrate spiritual experiences and bring them into the world. Internal examination is important, regarding questions of universal import, but also caring for the mundane is essential. Housecleaning is a continual need. Currents of energy flow more freely when stress, ego impediments, and the mire of unresolved issues are removed. Harmonizing relationships with others and growing into balance with all aspects of ourselves is very much a part of the UDV experience. This inner work is vitally important.

I received homework in sessions to strengthen my container, so that when I opened "doors of perception," I wouldn't be blown away. Usually this foundational work had to do with fine tuning myself in the day to day to receive more positive energy and ward off pejorative influences, as well as clearing away old baggage to make room in my heart and mind for Spirit. In one burracheira, I was literally shown a door begging to be opened, and when I did, I was transported to a realm of infinite possibilities. This powerful plant ally, when used in a reverential way, has the potential of being a conduit for Divine consciousness, stimulating us to reach our human potential. Hoasca facilitates clarity through the revelation of our true nature—the God and Goddess within, including our shadow. We must delve into the dark realms, as well as the glorious, to really know who we are. Hoasca unmasks the dark areas of our psyche and facilitates awareness of the emotions, thoughts, and actions that impede attunement with the higher self. She flashes light to the paralyzed areas of our psyche and body for healing. There is always more to know: the Universe, inner and outer, is infinite.

I have learned much with Hoasca regarding prayer and intention. At the culmination of the second conference on Hoasca sponsored by the UDV's Center for Medical Studies, I volunteered to assist three visitors on our way to a session. One of the visitors was from Spain and had her suitcase with her, as she was planning to catch a flight immediately after the session. We arrived at the temple only minutes before the session was to begin. I decided to leave the suitcase outside. I was sure it would be all right, as there was no threat of rain. I deposited her heavy suitcase at the base of a steep flight of stairs, and ran up the stairs to find seats for the guests. About forty-five minutes into the session, when I was beginning to feel the effects of the tea strongly, a gusty wind picked up and began to thrash against the building. Quite a storm was brewing, and the wind whipped and whirled in a wild, unpredictable way. It started to rain and I could hear the rain beating against the side of the building. I knew the suitcase was getting wet, and I was quite concerned. I had volunteered responsibility and had done a "half-ass" job. Now the visitor would have to lug a waterlogged bag back to Barcelona. Perhaps books, aside from clothes, would be damaged. I was in a predicament because I knew, given the physical condition I was in from the force of the tea, that it would be extremely difficult to get up, walk outside, go down the steep flight of stairs, and come back up with the heavy suitcase in hand. All I could do was remain in my chair with the sincere desire to do something. My heart and mind were clear with the intent to protect her bag. Suddenly, I felt an immense wing of energy sweep through the night sky and circle down, coming to rest with the suitcase nestled under it like the wing of a mother hen. The wind and rain stopped immediately. I breathed an incredulous sigh of relief. "So this is the way it works!"

"It is impossible to have a prayer without power. It is impossible to have a thought that is a secret, for all energy is heard," says Gary Zukav in *The Seat of the Soul*. "Aside from your level of the responsible choice of energy and how you form that into matter, the dependency on prayer assists you in pulling to yourself and invoking grace. Prayer is moving into a personal relationship with Divine Intelligence."

I had long wanted to drink Hoasca in an indigenous ceremony, and it was with the gentle Kulina that I had one of my best Hoasca sessions. Moacir Biondo, a botanist friend who is now a UDV mestre, invited me to travel with him to the Kulina reserve located in the state of Amazonas, bordering Acre. For over a decade the Kulina have been gathering medicinal plants and resin for Moacir, who is highly esteemed in their tribe. Thanks to Moacir's encouragement this group of Kulina has regained pride and appreciation for its heritage.

The Kulina ritual I participated in was held in a small hut and not outside on ceremonial ground due to torrential rains. Consequently, the number of participants was narrowed to thirteen men and women. All was silent until the effects of the tea were felt by the leaders of the ritual, by which time I was deep into the experience. An opening chant/invocation was sung, followed by continual chanting/singing for hours. First the men sang, then the women, then both . . . in the way Spirit moved them. In the session, whenever the force of the tea began to take a dip, the chanting lifted me up, keeping me in a high state of perception for hours. According to Terence McKenna, "people in the Amazon insist on the importance of chanting as a vehicle of expression when on tryptamine hallucinogens. This is a vital point, since in some way sound can control the topology of the hallucinations." This indeed has been my experience.

A vibrant macaw appeared in my vision three times in the ceremony. Each time the bird was larger than life, with feathers of brilliant shades of scarlet. After the session, I asked the *paje* (shaman) what the macaw signifies. He answered that *arara* (macaw) is the word given to the *Banisteriopsis caapi* vine they use the most in their preparation of *rami* (ayahuasca). The vine gathered from this region is known for its vision stimulating properties.

I saw rays of light emanating from the Kulina *paje* (shaman), pulsating upwards and outwards to the heavens as he sang. The *paje* also served as a focal point of reception for radiant beams of light being transmitted to the circle. (I have seen these light beams on several occasions in prayerful context, mostly in the course of sacred chanting.)

During the ceremony, I asked silently about the healing properties of several medicinal plants of the Amazon basin. As each plant presented itself to me, it revealed the wisdom of its healing power and showed how it functions on the material and spiritual planes. In a vivid image, I saw *Pau d'Arco* (*Tabebuia impetiginosa*) as an arc extending from the plant kindom (a term coined by Alan Kapuler) to the animal kindom. The energy of the plant opens a path of no resistance to the higher order of Divine Nature, allowing for the spirit of health to flow through the body/mind. I saw pipe cleaners cleaning, fine tuning, harmonizing, energizing . . . clearing channels, stimulating the immune system, going where needed to bring about balance. (*Pau d'Arco* is a plant I continue to use in tea, tincture, and flower essence form to empower the immune system.)

I went back in time in the burracheira, seeing dinosaurs in swamplands, and further yet to the time of the origins of the first organisms of plant life on this planet, then accompanied the force of vegetative evolution in fast-forward up to the present. It was fascinating and awe inspiring.

Continuing in a heightened state of awareness, I perceived the connection of native peoples to trees, and to a small degree witnessed the oppression of native peoples: enslavement and the crushing of their cultures. I perceived the improved quality of life that stems from community cooperation. An androgynous being appeared before me: two beings joined at the center, with painted faces one above the other facing each other. (To me, they represent the balance of the male/female within and the unification of opposites—the Andean ideal of balanced opposition.)

In the visionary state I witnessed the removal of a tumor (whose, I don't know) with a huge pair of tweezers. I saw native peoples, kneeling face down in a circle, with feathers on their heads converging in the center. First their headdresses were made of scarlet feathers, then exquisite blue ones. They were macaw feathers. (The Kulina I was with don't wear feathers—their adornments are made of reeds.) According to Wade Davis in *One River,* the feathers, including macaw, that are used in the headdresses of Kofan Indians represent "the memories of birds that can only be seen on yagé [Hoasca]. They [the birds] are the masters, the patrons of ecstatic intoxication."

In the burracheira I was taken to Machu Picchu and caught a glimpse of the Ritual of the Sun being celebrated during the reign of the first Inca King. Some say the royal family and those closest to the Inca King used Ayahuasca ceremonially. Ayahuasca is integral to the cultures of the Kulina, Ashaninka, and Kaxinawa, who are descendants of the Inca.

Many images flowed through my consciousness, responding to the invocation of Nature spirits and the energy circulating within me and the room—a weaving, intertwining, overlapping of images. I went outside to pee and to feel the fresh night air. It was still raining. An indigenous word for Divine Nature entered my thoughts, and at exactly that moment I saw a huge flash of light in the big night sky followed by two English words, which came to me: "drinking light."

In 1993, Dennis McKenna, Ph.D., and Charles Grob, M.D., invited me to participate in the Hoasca Research Project as an interpreter. The multinational research team investigated the psychological and biochemical effects of Hoasca on fifteen men who had been UDV members for ten or more years. Glacus de Souza, MD, UDV mestre, and consultant to the World Health Organization, coordinated the participation of hospital staff in Manaus, where the data collection took place. The study showed "remission of psychopathology (i.e., alcoholism, violent behavior, etc.) following the initiation of hoasca use along with no evidence of personality or cognitive deterioration" and in fact an increase in psychosocial skills.

For me, long-term effects include having been provided with keys to traverse portals and to penetrate some mysteries. For over eighteen years much Hoasca coursed through my body. The visions and insights I have had with this teacher and healer have ranged from simple, yet profound, to humorous, terrifying, or magnificently awe inspiring. I have seen and experienced many things, but most important to me is how I have integrated what I learned by embodying the lessons and valuable gifts from the spirit realm into daily life.

I credit entheogens with stimulating valuable insight that might have taken years or lifetimes to gain. In 1995, I left the União do Vegetal to focus on spiritual growth through dreamwork. To this day, I occasionally find myself drinking Hoasca in dreams and experiencing the burracheira. Several experiences I have had in the past few years, during which time I have not ingested entheogens, match the burracheiras in quality and content. These expanded states of consciousness have occurred spontaneously, while trance-dancing, in dreams, and in other situations. Once a relationship with a plant teacher has been established, ingesting the plant is not necessary to attain the effects. Hoasca is a good teacher: she not only opens us to what we need to know, but also teaches us how to open ourselves. Hoasca helps us to clear communication lines and access cellular memory. Expanded awareness is always present—it is simply a matter of tuning in. Life is a constant revelation of the power and brilliance of Creation. When our consciousness aligns with the creative force, and we act with integrity, clarity, and open heart, amazing things can happen. Opportunities abound in our daily lives, by centering our hearts and deepening our presence. By the gift of grace, and with conscious intent, veils can be lifted and portals opened, revealing mysteries right under the veneer.

11
A Scientist's View of Miracles and Magic

Alexander T. Shulgin

Alexander T. Shulgin, Ph.D., is a chemist/pharmacologist with academic training from Harvard and the University of California. His research, largely in the area of the creation and action of psychotropic drugs, has led to the appearance of about two hundred scientific publications and book chapters over the last fifty years. He and his wife, Ann, have coauthored the books *PIHKAL: A Chemical Love Story* and *TIHKAL: The Continuation,* which deal with the human dynamics of a number of psychedelic drugs.

◆

And then I actually saw it, right there in front of my eyes. It was . . . like a strip of water hanging in the air yet made of light and shimmering and it was at that moment I realized what had shot through me: it was the Holy Ghost.

"I saw this vision of the Cross," says Edward. "I say vision, not hallucination, because with a

hallucination—I've had plenty, what with the drugs—you see it yet you know it's false; but with this I saw it and I knew it was real. . . ."

From then on, the experience turned benign. "Put simply," said Edward, "God visited us for three hours."

For now that all-pervasive sense of wickedness was gradually replaced by the most profound joy either Edward or Jill had ever known. More, the voice of God Himself was in the flat there talking to them. Kindly, understanding, wise, telling them they'd be married eventually and have this wonderful life. Assuring them it would be Edward's calling to minister to adults, Jill's to help the young.

IAN COTTON, *THE HALLELUJAH REVOLUTION: THE RISE OF THE NEW CHRISTIANS*, 1996

Over the past several decades, I have given many lectures and addresses. Almost all of these have been to people with backgrounds in chemistry, pharmacology, or medicine, or to students who are intending to enter these fields. I was therefore expected to speak in chemical or pharmacological terms, using languages in which both they and I are reasonably fluent. My lecture material has always been shaped to fit a structure that was familiar.

I usually use the icons of brain, molecule, and receptor site. These are the "in" concepts in the world of pharmacology today. The description of what my research has been, what it presently is, and what I intend it to be in the future, would have to be cast in these images just to begin to open a door of communication. Normally I call heavily upon this vocabulary as a way of capturing the attention of my audience and so establishing a dialogue.

Today is different. For me, this invitation to talk to you here presents a rare opportunity to explore a different lecture format. Let me try to present my research work more in the form of the quest it really is. Let me risk using the icons of mind rather than brain, and spirituality rather than molecular structure.

HUMAN VERSUS ANIMAL MODELS

Almost all of the exploratory research that is being done today in pharmacology employs experimental animals. The use of human subjects, as experimental vehicles for new and known drugs, is considered medically unacceptable when an animal model can serve your needs. Research can run the entire range from cultures of single cells to the behavior patterns of intact animals.

If the goal of the research is to develop a drug to produce a change, then the before-and-after of that change is usually defined by the observation of an appropriate animal model. To assay a possible antibiotic, you would normally infect an animal. To assay a painkiller, you would normally hurt an animal. Then, the process of drug development can start moving through the many complex levels of evaluation such as toxicology, patent law, administrative approval, and marketing surveys, toward its first trial in a human being who is infected or hurting.

This process becomes a bit cloudier when the human malady cannot be demonstrated in an animal. An antidepressant would require that you know how to make an animal depressed. An antipsychotic would require that you have psychotic animals. It becomes essential that you use an euphemism for the illness. Call it something that it is not. Many of the classes of psychotropic drugs such as antidepressants or antipsychotics have been discovered from the observations of side effects of known drugs in clinical studies. The unexpected responses indicate to the careful observer new and possibly valuable potential uses. The drug is then put into animals, their behavior patterns are observed, and an effort is made to correlate these patterns to potential human application. This animal behavior pattern can then be used to titrate totally unexplored compounds as to their potential for producing that specific psychotropic effect in man.

But there are many, many aspects of the human mind that are simply not approachable in any way at all with animal modeling. Even the word "mind" is anathema to many researchers. They will say, "Oh, you mean the brain!" There is a consensus of denial of "mind pharmacology" by the scientific community. The chemistry of the mind is some-how considered outside the known medical disciplines.

I noticed an announcement at the Lawrence Berkeley Laboratory a few years ago, which said that a well-known pharmacologist from NIDA would be giving an hour's seminar on "How the Psychedelic Drugs Work." I attended with great interest, as this was the area of my own curiosity, and I was looking forward to, perhaps, finding some answers to my questions. The substance of the seminar was cast in terms of rat brains, state-of-the-art agonists, and beta-ray radiography of thin slices of tissue following the administration of labeled ligands. There was slide after slide of sections of cerebellum and cortex. Afterwards I asked him, "Shouldn't that lecture have been entitled, 'Where the Psychedelic Drugs Go?'" He admitted that that was a better title. "No one, of course, really knows how they work."

No, they don't, since they deal with things that are not easily locat-able in the rat's brain. How can one study the process of *deja vu*? Of telepathy or psi phenomena? Of memories of youth, or fear of death? What about human values that are spiritual or mystical, sacred or divine? What if a person were to find himself in a trance state? Or a near-death experience or a peak experience or a hypnotic trance? How does one communicate with one's own unconscious? How does one explain insight or conviction? Consider the simple parallel between the sleep state (and the insistent presence of a dreamworld) and the awake state (and the insistent presence of a real world).

Last summer I was sitting around a campfire with some conserva-tive friends who assured me that they would never expose themselves to an alteration of a state of consciousness. I asked the most vehement of them, "How can you go through the night without sleeping?"

"But I sleep, of course."

"But when you go from the awake state (with no awareness of your earlier dreams) into a sleep state (with no awareness of your earlier real-ity) is this not exactly that? An alteration of consciousness?"

"Sure, but it is a natural and normal process."

"And so are all explorations of alterations of consciousness.

Natural, normal, and very much a part of the human animal."

Not only is it natural and normal, but it is an inescapable part of our life process. It may be spontaneous, it may be induced, and it certainly will be a part of your own personal life experience. Consider the provocative description, by Vladimir Nabokov, obviously hypothetical, of the final two seconds of a man's life. The first of these two is taken up with memories. The last second is consumed by "The mysterious mental maneuver needed to pass from one state of being to another." What can be the research tool to study this inevitable alteration of consciousness? It is simpler just to deny death and turn to the study of depression and psychosis.

If, in my looseness of lecturing, I were to make a move yet further, from the arena of the mind to that of the spirit, the scientifically dedicated audience would simply get up and leave the room. Let me try the following questions. What is the biochemistry of your self-image? Where about you is God? Is there power in prayer? What is the neurochemistry of belief?

These are questions that the scientific technicians choose not to ask. Our technology today consists largely of manipulation of material things or entering keystrokes into a computer. To begin to explore these exquisitely human questions, we need tools that are just now beginning to be known and understood to reveal these answers.

THE ROLE OF TOOLMAKER

First, I must say that I truly believe that we have all of the answers to these questions right within us. It is just that we have not allowed ourselves access to them. We have not even acknowledged that they exist. The tools we need are those that would give us access to these answers. They may be processes such as meditation or dreaming. They may involve yielding to external forces through states of trance or coma. They may be in the form of materials such as certain plants or chemicals. Regardless of what vehicle is actually used, you must not lose sight of the fact that it is something that allows, not something that does.

Let me quote from the book that Ann and I wrote, on this very matter. This was my very first psychedelic experience, the swallowing of a capsule containing four hundred milligrams of mescaline sulfate. This is what convinced me that tools do exist.

The details of that day were hopelessly complex and will remain buried in my notes, but the distillation, the essence of the experience, was this. I saw the world that presented itself in several guises. It had a marvel of color that was, for me, without precedent, for I had never particularly noticed the world of color. The rainbow had always provided me with all the hues I could respond to. Here, suddenly I had hundreds of nuances of color, which were new to me, and which I have never, even today, forgotten. The world was also marvelous in its detail. I could see the intimate structure of a bee putting something into a sack on its hind leg to take to its hive, and yet I was completely at peace with the bee's closeness to my face. The world was a wonder of interpretive insight. I saw people as caricatures, which revealed both their pains and their hopes, and they seemed not to mind my seeing them that way. More than anything else the world amazed me, in that I saw it as I had when I was a child. I had forgotten the beauty and the magic and the knowingness of it and me. I was in familiar territory, a space wherein I had once roamed as an immortal explorer, and I was recalling everything that had been authentically known to me then, and which I had abandoned, then forgotten, with my coming of age. Like the touchstone that recalls a dream to sudden presence, this experience reaffirmed a miracle of excitement that I had known in my childhood but had been pressured to forget. The most compelling insight of that day was that this awesome recall had been brought about by a fraction of a gram of a white solid, but in no way whatsoever could it be argued that these memories had been contained within the white solid. Everything I had recognized came from the depths of my memory and my psyche. I understood that our entire universe is contained in the mind and the spirit. We may choose not to find access to it, we may even deny its existence, but it is indeed there inside us, and there are chemicals that can catalyze its availability.

There is a term in the sciences for something that allows something to occur, without a one-to-one correspondence, something that promotes something happening, but does not become part of the result. It is called a catalyst.

To me that day with mescaline still lives vividly in my memory. It was a day that confirmed the direction my life would take. Here was a simple material, the active component of a plant that has been used for countless years by countless people, for their own very personal needs, which can be of many types. Some will find mescaline, or peyote, an entertaining experience, with colors and motions of no profound value. Perhaps it might play for them a role of allowing a brief escape from the mundane or tedious. Others may participate in such use as a social vehicle, allowing interpersonal activities to be enhanced and opened up. This use can be extended to the role of information seeking, such as the search for the origins and explanations of illness or of sadness. But to me that day, as I know it has been with others, I found it to be the key to a magical discovery of my own personal spirituality. If this plain-looking white solid could play the role of being a catalyst, giving understanding of some part of the mind, what other materials could be created that might serve parallel roles?

I know that I have the art of the chemist in my hands, and I have the curiosity needed to explore this miraculous world of the mind. My role has evolved into that of conceiving, synthesizing, and personally evaluating new drugs that might alter the state of consciousness of man. In short, I have spent some thirty-five years inventing materials that can briefly and reversibly change a person's mental state.

I see myself as a toolmaker. I found it an exciting challenge to enter into the search for new and different catalysts. Many of the compounds that came from this search were inactive. Some were stimulants. One became an antidepressant and saw extensive clinical studies in a large pharmaceutical house. Some had toxic side effects. But some were magical catalysts, and many of them seemed to open the door to the unconscious.

I had hoped that some overall understanding of what was happening might come from studying the relationship between the molecule and what it allowed to occur. I have yet to make any sense from that correlation. Others, as curious as I, have added their input, and we all have the optimistic hope that it will come into focus some day. As I said, the answers are all up there in the mind—it is just that we still do not have much access to them.

CHEMISTRY OF GOD

But what does all of this, you might ask, have to do with churches and religion? Everything. You may have noticed that I have avoided using either of the two words, church or religion. I have the same vague discomfort about churches and their function that many people have about drugs. Many view the church as an entertaining experience with music and ritual but providing no profound value. To others, participation in church functions is used as a social vehicle allowing interpersonal activities to be enhanced and opened up. And yet to some, the relationship with a church offers precious insights and can provide the key to magical discoveries and personal spirituality.

It is just this quest, the search for understanding oneself, that defines, in my eyes, a religion. It is an inward quest, one that asks questions and seeks answers. I hope I do not offend too many, when I say that I believe that faith has nothing to do with true religion. The expression of faith is a statement of acceptance, acceptance of a system that is not of your own making. It is the placing of yourself in the hands of someone else, who might be anyone from a minister or rabbi to a Jesus or a Buddha.

As I continue my own personal search for my God, I am becoming increasingly convinced that he lies within me somewhere. Perhaps each person's own God lies within him; this is the meaning of the word entheogen. And if that internal God is the same God for all people, then we are all, in a sense, the same person. Perhaps the role of a sacrament in any religious practice has been, and is, to let a moment's light be shed on that part of reality. There is a remarkable congruity between changes of states of consciousness, religious experiences, mystical experiences, and personal miracles.

WHAT IS IN THE FUTURE?

It would be of the greatest value to humankind if these promising hints of synthesis between the body and the spirit could be pursued and extended. But I fear that in our present culture this may not be the way that things can develop.

Again, speaking as a chemist and explorer, I remember my earliest introduction to the thrill of the test tube. I had a Gilbert Chemistry Set in the basement of my home in Berkeley. It had remarkable things in it, like logwood and bicarbonate of soda. I could make things fizzle, and there was even an occasional controlled explosion. I would go down to the University Apparatus Company on McGee Street, and they would happily give me new things that had remarkable names, usually for free, and I would avidly read up on their properties from books that I accumulated as fast as I could. That basement was a smelly and magical place for me.

How many people who have enjoyed their lives as creative scientists have had their starts as mavericks in some rich learning environment such as this? I fear that this type of introduction cannot be repeated in our present generation. Today, the presence of a "basement" smelling of strange chemicals would be seen as a drug laboratory, or as an environmental hazard, or as being in some other way socially unacceptable. Today, no one would sell, let alone give, a chemical to a child. Even adults can no longer buy chemicals from the major supply houses; most will only sell to businesses. In several states, one cannot even buy a beaker or glass tubing without a state permit in hand.

And there has been an avalanche of other legal impediments to these forms of free behavior. The laws have robbed us of all the sacred materials that might be used for sacramental purposes: and robbed us of the right to explore new and unknown materials that might have potential sacred properties. The enactment of the analog substances law has made it a crime to explore any substance that might be a catalyst in opening a door to one's own psyche. The chemical induction of a change of one's state of consciousness is now illegal.

I feel saddened that what little work is being done, in our culture at least, is underground. Much of it will never be made public and will remain unavailable. It therefore cannot become part of a research process that I feel is absolutely essential for the development of humanity.

But let me close on a somewhat more upbeat note. A synthesis of religion and pharmacology lies just below the surface of this meeting. This union must be explored with the acceptance of the personal right to believe as one chooses.

There must come a parallel acknowledgment of the individual's right to explore his own mind as he chooses. This meeting just may lay the groundwork for starting the search for a solution to this dilemma.

12
LSD as a Spiritual Aid

Albert Hofmann

Albert Hofmann, Ph.D., Dr.Pharm.H.C., Dr.Sc.Nat.H.C., is best known for his serendipitous discovery of LSD and for his chemical work identifying the active principles of the sacred mushroom of Mexico. He was the retired director of research for the Department of Natural Products at Sandoz Pharmaceutical Ltd. in Basel, Switzerland. Dr. Hofmann was a fellow of the World Academy of Science and a member of the Nobel Prize Committee, the International Society of Plant Research, and the American Society of Pharmacognosy. He wrote many scientific papers and several books: *The Botany and Chemistry of Hallucinogens* and *Plants of the Gods* with Richard Evans Schultes, *The Road to Eleusis* with R. G. Wasson and Carl Ruck, *LSD: My Problem Child*, and *Insight/Outlook*.

Born January 11, 1906, Albert celebrated his 100th birthday in excellent health with thousands of grateful admirers at the Spirit of Basel—a celebration of his life's work (www.lsd.info/en/home.html). Albert died two years later, on April 29, 2008, four months after his wife, Anita, had passed away. His archives and legacy are managed by Dieter Hagenbach at www.gaiamedia.org.

———————— ◈ ————————

The use of soma (which is the Iranian haoma) is one among many examples of the religious use of drugs and intoxicants that have strange psychological effects. In our own day, Aldous Huxley has advocated the use of mescaline. The weird and glorifying properties of such plants and concoctions have given man a heightened religious experience, a window, as it were, on a world that is normally beyond the range of humdrum senses.

NINIAN SMART, *THE RELIGIOUS EXPERIENCE OF MANKIND,* 1984

Before I start with the report on the role LSD has played in my spiritual development, some general remarks on this very special psychopharmacon are appropriate.

LSD is not a product of planned research. I did not look for it, it came to me. This means to me that a higher authority thought it was necessary now to provide mankind with an additional pharmacological aid for spiritual growth.

LSD is not just a synthetic substance from the laboratory. After the discovery of lysergic acid amide and lysergic acid hydroxyethylamide (very closely related to lysergic acid diethylamide) as the entheogenic principles of *Ololiuqui,* an ancient sacred plant of Mexican Indians, LSD had to be regarded as belonging to the group of natural entheogenic drugs of Mesoamerica.

These two characteristics of LSD legitimate its use in a religious framework.

Now I come to the report of how LSD was a spiritual aid to me and how it influenced my worldview (*Weltanschauung*).

After my first experiences with LSD, the question arose for me: Which is true, the picture of the world as we perceive it with our everyday consciousness or the overwhelming image under the influence of entheogens?

This caused me to analyze what we know about the mechanism of perceiving reality.

Perception presupposes a subject that perceives and an object that is perceived. In human relations the subject that perceives is the individual human being, more exactly his consciousness, and the object perceived is the outer material world.

It is of the greatest importance to be aware of the fundamental fact that the outer world consists *objectively* of nothing more than matter and energy.

In order to make conspicuous the mechanism of our experiencing reality, I have chosen a metaphor from television. The material world functions as transmitter, emanates optical, acoustical, gustatory, olfactory, and tactile signals that are received by the antennae, by our sensory organs, eyes, ears, tongue, nose, and skin and are conducted from there to the corresponding center in the brain to the receiver. There these *energetic* and *material signals* are transformed into the *spiritual phenomena* of seeing, hearing, tasting, smelling, and touching. One does not know how this transformation of material and energetic impulses into the psychic dimension of perception takes place. It includes the mystery of the connection between the material and the spiritual world.

The transmitter-receiver metaphor of reality makes evident that the picture of the outer world comes into existence inside, in the consciousness of the individual.

This fundamental fact signifies that the screen on which the colorful world is perceived is not in the outer but in the inner space of every human being. There are no colors, no sounds, no taste, no odors in the outer world. Everyone carries within himself his own personal image of the world, an image created by his private receiver. There is no common screen outside. This makes us fully aware of the cosmogenic (world-creating) power invested in every human.

Before making use of these considerations to explain the ability of LSD and the other entheogens to change the experience of reality, our knowledge about the essence of consciousness must be reviewed.

Consciousness defies a scientific definition and explanation; for it is what is needed to contemplate what consciousness is. It can only be circumscribed as being the receptive and creative center of the spiritual ego, which has the faculties of perceiving, thinking, and feeling, and which is the seat of memory.

It is of fundamental importance to be aware of how consciousness originates and develops.

The newborn human possesses solely the faculty of perceiving—possesses, or more correctly, is this mystic nucleus of life. He owns—to use again the metaphor of television—a blank videocassette, where the incoming stimuli from the outer world are transformed into images and sensations that can then be stored in the memory, providing the groundwork for thinking. Without these signals from outside, no consciousness could develop.

There is common consent that the *evolution of mankind is paralleled by the increase and expansion of consciousness.* From the described process of how consciousness originates and develops, it becomes evident that its growth depends on its faculty of perception.

Therefore every means of improving this faculty should be used.

The characteristics of entheogens, their faculty to improve sensory perception, makes them inestimable aids in the process of expanding consciousness.

It was LSD, the most potent entheogen, that, to use Blake's famous line, cleansed my doors of perception and made me see every thing as it is, infinite.

In my childhood I experienced spontaneously some of those blissful moments when the world appeared suddenly in a new brilliant light, and I had the feeling of being included in its wonder and indescribable beauty. These moments remained in my memory as extraordinary experiences of untold happiness, but only after the discovery of LSD did I grasp their meaning and existential importance.

As mentioned at the beginning of this short essay, it was my experiences with LSD that caused me to think about the essence of reality. The insights I received, as described, increased my astonishment about the wonder of existence, of which we become conscious in enlightened moments.

13

Strychnine and Other Enduring Myths

EXPERT AND USER FOLKLORE SURROUNDING LSD

David E. Presti and Jerome Beck

David E. Presti, Ph.D., is a clinical psychologist and neuroscientist who teaches neurochemistry and neurobiology at the University of California at Berkeley. For many years he worked in the treatment of drug and alcohol addiction and post-traumatic stress disorder at the Veterans Administration Medical Center in San Francisco. He holds doctorates in Clinical Psychology from the University of Oregon and Molecular Biophysics from the California Institute of Technology. He may be contacted at the Department of Cellular and Molecular Biology, University of California, Berkeley, California, 94720–3200, or presti@socrates.berkeley.edu.

Jerome Beck, Dr.P.H., has extensive experience as both an educator and researcher in the substance-abuse field. A strong interest in entheogenic substances has resulted in a number of publications on various facets of the subject. Research conducted under the auspices of the federally funded "Exploring Ecstasy" study in the late 1980s culminated in his dissertation, *The MDMA Controversy: Contexts of Use and Social Control,* for the UC Berkeley School of Public Health as well as *Pursuit of Ecstasy: The MDMA Experience* (coauthored with Marsha Rosenbaum), published by the State University of New York (SUNY) Press in 1994. In addition to teaching, he has worked as a Research Administrator at the University of California Tobacco-Related Disease Research Program. He may be contacted at jerome .beck@home.com.

Medical evidence, based on the opinion of scientists and other experts, including medical doctors and anthropologists, is that peyote is not injurious; . . . The carefully circumscribed religious context in which peyote is used by Indians is far removed from the irresponsible and unrestricted recreational use of unlawful drugs. . . .

UNITED STATES HOUSE OF REPRESENTATIVES,
REPORT 103–675, TO ACCOMPANY AMERICAN INDIAN
RELIGIOUS FREEDOM ACT AMENDMENTS OF 1994

LSD (lysergic acid diethylamide), like many hallucinogenic, visionary, or entheogenic chemicals, is classified by the United States government as a Schedule 1 controlled substance. Such substances are deemed to have no medical applications and are not legally available for human use in the United States. As such, LSD is available to users only as an illicit "street drug" of unknown purity and potency. Many so-called street drugs have an associated corpus of myth, but nowhere is this more dramatic and fantastic than with LSD. Although unknown prior to its synthesis in 1938 and characterization in 1943 by Albert Hofmann (Hofmann 1983), LSD represents to many the prototypical hallucinogen. The remarkable folklore associated with LSD is perhaps to be expected, given its highly controversial nature and its powerful and profound effects on consciousness.

A particularly noteworthy aspect of LSD mythology is its existence among both users of the drug and experts in the substance-abuse field. Among professionals, some of these myths are pervasive enough to have received mention as "facts" in prominent professional publications. Although the general public and the media may be hoodwinked by misinformation, users of hallucinogens are often well informed about the substances they use. Despite this, some myths are still widely believed by users of LSD.

Most of the LSD myths began in the politically charged era of the 1960s and have multiple origins and methods of propagation, among which have been the media, street-user subculture, and scare tactics by the government and law enforcement. In this chapter we address the prominent folklore associated with LSD, giving particular attention to the prevalent belief held both by users and by professional experts that strychnine is a common adulterant of LSD. In addition to this prototypical myth, we reflect briefly on several other widely held beliefs.

STRYCHNINE AND OTHER ADULTERANTS

That LSD is frequently adulterated ("cut") with a number of toxic substances is a long-standing belief that has permeated user and professional networks for more than three decades, despite the lack of any supporting evidence. Prominent among the believed additions to LSD are methamphetamine (the popular synthetic street drug known as "speed") and strychnine (an alkaloid from the seeds of a tree native to India, *Strychnos nux-vomica,* historically used as a rodent poison and having nervous-system stimulant properties [Hardman et al. 1996, 1689–90]). Users will sometimes attribute characteristics of an LSD experience as much to these adulterants as to the LSD itself. For example, an LSD experience may be described as "speedy" due to methamphetamine presumed to be present in the sample. LSD thought to be adulterated with strychnine is sometimes claimed to be the basis for an unpleasant experience or "bad trip," or as the source of gastrointestinal distress experienced by some users on LSD. Even *High Times* magazine—a standard reference among users—has reported that "common adulterants [to LSD] are strychnine, amphetamines, and whatever else was lying around the bathtub" (Weasel 1993). In a survey administered to over four hundred university undergraduates in a required health class, students who had used LSD commonly believed that strychnine and methamphetamine were frequent adulterants, while those who had not used LSD were largely unaware of this myth (Beck 1980).

It is also widely believed among drug-treatment professionals that LSD is frequently adulterated with strychnine. Even the *DSM-IV (Diagnostic and Statistical Manual of Mental Disorders, 4th Edition)*— the standard reference in the United States on the diagnosis of mental disorders (including drug abuse)—mentions strychnine as an adulterant to LSD (APA 1994, 231). *Psychiatric Annals,* a professional journal of continuing education for psychiatrists, devoted an issue to hallucinogens in 1994. Among the numerous inaccuracies in this issue of the journal was a reference to strychnine being added to LSD in order "to increase the potency of its hallucinatory experiences" (Giannini 1994, 134). This article continued with a description of the procedure for the treatment of strychnine poisoning, indicating that this is likely to be an emergency medical need for anyone presenting acute distress after having ingested LSD.

Strychnine contamination of LSD is also mentioned in leading professional books on substance-abuse treatment (Pechnick and Ungerleider 1997, 234), as well as recent drug-education textbooks (Carroll 1989; Hanson and Venturelli 1995; Kuhn et al. 1998). Thus educational texts continue to propagate the strychnine myth, without reference to any documented analyses or cases.

Compilations of drug slang published by the United States Department of Justice (DOJ 1994) and professional medical journals (JEM 1988) list terms that describe combinations of LSD and strychnine, such as "backbreaker," "white acid," and "four way." However, there is no evidence whatsoever that this chemical combination ever existed under any name. The extent of this belief among experts is impressive and makes the strychnine myth unique in the corpus of LSD folklore.

The strychnine myth may have been fortified by Albert Hofmann's report of an analysis (conducted in 1970) of a powder sample purported to be LSD, which turned out to be nothing but strychnine (Hofmann 1983, 71–72). However, all other analyses of a large number of street samples of LSD over the years have consistently revealed that products sold on the street as LSD seldom contain adulterants and have never been found to contain strychnine (Ott 1993, 134–35; Grinspoon & Bakalar 1997, 76).

Thirty years ago, in the few cases where adulteration was detected, the adulterant was either PCP or methamphetamine. Of 581 street samples of purported LSD analyzed by Brown and Malone (1973), results showed that 491 (84.5 percent) contained LSD alone; 31 (5.3 percent) contained LSD and PCP; 11 (1.9 percent) were PCP alone; and 5 (0.9 percent) contained LSD plus amphetamine or methamphetamine. Brown and Malone stated: "We have analyzed several samples thought to contain strychnine on the basis of toxic symptoms, but in each case only LSD was detected. . . . None of the other groups doing street drug analyses has reported strychnine in any LSD-containing sample" (Brown and Malone 1973).

Even if, historically, adulterants were infrequently detected in street samples of LSD, this possibility has been rendered even more unlikely in recent times by the introduction of blotter paper, which has been by far the most common carrier medium for the distribution of LSD for more than twenty years. This medium evolved because the high potency of LSD demands that a reliable method be used to partition small quantities of the chemical into uniform doses. Exposing absorbent paper to solutions of known concentration works quite well for this. However, in order to produce any significant psychoactivity, the five-millimeter-square dosage units of blotter paper cannot contain sufficient amounts of strychnine or other substances claimed to be adulterants. In addition, the very high potency and continued low cost of LSD make it unnecessary to add adulterants to enhance its effects.

In *Licit and Illicit Drugs,* Brecher claims that strychnine may have been added to LSD as a "bulking agent" and possibly to increase the immediacy of psychoactive effects (Brecher 1972, 376). Another reason offered for the presumed presence of strychnine in LSD is that it is required to facilitate the bonding of LSD to blotter paper. None of these are true. Other stories say that strychnine is a contaminant of the synthesis of LSD, a breakdown product of LSD, or a metabolite produced after ingestion. These are also mythos. While both strychnine and LSD are complex carbon-based compounds, their molecular structures are quite different. Strychnine is not a chemical precursor, byproduct of synthesis, degradation product, or metabolite of LSD. There simply has been no strychnine found in street samples of LSD or any reason to expect its presence.

The origin of the strychnine-in-LSD myth is obscure. It was already well established by the late 1960s. In their otherwise excellent historical review of LSD use, Lee and Shlain state: "Much of the LSD turning up on the street [in San Francisco's Haight-Ashbury neighborhood in the late 1960s] was fortified with some sort of additive, usually speed or strychnine, or in some cases insecticide. But where did this contaminated acid come from?" (Lee and Shlain 1985, 188). The authors go on to say that this contaminated LSD was manufactured and distributed by organized crime and came to be called "syndicate acid," a name that was at the time synonymous with bad LSD. The late 1960s were chaotic times in the hippie scene of San Francisco. Alcohol, heroin, and methamphetamine were increasingly used, and this, together with the influx of large numbers of clueless youth, was rapidly contributing to the demise of the formerly idyllic scene. The resultant chaos undoubtedly added a powerful negative component to the set and setting of the LSD experience. However, there is no evidence from that time indicating the actual presence of strychnine in LSD samples. We suspect that the strychnine myth evolved in the late 1960s to help explain negative aspects of the LSD experience related to the degenerating social scene.

There are claims from experienced users that different samples of illicit LSD may produce subtly different effects. Although such differences might be accounted for by variations of mental set and physical setting, there may also be chemical mechanisms at work. Other ergot alkaloids and chemical relatives of LSD present in an incompletely puri-fied preparation could have psychoactive effects (Shulgin and Shulgin 1997). Breakdown products and metabolites of LSD might also con-tribute to such reported differences. However, this remains speculation at this point in time. Clinical study of such possibilities has not been conducted and, indeed, would be virtually impossible to conduct at the present time, given the difficulty of doing human research with LSD and related chemicals.

From the perspective of the government, law enforcement, and the substance-abuse treatment community, the myth of strychnine as an adulterant remains a convenient scare tactic to dissuade users from experimenting with LSD. From the perspective of the user, this myth remains a convenient external explanation for those experiences that are significantly unpleasant (i.e., the "bad trips").

TATTOO ACID

Another myth has been passed around so often between the media, law enforcement, and parents' groups that it has been described as "the most insidious urban drug legend" (Brunvand 1984). This is the ever-surfacing myth of "tattoo acid." Because blotter-paper LSD is frequently illustrated with cartoon characters or other artistic designs, some folks have found them to resemble transfer tattoos. This has resulted in the periodic appearance in communities throughout the United States of anonymous fliers warning of the threat this brings to children. One such police bul-letin stated: "A new danger has entered our community. . . . This is a new way of selling acid by appealing to our young children. A young child could happen upon these and have a fatal 'trip.' It is also learned that little children could be given a free 'tattoo' by older children who want to have some fun or by others cultivating new customers." The bulletin con-cludes by warning people not to handle these tattoos because "these drugs are known to react very quickly and some are laced with strychnine." (Emeryville California Police Department Bulletin, March 31, 1987).

This particular myth is the only one that has been officially dis-

credited by the Drug Enforcement Administration (DEA). In a memo-
randum issued in 1991, the DEA states:

> Fliers with warnings against a claimed "new form" of LSD have been
> circulating throughout the United States for more than a decade.
> Typically, the warnings, which are usually addressed to parents . . .
> warn of the dangers of LSD-impregnated decals or tattoos deco-
> rated with cartoon characters or other pictures designed to appeal to
> children. . . . It is claimed that, by licking the decals and apply-
> ing them to the skin, a child could suffer an hallucinogenic high.
> . . . The warnings, which have been found on letters, posters, and fli-
> ers, have been reproduced countless times by well-meaning persons,
> school systems, private companies, and the press. The warnings can
> be particularly troublesome and confusing because they do contain
> some accurate information about LSD, its forms, and effects. . . . The
> accidental similarity between children's decals and decorated blotter
> acid was probably the basis for the erroneous presumption made by
> some well-meaning individuals that there was a particular danger to
> small children. Although some high school and college-age youth may
> be purchasing blotter acid and getting high on it, no, repeat, no DEA
> or state or local authorities have ever, to date, reported any instance
> of children's decals or tattoos with LSD. . . . It is a hoax. (DEA 1991)

CHROMOSOME DAMAGE AND BIRTH DEFECTS

One of the preeminent myths of the late 1960s, and one that contributed significantly to the fear and condemnation of LSD, was the belief
that LSD use produced chromosomal breakage, other genetic damage,
and birth defects (teratogenicity). This story began with a short publication in the reputable journal *Science* in 1967 claiming that LSD
added to cultured human white blood cells produced chromosomal
abnormalities (Cohen, Marinello, and Back 1967a). The primary author
of this article published a similar report in the prestigious medical
journal *The New England Journal of Medicine* a few months later

(Cohen, Hirshhorn, and Frosch 1967b). The same issue of this latter journal also contained an editorial article highlighting the discovery of birth defects and genetic damage caused by LSD, emphasizing that the effect of LSD on chromosomes was similar to the damage produced by ionizing radiation (NEJM 1967). These publications were followed by a spate of work by various researchers claiming more of the same. Such findings were given front-page attention by the media and became a prominent aspect of the public perception of LSD.

Later and more careful studies demonstrated that the conclusions drawn from the initial research were ill-founded. A comprehensive review of sixty-eight studies and case reports published in the four years following the initial 1967 article appeared as a major article in *Science* in 1971. The review concluded, "pure LSD ingested in moderate doses does not damage chromosomes in vivo, does not cause detectable genetic damage, and is not a teratogen or a carcinogen in man" (Dishotsky et al. 1971).

Unfortunately, these refutations of earlier claims were ignored by the media and government purveyors of drug information. As a result, the myth of LSD as a promoter of genetic damage is still very much alive. One of the better contemporary drug-education textbooks opens with the results from a series of true/false questions on drugs. The questions were presented to a drug-education class taught by the author of the book at the State University of New York at Stony Brook. One question states, "women who take LSD during pregnancy, even once, have a significantly higher likelihood of bearing children with birth defects than women who do not take LSD." The answer is false. In a class of 223 students given this question in 1991, only 6 percent chose the correct answer (Goode 1993); and in a class of 200 students given this question in 1996, only 9 percent answered correctly (Goode 1999). The myth lives on.

GOING CRAZY: ACUTE AND LONG-TERM ADVERSE REACTIONS

LSD, as well as many other psychoactive drugs, can produce a variety of acute (short-term, during the period of intoxication) behavioral effects.

These may include anxiety, euphoria, dysphoria, paranoia, hallucinations, other alterations of perception, and so forth. Alterations of perception and consciousness are, not surprisingly, an anticipated part of the experience. In addition, the initial mental set (mood, expectations, etc.) of the user may profoundly influence the nature of the experience. Someone who is depressed or anxious and takes LSD may experience an exacerbation of depression or anxiety. Someone who is in a positive mental space may have an ecstatic experience, although not necessarily so. Any single experience with LSD can include both positive and negative mood states. Even negative mood states can be psychologically beneficial, if material that emerges is therapeutically processed or integrated within a spiritual framework. This is one facet of the psychotherapeutic value of LSD and similar substances (Grof 1994; Stolaroff 1994).

Lasting (chronic) negative psychological sequelae are a different story. LSD and other hallucinogens are frequently discussed as being associated with a significant and unpredictable risk of "going crazy," as well as a haunting fear of "permanent brain damage." Such folklore includes outrageous statements like "use LSD seven times (or five times or ten times or whatever . . .) and you are legally insane," or "I know someone who took LSD and felt like they turned into an orange and they still feel like they are an orange." Other effects spoken of are the development of chronic anxiety, depression, paranoia, psychosis, or suicidal and violent behavior, to name but a few. While we are not disputing the possibility that lasting negative sequelae of LSD use might occur in particular individuals, reviews of the clinical literature suggest that chronic problematic effects, when they do occur, are most often associated with psychological instability that was present prior to LSD use (Strassman 1984; Grinspoon and Bakalar 1997). For example, persons with borderline personality functioning (in the language of the *DSM-IV* [APA 1994, 654]) or latent mental disorders (e.g., having a positive family history for schizophrenia) may experience activation of symptoms from LSD use and chronic problems thereafter. Such individuals would also be at risk from exposure to a variety of other environmental stressors.

A comprehensive review by Dr. Sidney Cohen of the use of LSD in psychotherapeutic environments during the 1950s (including approximately twenty-five thousand administrations, given to five thousand recipients) reported that the incidence of acute and chronic problematic reactions was extremely low when LSD was administered under controlled therapeutic conditions to individuals not having pre-existing severe psychopathology (Cohen 1960). This argues for psychological screening of potential users (it may be safe for most people, but it is not for everyone), as well as careful attention to the set and setting of the drug session.

Human death from toxic pharmacologic effects of LSD has never been documented (Gable 1993). The pharmacologic therapeutic index (the ratio of lethal dose to therapeutically effective dose) for LSD is undoubtedly very large. There is an infamous case of some "scientific research," published in *Science* (West, Pierce, and Thomas 1962), in which an elephant who received a very large dose of LSD subsequently died. However, in this situation the elephant was also administered other potent substances, including barbiturate and anti-psychotic drugs, which likely contributed to its demise.

We have heard claims that LSD sequesters in the brain, spinal cord, and body fat, and can leak out at later times—even years later!—to produce adverse effects (such as flashbacks, which are the re-experiencing of some aspects of the drug-intoxication experience in the absence of the drug). Recently we heard from a medical student that she learned this "fact" in a class at one of the country's leading medical schools. There is no basis in reality for this, as there is absolutely no evidence suggesting that LSD remains in the body for extended periods of time.

The notion of "flashback" is probably one of the more muddled concepts in the literature about hallucinogenic drugs. In their excellent discussion of this phenomenon, Grinspoon and Bakalar have this to say:

> Studies of flashbacks are hard to evaluate because the term has been
> used so loosely and variably. On the broadest definition, it means
> the transitory recurrence of emotions and perceptions originally

experienced while under the influence of the drug. It can last seconds or hours; it can mimic any of the myriad aspects of a trip; and it can be blissful, interesting, annoying, or frightening. Most flashbacks are episodes of visual distortion, time distortion, physical symptoms, loss of ego boundaries, or relived intense emotion lasting a few seconds to a few minutes. Ordinarily they are only slightly disturbing, especially since the drug user usually recognizes them for what they are; they may even be regarded lightheartedly as "free trips." Occasionally they last longer, and in a small minority of cases they turn into frightening images or thoughts. (Grinspoon and Bakalar 1979, 159)

One framework for thinking of flashbacks is as a kind of memory that is robust and easily activated. Another conceptualization of flashbacks is a psychodynamic one that views them as related to a re-emergence of conflictual material released from the unconscious mind during the time of the drug action and not fully processed at that time. Stanislav Grof, one of the world's most experienced LSD therapists, makes the following statement about flashbacks and other adverse reactions in his classic book on LSD *Psychotherapy*.

Sessions in which the drug activates areas of difficult emotional material and the individual tries to avoid facing them can lead to prolonged reactions, unsatisfactory integration, subsequent residual emotional or psychosomatic problems, or a precarious mental balance that becomes the basis for later "flashbacks." (Grof 1994, 134)

The *DSM-IV* terminology for flashbacks associated with LSD use is "Hallucinogen Persisting Perceptual Disorder," abbreviated HPPD (APA 1994, 233–34). The *DSM-IV* takes a particularly narrow definition that focuses on persistent visual perceptual phenomena that cause significant distress to the individual. This condition may be a real but rare occurrence among individuals who have used LSD (Abraham and Aldridge 1993). However, the condition has received only very limited study, and its claimed association with LSD use is confounded by poly-drug use as well as other variables (Myers, Watkins, and Carter 1998).

A major factor in determining the intensity—either ecstatic or problematic—of an LSD experience is the quantity of drug ingested. Along these lines it is important to note that the average dosage contained in street samples has declined dramatically since the early 1970s. While dosage units of street LSD in the 1960s were generally upwards of two hundred micrograms, the reported average dose of street samples in the 1990s was closer to sixty micrograms (DEA 1991; Henderson and Glass 1994, 52).

Acute adverse psychological reactions are certainly the most significant concerns associated with LSD use. Unfortunately, these dangers are also the ones that are most enhanced by the myths and dire warnings. The LSD experience is shaped not only by the pharmacology of the drug itself, but also by the beliefs that accompany the experience. Because of the highly suggestive nature of the LSD experience, belief in the myths can contribute to self-fulfilling prophecy and increase the likelihood of having an adverse reaction. Cohen called this the phenomenon of "excessive initial apprehension" and cited it as a significant factor contributing to bad trips (Cohen 1960). Given this, it is perhaps not surprising that the number of reported bad trips increased markedly during the media blitz of the late 1960s. After media coverage died down at the close of the decade, so did the number of negative experiences. This occurred despite the fact that the total number of LSD users was still increasing into the early 1970s (Brecher 1972; Bunce 1979; Zinberg 1984; Grinspoon and Bakalar 1997). An increasingly informed user culture and the predictably lower dosages of street LSD have been among the most significant contributors to this decline in negative experiences.

Henderson and Glass, in their book on the recent history of LSD, summarize the relationship between adverse reactions and mythos in the following way:

> In the popular mythology, LSD users are prone to violent outbursts
> and bizarre behavior. They may jump off buildings believing they

can fly, stare at the sun until they go blind, tear their eyes out, or even become homicidal. It is widely believed that an LSD user may at any moment experience a drug flashback during which any of these events may recur. The literature on LSD does document some bizarre episodes. Given the millions of doses of LSD that have been consumed since the 1950s, however, these are rare indeed. (Henderson and Glass 1994, 55)

SPIRITUAL DEVELOPMENT

A central theme of this book is the entheogenic potential of LSD and similar substances. Indigenous cultures around the world and throughout history have used psychoactive plants as sacramentals in religious rituals that have served to facilitate their connection to the transpersonal. This notwithstanding, it is a myth that the use of these substances will automatically lead to a higher degree of spiritual or religious development. Entheogen use does not necessarily make spiritual development any easier. Skillful and respectful use, with careful attention to intention, set, and setting may help to foster the spiritual path.

CONCLUSION

There is more to these myths than simply inaccurate information. They have had a major impact on public, scientific, clinical, and governmental perceptions of hallucinogens as well as on user experiences. These myths were a primary factor in the termination of the clinical research thirty years ago and continue to interfere with the resumption of legitimate investigation of the therapeutic and entheogenic properties of LSD and similar substances.

Searching for the origins of these enduring drug mythologies often proves to be both a fascinating and frustrating experience that only rarely yields complete elucidation. Possessing a life of their own, these hoary myths are hardly static as they journey through space and time. Reflecting the dynamic and adaptive nature of myths, their elements often undergo changes and embellishments over time as a result of faulty memories or the emergent needs of various interest groups.

The Internet has assumed a central role in the diffusion of drug mythology. While the potential exists for the Internet to further propagate these as well as other myths to a wider population, it appears that the opposite may actually be occurring. Electronic mail exchange, newsgroup discussions, and the information-rich World Wide Web have emerged as correctors of myths that have remained largely unchallenged for decades. Websites such as those of *Erowid* (www.erowid.org), the *Multidisciplinary Association for Psychedelic Studies* (www.maps.org), *The Psychedelic Library* (www.psychedelic-library.org), *The Lycaeum* (www.lycaeum.org), and the *Council on Spiritual Practices* (www.csp .org) are exemplars of such founts of accumulated knowledge.

More than half a century after its discovery by Albert Hofmann, LSD remains one of the most powerful and profound psychoactive substances known. The folklore surrounding LSD reflects, in part, fears of this power. LSD has the potential to produce extraordinary effects on consciousness, stripping away psychological defenses and bringing users into contact with the gods and the demons of their own psyches. It deserves the utmost respect for the powerful effects it can produce. There is power enough in this truth.

REFERENCES

Abraham, H. D., and A. M. Aldridge. 1993. "Adverse consequences of lysergic acid diethylamide." *Addiction* 88: 1327–34.

APA. 1994. *Diagnostic and Statistical Manual of Mental Disorders, Fourth Edition (DSM-IV)*. Washington, D.C.: American Psychiatric Association Press, 231–34, 654.

Beck, J. E. 1980. "Drug use trends and knowledge among students enrolled in a required health course at the University of Oregon, winter 1980." Unpublished honors thesis. University of Oregon, Eugene.

Brecher, E. M. 1972. *Licit and Illicit Drugs*. Boston: Little, Brown and Company, 376.

Brown, J. K., and M. H. Malone. 1973. "Status of drug quality in the street-drug market." *Pacific Information Service on Street Drugs* 3(1): 1–8.

Brunvand, J. H. 1984. *The Choking Doberman and Other "New" Urban Legends*. New York: Norton.

Bunce, R. 1979. "The social and political sources of drug effects: the case of bad trips on psychedelics." *Journal of Drug Issues* 9: 213–33.

Carroll, C. R. 1989. *Drugs in Modern Society*. Dubuque, Iowa: Wm C. Brown.

Cohen, M. M., M. J. Marinello, and N. Back. 1967. "Chromosomal damage in human leukocytes induced by lysergic acid diethylamide." *Science* 155: 1417–19.

Cohen, M. M., K. Hirshhorn, and W. A. Frosch. 1967. "In vivo and in vitro chromosomal damage induced by LSD-25." *The New England Journal of Medicine* 227: 1043–49.

Cohen, S. 1960. "Lysergic acid diethylamide: side effects and complications." *The Journal of Nervous and Mental Disease* 130: 30–40.

DEA. 1991. *LSD: A Situation Report*. Washington, D.C.: Drug Enforcement Administration.

Dishotsky, N. I., W. D. Loughman, R. E. Mogar, and W. R. Lipscomb. 1971. "LSD and genetic damage." *Science* 172: 431–40.

DOJ. 1994. "Street terms: drugs and the drug trade." Rockville, Maryland: United States Department of Justice.

Gable, R. S. 1993. "Toward a comparative overview of dependence potential and acute toxicity of psychoactive substances used nonmedically." *The American Journal of Drug and Alcohol Abuse* 19: 263–81.

Giannini, A. J. 1994. "Inward the mind's I: description, diagnosis, and treatment of acute and delayed LSD hallucinations." *Psychiatric Annals* 24: 134–36.

Goode, E. 1993. *Drugs in American Society* (4th edition). New York: McGraw-Hill.

———. 1999. *Drugs in American Society* (5th edition). New York: McGraw-Hill.

Grinspoon, L., and J. B. Bakalar. 1997 originally published 1979. *Psychedelic Drugs Reconsidered*. New York: Lindesmith Center, 76, 159.

Grof, S. 1994, originally published 1980. *LSD Psychotherapy*. Alameda, Calif.: Hunter House, 134.

Hanson, G., and P. J. Venturelli. 1995. *Drugs and Society*. Boston: Jones & Bartlett.

Hardman, J. G., et al. 1996. *Goodman & Gilman's The Pharmacological Basis of Therapeutics* (9th edition). New York: McGraw-Hill, 1689–90.

Henderson, L. A., and W. J. Glass. 1994. *LSD: Still With Us After All These Years*. New York: Lexington Books, 52–55.

Hofmann, A. 1983 originally 1979. *LSD, My Problem Child: Reflections on Sacred Drugs, Mysticism, and Science*. Los Angeles: J. P. Tarcher, 71–72.

JEM. 1988. "Street names for common drugs." *Journal of Emergency Medicine* July: 46–47.

Kuhn, C., et al. 1998. *Buzzed: The Straight Facts about the Most Used and Abused Drugs*. New York: Norton.

Lee, M. A., and B. Shlain. 1985. *Acid Dreams: The CIA, LSD, and the Sixties Rebellion*. New York: Grove Press, 188.

Myers, L. S., S. S. Watkins, and T. J. Carter. 1998. "Flashbacks in theory and practice." *The Heffter Review of Psychedelic Research* 1: 51–55.

NEJM. 1967. "Radiomimetic properties of LSD." *The New England Journal of Medicine* 227: 1090–91.

Ott, J. 1993. *Pharmacotheon: Entheogenic Drugs, Their Plant Sources and History*. Kennewick, Wash.: Natural Products Company, 134–35.

Pechnick, R. N., and J. T. Ungerleider. 1997. "Hallucinogens." In J. H. Lowinson et al., eds. *Substance Abuse: A Comprehensive Textbook*. Baltimore: Williams & Wilkens, 230–38.

Shulgin, A., and A. Shulgin. 1997. *TIHKAL: The Continuation*. Berkeley: Transform Press.

Stolaroff, M. J. 1994. *Thanatos to Eros: 35 Years of Psychedelic Exploration*. Berlin: Verlag fur Wissenschaft und Bildung.

Strassman, R. J. 1984. "Adverse reactions to psychedelic drugs: a review of the literature." *The Journal of Nervous and Mental Disease* 172: 577–95.

Weasel, P. 1993. "Trans-high market quotations." *High Times,* May 1993: 72.

West, L. J., C. M. Pierce, and W. D. Thomas. 1962. "Lysergic acid diethylamide: its effects on a male Asiatic elephant." *Science* 138: 1100–3.

Zinberg, N. E. 1984. *Drug, Set, and Setting*. New Haven: Yale University Press.

14

Manna, the Showbread, and the Eucharist

PSYCHOACTIVE SACRAMENTS IN THE BIBLE

Dan Merkur

Dan Merkur, Ph.D., underwent an LSD-induced religious conversion and spiritual emergency in 1971 and acquired a permanent interest in the history, theoretical understanding, and spiritual direction of psychedelic experiences. He earned a Ph.D. in the history of religions in 1985. His scholarship discusses religious experiences historically, cross-culturally, and psychoanalytically. Married and the father of four children, he lectures at the University of Toronto and is a psychoanalytic psychotherapist in private practice. The author of eight scholarly books and several dozen articles, his writings on psychedelics and religion include: *The Ecstatic Imagination: Psychedelic Experiences and the Psychoanalysis of Self-Actualization* (1998); *The Mystery of Manna: The Psychedelic Sacrament of the Bible* (2000); and *The Psychedelic Sacrament: Manna, Meditation, and Mystical Experience* (2001).

❖

*The thunderbolt of Zeus was itself a mediation between
the Father God's realm and earth, as the ethnomycologist
R. Gordon Wasson has shown in demonstrating the widespread belief that mushrooms appear where lightning
strikes the earth. Amanita was divine food, not something
to be indulged in lightly, not something to be profaned. It
was the food of the gods, their ambrosia, and nectar was
the pressed sap of its juices.*

C. A. P. RUCK AND DANNY STAPLES,

THE WORLD OF CLASSICAL MYTH:

GODS AND GODDESSES, HEROINES AND HEROS, 1994

There are two unequivocal references to the psychoactivity of manna
in the Hebrew Bible. In Exodus 16, the Israelites are told that in the
morning, when they are to eat the manna, they will see the glory of
Yahweh. "Glory" was a technical, theological term that referred to the
visible form that represented Yahweh in dreams and prophetic visions.
Theological views differed on whether the glory was an aura emitted by
Yahweh's being, a hypostasis or independent angel, or an anthropomor-
phic mental image that accompanied and was envisioned as the speaker
of Yahweh's revelation. Whatever nuance the priestly writer intended in
his concept of Yahweh's glory, his text is unequivocal that eating manna
was the occasion of the vision. Manna was an entheogen. The ingestion
of manna induced religious experiences.

The second passage that refers to manna as an entheogen occurs
in the book of Isaiah. It reads: "And my Lord will give you the bread
of hardship and the water of affliction, and your teacher will no longer hide himself, and your eyes shall see your teacher" (Isaiah 30:20).
In amplification of the hope for universal prophetism in Numbers
12:29 and Joel 3:1, the passage associated manna with visions of God
in the future era of Israel's redemption.

Beyond these two references, I have found no further references to entheogens in the Hebrew Bible that are explicit, conclu-
sive, and unarguable. Many previously obscure passages become

comprehensible, however, when manna is understood as an entheogen.

In Exodus 16:32, Moses reported Yahweh's commandment that an omer of manna be on permanent display to the people of Israel. In verses 33–34, by contrast, Moses instructed Aaron to put an omer of manna in a jar in front of the ark of the testimony in the Tabernacle, where none might enter but a priest. The first version, deriving from the Yahwist (J) source document in the tenth century BCE, advocated public knowledge of manna and reflects a practice that dates early in the history of biblical Israel. The second version, composed by the Priestly (P) author in the late eighth century as part of Hezekiah's reformation, instead restricted access to manna to the priesthood.

How did Jerusalem's priests fulfill the commandment to keep manna on display? Or, to put the question another way: What among the ritual or sacramental objects of Solomon's temple was euphemistically described in biblical narrative as manna? The answer is not far to seek. According to Joshua 5:11–12, on the day after the first Passover in Canaan unleavened bread was substituted for the manna of the wilderness years.

Further parallels support the equation. Both manna and the showbread were placed "before Yahweh" (Exodus 16:33–34; Leviticus 24:8) on a table in the sanctum of the Tabernacle. Manna was "a fine, flake-like thing" (Exodus 16:14), evidently a biscuit or flaky pastry; the showbread was made of unleavened bread and still edible a week after it was baked (Leviticus 24:9). Manna tasted like "cakes baked with oil" (Numbers 11:8) or "wafers made with honey" (Exodus 16:31); the showbread was made with "fine flour and oil and honey" (Exodus 16:19) and a bit of coriander seed (Exodus 16:31). Presumably we are dealing with something like baklava, but flavored with seeds rather than nuts.

Like manna, the showbread was on public display early in Israel's history, for example, when David and his men ate the showbread at the Gibeonite shrine at Nob. However, again like manna, the showbread was later reserved to an inner location in the Jerusalem temple, where only priests had access to it. Hezekiah's celebration of a great Passover, as had not been celebrated since the time of Solomon (2 Chronicles

30:26), was presumably an effort to restore the original custom.

The botanical identification of manna is suggested by the draught ordeal in Numbers 5:11–31. Women who were accused of adultery were required to drink a poison that was prepared with dust from the floor of the temple. Since the temple had originally been a threshing floor, the dust on its floor presumably included ergot; and the women's symptoms were consistent with ergotismus.

A considerable number of passages describe Moses extracting water from a rock, honey from a rock, oil from a rock, or the milk of wheat from a rock. These motifs, which always invoke the ingredients common to manna and the showbread, typically had Moses strike a rock with a stick, staff, or rod before the fluid flowed. The earliest variant simply had Moses throw a stick into bitter waters, causing them to become sweet. So we are dealing with a vegetable ingredient that was added to water, but in such a fashion that water was metaphorically said to have been drawn out of stone.

According to Albert Hofmann, the psychoactive factors in ergot are soluble in water, whereas the toxic factors are not. What I suggest is that the Israel draught ordeal was dangerous because solid vegetable matter was consumed along with the water. The sweet waters that Moses prepared were safe because only fluids were swallowed. This circumstance explains the transparency of the deceptions concerning the identity of manna. The tales were presumably intended to avoid encouraging children to experiment with ergot on their own. However, through increased secrecy regarding the meaning of the stories, the deception later extended to adults as well.

More stories: In Exodus 16, the miraculous capacity of manna to satiate in all quantities great or small, may be understood not as a fabulous motif, but as a straightforward discussion of the recommended dosage. No matter how little or how much people gathered and consumed, they ate neither too little nor too much. Apparently, a very small quantity of manna sufficed to produce the desired visionary state, while a large dose was superfluous.

An equivalent story was told of the prophet Elijah in I Kings 17, where a minute amount of meal and oil lasted until the rainy season. A few details of the story are notable. At the start, when the widow proposed to bake the meal and oil, so as to eat and die, Elijah told her to have no fear because he would eat the cake first. In the sequel, Elijah and the widow were fine; but because the widow's son died, Elijah was obliged to facilitate his resurrection. I suggest that the "bread of hardship" was feared both for its possible toxicity and for its capacity to induce acute adverse reactions of the type that have variously been termed "death-rebirth" experiences, "ego-death," "acute panic states," and, by Grof, "perinatal matrix IV."

Ergot may again be implicated in the legend of Gideon. Gideon was threshing grain when he first encountered an angel of Yahweh. After the angel touched his staff to food that Gideon shared with him, Gideon engaged Yahweh in a prophetic dialogue and went on to become the savior of his people. The designation of a moldy barley bread as the "sword of Gideon" in Judges 7 renders the motif unequivocal, and incidentally clarifies the meaning of the swords held by angels in Numbers 22 and Joshua 5 and by Levites in Exodus 32.

A similar tale concerns the selection of the site of Solomon's temple. In the days of the wheat harvest, a plague killed seventy-seven thousand men (2 Samuel 24:15). As the plague, which presumably infested the wheat, approached Jerusalem, David saw the destroying angel by the threshing floor of Araunah the Jebusite, and he prayed to Yahweh (verses 16–17). Yahweh commanded the destroying angel to desist; and the prophet Gad, whose name means "Coriander," instructed David to raise an altar to Yahweh on the threshing floor (verses 16b, 18).

Jeremiah commenced his book with the following account of his divine call to become a prophet: "Then Yahweh put forth his hand and touched my mouth; and Yahweh said to me, 'Behold, I have put my words in your mouth. . . .'" And several lines later, he wrote: "And the word of Yahweh came to me, saying, 'Jeremiah, what do you see?' And I said, 'I see a stick of almond.'" Jeremiah's sight of an almond stick alluded to the legend of Aaron's rod, which Moses had employed to produce water from the rock at Meribah and which had thereafter been kept in the temple sanctum. In one tale, the rod "sprouted and put forth buds, and produced blossoms, and bore ripe almonds" (Numbers 17:23). Jeremiah was evidently shown the rod at the time of his initiation.

We learn more about Jeremiah's call from a later prophecy. He wrote:

> *Your words were found,*
> *and I ate them;*
> *and your word became for me a joy*
> *and the delight of my heart;*
> *and I was called by your name:*
> *Yahweh of hosts.* (Jeremiah 15:16)

The Yahweh who touched Jeremiah's mouth at his initiation (Jeremiah 1:9) was presumably a priest who acted in a ritual capacity on behalf of Yahweh. The touch that Jeremiah felt on his mouth and his experience of eating the words of Yahweh (Jeremiah 15:16) may be taken at face value, as references to his ingestion of an edible substance. Because eating the substance gave Jeremiah access to Yahweh's words, the sacrament must have been psychoactive. If the substance was prepared in water, the role of Aaron's rod in the initiatory procedure may be explained.

Closely similar motifs occur in Ezekiel's account of the vision during which he received his prophetic mission. In the vision, he eats a scroll that is filled with "lamentation and mourning and woe" (Ezekiel 2:10c) that nevertheless tastes "as sweet as honey" (Ezekiel 3:3c). Here Ezekiel acknowledged the dangers of manna even as he boasted its sweetness.

NEW TESTAMENT MANNA TRADITIONS

Four passages in the New Testament provide unequivocal indication that the traditional association of manna with ergot continued into Christianity. The Gospel of John states that Jesus turned water into wine as "the first of his signs, in Cana of Galilee, and revealed his glory"

(John 2:11). The wine that revealed the glory was evidently an entheogen. According to Paul, the glory of Jesus was to be beheld in this life, following a visionary's ascension to heaven, where the glorified Jesus sat enthroned in Paradise. The intoxicating water that produced visions of the glory is described in John as wine because the gospel writer wished to associate it with the sacramental wine of the mass.

In all four gospels, Jesus fed the five thousand with loaves and fishes (Matthew 14:15–21; Mark 6:35–44; Luke 9:12–17; John 6:1–15). This motif alludes to the miracle of manna and quail in Moses' time. The motif of fraction simultaneously alludes to the sacramental fraction of the host during mass. The manna tradition was thus associated with communion in the very earliest stratum of Christian tradition. Significantly, the fraction of the five loaves into enough pieces to feed five thousand people expressed, in a completely original way, the sufficiency of a minute quantity of heavenly bread. However, it was only the author of John who explicitly disclosed the meaning of the narrative. He had Jesus state, "You are looking for me, not because you saw signs, but because you ate your fill of the loaves" (verse 26). Here it is the eating of the miraculous bread that encourages a person to look for Jesus, implicitly, through a vision of moving about in New Jerusalem in search of the enthroned Glory.

Another explicit allusion to the manna tradition occurs in Hebrews 6:4–6, where the author speaks of Christians as "those who have once been enlightened, and have tasted the heavenly gift, and have shared in the Holy Spirit, and have tasted the goodness of the word of God and the powers of the age to come." Here eating manna permits a Christian to experience the Holy Spirit, to hear the word of divine prophecy, and to know, presumably through a vision, the angelic powers presently in New Jerusalem who are to become active on earth in the new age to come.

In 1 Corinthians 10:1–5, Paul refers to manna as "spiritual food" and to the water that flows from "the spiritual rock" as "spiritual drink." Scholars who assume that Paul was incapable of speaking well of Judaism reject the literal interpretation, that the manna and water rendered the Jews spiritual. I see no reason not to take Paul at his word.

A further allusion to the manna tradition occurs in another tale, uniquely transmitted by Luke. The resurrected Jesus accompanied two disciples on a walk from Jerusalem to the village of Emmaus but went unrecognized by them until he broke bread. "When he was at the table with them, he took bread, blessed and broke it, and gave it to them. Then their eyes were opened, and they recognized him; and he vanished from their sight" (Luke 24:30–31). The disciples were apparently able to see Jesus in his glory only after eating the fractured host.

In closing, I note that the priest who initiated Jeremiah, and every priest who officiates at a Christian mass, performs the role of God; and after having eaten, Jeremiah achieves union with God, as does every communicant. It is possible that Christianity was heir to the manna tradition, as the tradition descended specifically from Jeremiah. May we conclude that Jesus and his followers were persecuted, among other reasons, because it was the temple's own secrets that they were attempting to publicize?

15
What Is Entheology?

Rev. Aline M. Lucas

Aline M. Lucas, a graduate of Harvard University (the Divinity School), is a priest on staff at Saint Mary of Magdala Cathedral in Fresno, California. She is also the dean of St. Thomas College, a diocesan training school for the ministry. She is an adjunct professor in the Philosophy Department at the Clovis Center, one of the several colleges of the State Community College District in Fresno.

Then later when questioned about LSD by some of the young Westerners that were with him, he [Maharaja-ji] said, "If you're in a cool place and you're quiet and you're feeling much peace and your mind is turned toward God, it's useful." He said that it will allow you to come in and have a visit—the darshan—of a saint, of a higher being of a higher space—higher consciousness is how you can translate it. But he says you can't stay there— after a couple of hours you gotta come back. He said, you know, it would be much better to become

a saint, rather than to go and have this visit; but having this visit is nice. He said it strengthens your faith in the possibility that such things exist.

RAM DASS, *THE ONLY DANCE THERE IS*, 1974

WHAT IS ENTHEOLOGY?

When we practice entheology or when we are willing to call ourselves entheologians, we are discussing our experiences of the divine, and of the revelation of that divine source through the agency of psychoactive sacramentals, be it a revelation of the "divine spark" within (to use Meister Eckhart's term) or without, that is, the reception of a revelation, which is located outside the mystic him/herself.*

Although the term is new, entheology as a science is not. We know, from the great researchers like Wasson, Yensen, and Metzner that entheology has been practiced by many non-Christian and indigenous-based Christian groups (for example, the Mazatec visionary Maria Sabina, and as we have heard this morning, the Peyote Way Church, Santo Daime, and UDV) for many years. This can be more appropriately called non-Western entheology, practiced by cultures from which we have much to learn.

My personal interest, however, lies in Western, Christian entheology, partly because Western Christian traditions tend to reject any assimilation of entheogens into their theological and liturgical paradigms.

ENTHEOLOGY AND LITURGY

I will ask you to keep in mind the two following definitions:

---

*Since the conference, I have reworded the definition of "entheology" so that it now reads: "Entheology is that branch of theology, which deals with the experience and/or knowledge of the divine, and of the revelation of that divine, through the agency of psychoactive substances (used as sacraments), be it at a revelation of the divine within and/or without the individual."

1. A sacrament is an outward and visible sign of an inward and spiritual grace.
2. Liturgy, to quote from Aidan Kavanagh's *On Liturgical Theology,* can be defined as "any ceremonialized human gathering, sacred or secular."

As we begin examining the question of entheology and liturgy from the mainline Christian perspective, we are confronted with a virtual conundrum—a chicken/egg dilemma in a sense. Which comes first? Do we begin with a liturgical paradigm that includes entheogens as sacramental agents and then design a theology based on that experience? Or, do we begin by thinking theologically and then act liturgically? In other words—words Mr. Sartre could have used had he been a liturgical theologian—does liturgy precede theology or does theology precede liturgy?

I used to think the latter. Having read the reports of the Harvard Agape, I altered my perspective. I would now opt for the former—liturgy precedes theology.

As Urban Holmes wrote:

Liturgy leads regularly to the edge of chaos, and from this regular flirt with doom comes a theology different from any other.* One such insight in that theology is not the very first result of an assembly's being brought by liturgical experience to the edge of chaos. Rather it seems that what results in the first instance from such experience is deep change in the very lives of those who participate in the liturgical act. And deep change will affect their next liturgical

---

*This idea of liturgy bringing us to the "edge of chaos" reminds me of Otto's concept of *mysterium tremendum et fascinans*—the awe-full encounter with God. It is also interesting that Holmes, speaking of traditional liturgical expression, would use the word "chaos." Indeed, one hardly thinks of chaos when one recalls any mainline Christian service. However, the reports of people who have experimented with entheogens, and LSD in paticular, give us a better sense of what standing at the edge of chaos may be. I strongly believe that the use of entheogens within a liturgical paradigm, be it traditional or innovative, would bring the participants to that edge.

act, however so slightly. To detect that change in the subsequent liturgical act will be to discover where theology has passed. (quoted in *On Liturgical Theology,* Kavanagh, 1984)

To use the famous Anglo-Catholic statement of the Oxford Movement: *lex orandi, lex credendi*—the law of prayer is the law of belief.

One must act first and then reflect upon that action. Because one of the characteristics, or perhaps effects, of the liturgical act is the building of community, our primary concern should be for liturgical expression. Gather people together in corporate worship, gather people together in community, gather people together in peace, in trust, in love, and you will witness the birth and growth of communion. And it is in communion that the sacrament becomes efficacious, becomes the agent or channel of revelation, the transformer of visibility into invisibility, of sign into grace. From revelation we come to the knowledge of the divine. And from that knowledge comes theological reflection and change.

THE HARVARD AGAPE

As a working example, I will share with you some thoughts on the Harvard Agape, but first I want to summarize, according to the categories drafted by Evelyn Underhill in *Worship,* what constitutes a liturgical event, or *cultus.* She offers four elements:

1. Ritual, or liturgic pattern
2. Symbol or significant image
3. Sacrament, in the general sense of the use of visible things and deeds, not merely to signify, but also to convey invisible realities
4. Sacrifice, or voluntary oblation

These four elements were operating in the Harvard Agape at various levels.

1. I had designed a very loose ritual because of the religious diversity of the people in our group and our opposing views on liturgical structure. We gathered together a couple hours before the Agape was to start. At 5 p.m., we began the service with one participant leading us into the sacred time and space through a Buddhist meditation. A few words of dedication were said by all and we communicated. After a long period of silent meditation, I chanted the Agape Hymn and the service was open to all, to share their spiritual stories if and when moved by the Spirit. And they did: some sang, others read poetry, and others shared meaningful stories by speaking or listening.

2. The most significant symbol was a single red rose. It was brought by the entheogenic "father" of the group. He always entered entheogenic events with a red rose, in memory of Walter Huston Clark. I think that after the Agape, we all understood the red rose to be our icon. Other images were brought by each participant—someone brought a statue of Buddha, I brought an icon of the Mary Magdalene, we all brought pictures of our loved ones, and so forth.

3. The sacrament was MDMA.

4. By sacrifice/oblation, I understand a personal gift to a greater reality. In the case of the Agape, we all had to give up a bit of our individual selves to be there and to make the service happen. Cost, illegality, and personal religious differences that had to be overcome all constitute sacrifices. But to that must be added spiritual sacrifices—like the prayers we offered, the stories we shared, and the objects we placed on the altar.

Now remember what I said earlier. Before the Agape, I was operating according to the "theology precedes liturgy" model. Since I sensed that everybody was somewhat nervous about this great event, I decided to write them all an introductory/explanatory note, which I distributed a day before the event. I wanted to explain the theory behind the deed. Let me read you a short passage:

What is more, in the liturgical moment, we encounter each other as well as the whole communion of saints. What we do in that time and in that space links us to another group celebrating the same mystery somewhere else, in California or in the New Mexico desert or in the suburbs of Rio. In the liturgical moment we transcend our sarcic limitations and are transformed into psychic travelers, psychic guides, psychic worshippers, psychic priests. In our liturgical epiphanies we join in with Maria Sabina chanting, with Hofmann on his bicycle, with Bach on the harpsichord, with a child being born, with the moon slowly rising over a Tibetan monastery . . . in a sense the liturgical moment serves as axis mundi, as that one unique point of gathering.

Something like this:

> *Tao produced the one.*
> *The one produced the two.*
> *The two produced the three.*
> *And the three produced the ten thousand things.*
> *The ten thousand things carry the yin and embrace the yang,*
> *and through the blending of the material force they*
> *achieve harmony.*

In the liturgical moment we are the 10,000 things—achieving harmony.

My goal in the Agape is to capture (on a smaller scale of course) that pattern. Also, we must remember the meaning of sacrament: an outward and visible sign of an inward and spiritual grace. The grace received through the agency of the entheogen is simply that sense of participation in the divine harmony. When our little community gathers in silence, surrounded by the fire of the spirit, when it opens its heart to the moving of the Ruach, then it produces the 10,000 things.

I read you this passage because I want you to understand that, although we were all more or less involved in religion, there was a great deal of doubt in the minds of the participants. I am lucky to have gotten honest reports back from most of the people involved. Let me read from a couple of them so that you can judge for yourselves:

From Report 1:

Of all the people who participated in our agape, I am probably the most skeptical about the value of structured ritual for spiritual development, and certainly the most cynical. So I was a little concerned at first that the whole affair would turn into some ghastly approximation of church, which I had enough of when I was an altar boy. . . . I also didn't want to end up in the middle of some goofy hippy [*sic*] love fest where we all sat around saying prayers to "holy entheogenos" and chanting for five hours until the effects of the drug wore off.

From Report 2:

I had many reservations from the time of the first invitation to the moment I entered the apartment kitchen. . . . My reservations stemmed from the important differences between the other participants and me, and because I naturally hesitate to place myself in situations that might require me to be more open with people than my stoic Irish-Catholic roots have inclined me. I was also concerned about an implied quest for spirituality.

Now you understand what I was dealing with! But not everybody was so skeptical. Some people were actually excited! So the Agape took place . . . and the sacrament did impart grace. That grace took on different forms for different people: communion, healing, salvation, exhortation, admonition, revelation, confirmation, and so forth, to use classical terms. Let me read you the concluding thoughts from the same two reports:

From Report 1:

We were continually possessed by a spirit of community, as chan-
neled through each of us as individuals. I strongly feel that each of
us got out of it what we wanted and needed from it, and that we
all became better people, and certainly closer friends through our
common experience of the agape. . . . I have been convinced from
my experiences of January 21, 1995, that using entheogens within
a loosely-structured ritual setting does not restrict the individual's
opportunities for personal enlightenment. Rather, when this ritual
takes place among a group of closely-knit friends, I think it fosters a
deeper sense of belonging to a community and allows each individual to express their own identity strongly in a way that invigorates
the community in which it takes place.

From Report 2:

Two important qualities are clear when I think of the experience.
The first is that the entire event occurred in a nonjudgmental
ambience. . . . The second is the connection between inspiration
and spirituality. . . . The words, whether their own or the words of
others, were expressed as the extension of their souls. Finding the
place in which and the people with whom this could be acted out is
the key to spirituality. The lessons of inspiration as well as the sense
of communal responsibility conjured by the agape will remain key
tools in my forming search for spirituality.

Very potent words!

CONCLUSION

I engaged in the Harvard Agape as a committed Christian. I think that
it is time for the Westerner to stand up and dare to speak against the
oppressive status quo, the status quo he/she has created or let happen. It

is time for religious leaders to get informed about the power of entheo-gens, to experience the power of the spirit. Christianity, historically, is a pneumatic religion. It believes in open revelation, in the presence of God made known in the world here and now (as well as in the tradition of the Church and in the biblical record). What happened at Pentecost? It is time for believers to demand—from their churches, temples, synagogues—to demand the space, the possibility, the latitude for a new Pentecost.

I'll end with a word of wisdom from another Harvard trouble-maker, Mr. Emerson:

> Yourself a newborn bard of the Holy Ghost, cast behind you all con-formity, and acquaint people at first hand with deity.

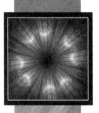

16

A Protocol for a
Sacramental Service

Myron J. Stolaroff

Myron Stolaroff, M.A., studied Electrical Engineering at Stanford. In 1961 he founded the International Foundation for Advanced Study in Menlo Park, California, where research was conducted with LSD and mescaline for three and a half years. This work resulted in a number of papers published in medical journals, including a well-received paper on creativity. He conducted two decades of research on promising phenethylamines. He is author of *Thanatos to Eros: Thirty-five years of Psychedelic Exploration,* published in 1994, and *The Secret Chief: Conversations with a Pioneer of the Underground Psychedelic Therapy Movement,* published in 1997.

❖

We saw that the human being is at first biocentric and egocentric, lost in its own impulses and incapable of taking the role of other. As egocentric gives way to sociocentric, the human being starts to treat others of its group with the same courtesy it extends to itself. And then with worldcentric morality, the human being attempts to treat all

humans with equal dignity or at least equal opportunity.
(And with further development into the World Soul, all
sentient beings are extended this courtesy, even if they can't
respond.)

KEN WILBER, *A BRIEF HISTORY OF EVERYTHING*, 1996

This chapter relates the wisdom gathered from the supervised, structured use of various entheogens before the substances were made illegal. This information is presented to preserve it for the benefit of future students of the entheogens at a time when such use is once again permitted.

A variety of protocols may be employed in using entheogens in sacramental services. These can include using different psychoactive substances, varying dose levels, or different combinations of participants. The protocols may vary as the experience of the participants broadens.

Ideally, individuals will be introduced to group participation as they gain the ability to be at ease with and best make use of the experience, or as they develop some of the attributes of "the trained user" (see below). One approach is to work individually with a person until he/she is ready to join a group. Another approach is to use less challenging entheogens, such as MDMA, with the whole group participating from the beginning. A third variation is to use either of these approaches but start with a low dose level and work up to larger doses. Each of these approaches has specific advantages and disadvantages.

To bring into focus the various considerations governing these choices, I will use as a model the most intense case, that of introducing a novice with a full dose of one of the powerful entheogens, such as LSD. This example will allow us to examine important aspects of achieving the most favorable result in the most demanding situation likely to be encountered in sacramental use.

WHAT DO ENTHEOGENS DO?

In order to determine how best to conduct a ceremony, we must understand the parameters of the experience. A simplified description of the action of the sacrament is that it dissolves the barrier to the unconscious mind, making the unconscious contents available. This can reveal buried painful memories and repressed feelings, values, and drives as described by Freud, which parallel the human archetypes and collective unconscious postulated by Carl Jung. Beyond these descriptions, vast ranges of mind become evident, including esoteric concepts of universal mind, remarkable floods of imagery, and an overflowing source of fresh thoughts, intuition, and creative ideas. Ultimately one can find at the heart of being an awesome source of light, energy, beauty, meaning, and unsurpassed love that is the very revelation of Divinity. Such discoveries have been described as reaching the supreme mystical experience of Union with God. Here the harmony, beauty, wholeness, and unity of all of creation are self-evident.

It is clear that the most desirable outcome of a sacramental experience is to reach the transcendental levels of consciousness. Unfortunately such an objective cannot be produced on demand. It may first be necessary to encounter and resolve important unconscious contents of the mind. Subjects who are healthy-minded, well motivated, flexible, and who generally appreciate life in its manifold facets may be propelled directly into transcendental realms, experiencing great joy, bliss, and realization.

However, persons who carry heavy psychic loads, and who are rigid or judgmental in their approach to life may have to spend a fair amount of time resolving such difficulties before entering the Promised Land of transcendental experience. The following suggestions are offered to facilitate a safe and comfortable passage through whatever may be encountered, with the objective of achieving a rich, helpful, and satisfying experience.

SELECTING CANDIDATES

Motivation is the single most important characteristic for one who wishes a fulfilling sacramental journey. Deep intention for a positive outcome can dissolve many barriers and resistances. Psychological health eases the passage, but much valuable work can be done by those with emotional and psychological problems if they are well motivated and prepared to confront and deal with whatever they encounter in the experience. Therefore openness and ability to surrender to the experience help greatly to ease the passage. Resistance, on the other hand, increases discomfort and can prevent many rewarding discoveries.

Honesty is another important requirement for a successful journey. Honesty encourages the subject to face whatever is occurring, even if unpleasant; strengthens his or her resolve to persistently pursue the truth; and helps enormously after the experience in assimilating what has been learned and applying it to everyday living.

PREPARATION

Since motivation is the single most important factor affecting the outcome, subjects should thoroughly examine their objectives. It is advisable for each participant to make a list of questions to which answers are sought and to review the questions with a knowledgeable guide prior to the experience. The guide can help the subject focus his or her intent and may suggest worthwhile topics for exploration that the subject may have overlooked. See below for a more detailed description of the guide role.

CONDUCT OF THE SESSION

The Guide. A knowledgeable guide is the most important element of the environment in which the experience takes place. This should be someone who has a great deal of personal experience in using entheogens and is quite familiar with the substances and their application. The guide should be sensitive, caring, and supportive, with experience handling the great variety of circumstances that can appear in a session. Most important, the subject and guide shall have established good rapport.

The Setting. The place where the experience takes place should be comfortable, well appointed, quiet, and free from distractions. Also important is ready access to natural beauty such as a view, a garden, or beautiful grounds. There should be a comfortable place to recline, and a good music system should be available. The room should have inspiring pictures and a collection of interesting artifacts available for examination: art books, crystals, and intriguing objects.

Dose Level. This protocol follows the overwhelming-dose technique, where the dose administered is sufficient to overcome the resistance of the ego. The guide or director of the session recommends the dose based on body weight and, what may be even more important, the psychological armor of the subject. After a sufficient length of time has transpired for the initial dose to take effect time (depending on the material used), the subject can be asked if he/she is responding satisfactorily. If the participant is sure, the experience may proceed. If not sure, the guide should check again after fifteen or twenty minutes. If the subject is not satisfied, add a supplement. Supplements can be added at about half-hour intervals up to two or so hours, again depending on the material used, until the subject is satisfied that the dose is adequate.

Trust. In order to trust, the subject must have a concept of something in which to trust. Preferably those undergoing sacramental experiences will have some personal notion of the reality of God. Pre-session discussions can cover various relevant aspects of the Godhead—the existence of an all-wise Inner Teacher, a Source of life that best understands the requirements for growth and fulfillment, the Redeemer, the Healer, the Comforter. The stronger one's experience of such realities, the easier it is to let go and trust completely in the process, regardless of how uncomfortable, joyous, or unusual the experience may be. Most of us have apprehension of the unknown, and an effective sacramental experience will provide a great deal of previously unknown material. The more one can trust and let go, the smoother will be the journey through any rough places and the more fruitful the outcome of the experience.

The person who I believe to have been the world's greatest entheogenic therapist introduced over three thousand subjects and over one hundred therapists to properly conducted fruitful sacramental experiences. At first he had clients read various kinds of spiritual literature as preparation. In the end he gave up the idea of preparatory reading and simply had clients recite twice at the beginning of their experience the following prayer:

> *Lord, I know not what I ought to*
> *ask of thee; Thou only knowest*
> *what I need; Thou lovest me better*
> *than I know how to love myself.*
> *O Father, give to Thy child that*
> *which he himself knows not how to*
> *ask. I dare not ask either for*
> *crosses or for consolations; I simply*
> *present myself before thee, I open*
> *my heart to Thee. Behold my needs which*
> *I know not myself; see and*
> *do according to Thy tender mercy.*
> *Smite, or heal; depress me or raise*
> *me up; I adore all Thy purposes*
> *without knowing them; I am silent;*
> *I offer myself in sacrifice; I yield*
> *myself to Thee: I would have no*
> *other desire than to accomplish*
> *Thy will. Teach me to pray. Pray*
> *Thyself in me. AMEN.*
>
> FRANCOIS DE SALIGNAC FENELON

The Inner Journey. The first several hours are spent encouraging the subject to search deeply within her/himself. This is facilitated by having the subject lie down and put on a good pair of stereo headphones, then covering his/her face with a velvet cloth. The first few hours are spent listening to music, which greatly encourages the unfolding and focusing of the experience. The beauty and wonder of music as experienced under the sacrament eases any encounter with unpleasant material and is often in itself a source of extreme enjoyment and even amazement. The subject should bring favorite and meaningful selections. The initial musical selections are quiet, lyrical compositions that encourage relaxation and sentimentality and convey a sense of mystery, such as Respighi's *Fountains of Rome* or Ibert's *Ports of Call.* As the subject goes deeper into the experience, more dramatic music can be introduced. Toward the end of the inward exploring period, and especially if the subject approaches transcendental levels, spiritual music is compelling. In the research days of our Foundation,* almost all who began the experience with a dislike of classical music ended up preferring it.

Outer Resolution. After four or five hours of inner exploration, the subject is ready to sit up and observe the surrounding world and to begin relating the inward journey to life circumstances. At this point photographs of intimate partners, close family members, and friends are most helpful. These can be examined with heightened insights and understanding. Outstanding works of art and objects of physical beauty are also fruitful. The beauty of living things in nature is most compelling at this point. One of the most influential artifacts during the research conducted by our Foundation was a fresh red rose. This was often overpowering, and it seemed an especially appropriate symbol of femininity. At the completion of these activities is a good time to review the list of questions to see if everything was answered. Participants are often amazed to see how many questions were answered that had not been consciously addressed during the experience. Even when it seemed that questions were not answered, the passage of time after the session revealed that they had indeed been answered. Toward the end of the experience, intimate partners, family members, or friends may be brought in for direct interaction.

Handling Stuck Areas. There are times when the subject may be resistant to encountering repressed, highly charged, or painful material. Insofar as possible, the subject should be encouraged to continue lying

---

International Foundation for Advanced Study, Menlo Park, California

down and to proceed with the inner journey, whereby such areas are confronted and resolved. If the subject is too frightened to continue the inner search, he or she should be encouraged to sit up and describe what is happening, including the accompanying feelings. Often simply talking relieves much anxiety. If too disturbed to talk, the subject can be shown pictures or objects to take his or her attention off of the discomfort. A walk in nature can be quite helpful, providing that privacy is available. The guide should continually remind the subject that the effects of the drug will wear off in due time and that the subject will be freed from the pressures he or she is feeling. If the subject is still unsettled at the end of the day, provisions must be made for companionship until he or she can fall asleep. The compelling feelings released by the action of the sacrament are almost always dissipated by the following morning. The subject will then either be at ease, or find it much easier to interact.

Asking for Help. The act of asking is often overlooked in a session. Many of us are reluctant to ask for help and feel that we should work everything out for ourselves, especially if we have had any realization of the enormity of the Self. The concept that we have within us the Ultimate Teacher is useful in undertaking a sacramental journey. This all-wise Knower is most happy to help us in any way possible. It must be remembered that Free Will is an ultimate cosmic law that will not be violated. Consequently if we wish for help, we must make it clear. Many have been surprised, even shocked, at how readily an answer came when a question was seriously asked.

One cannot guarantee that this will happen every time, as a number of factors affect the situation. For example, do you really wish to know the answer to your question? Sometimes it takes enormous fortitude to be willing to be still and experience the answer, particularly if the answer is in conflict with pet beliefs or heavily defended feelings. Consequently the question must be asked with the entirety of our being. Like intent, the deeper the desire to know, the more the scattered or opposing elements of our inner being will be drawn into alignment, like the molecules in a magnetized rod of iron, facilitating the appearance of the answer to our question. Much can be learned by asking and being completely receptive to whatever may come.

FOLLOW UP

Written Report. Subjects should be encouraged to write a detailed account of their experience. This will aid in recall and serve as a valuable reference as changes in personal dynamics take place in subsequent weeks and months.

Action. It is extremely vital to put important learning into action in daily living. This is the best way to retain the new learning that has taken place. Failure to act upon what one has learned can permit the new truths to dissipate, and in time powerful habits can reestablish themselves. The best way of preventing this is to express newly found energy in new modes of functioning.

THE TRAINED USER

Undertaking the procedure described above allows participants to work through and resolve much material that has been stored in their unconscious as well as discover much about themselves, their personal dynamics, their relationships, the nature of mind, and the nature of reality. All of these discoveries assist persons to more readily undertake subsequent experiences (either individually or when appropriate in group settings), to make their way through them more comfortably, and to learn more rapidly. As the participants gain experience they "learn how to learn" more and more until ultimately they begin to take on the characteristics of a "trained user." I use quotation marks here because the term "trained user" has not been used in the literature to my knowledge, thus leaving out a very significant aspect of employing entheogens. The most important ability of a trained user is to hold one's mind perfectly steady so that attention may be fixed on a chosen object and held until the object of attention reveals itself in its various aspects and dimensions. One must also learn patience, acceptance, detachment, and courage in facing whatever is being presented. A loving attitude toward the object of attention is also helpful.

Mental stability is a most valuable asset. The practice of meditation as a means of achieving mental stability is one of the outstanding contributions of Buddhism. When one develops the ability to hold the mind absolutely still, one creates the most favorable condition for nonordinary aspects of reality to become apparent. The flow of imagery, thoughts, and energy that results from a significant dose of an entheogen substantially interferes with holding the mind steady. However, the pressure of the mind stream diminishes as repressed unconscious material is relieved, and it becomes easier to hold the mind steady. With progressive clearing and steady practice, which strengthens the ability to become free of distractions, one can develop considerable skill in making full use of the potential that entheogens offer. Then the enormous value of entheogens as means of learning and of directly apprehending Divinity can be fully appreciated.

17

A Theology of Human Liberation and Entheogens

REFLECTIONS OF A CONTEMPLATIVE ACTIVIST

Rev. George F. Cairns

George F. Cairns, M.Div., Ph.D., is trained as both an experimental and clinical psychologist. He received his B.A. from Rutgers University in 1967, and his M.A. and Ph.D. from Emory University in 1969 and 1971. He received his M.Div. degree from Chicago Theological Seminary in 1989, where he is now Assistant Professor of Practical Theology and Spirituality. He teaches courses in psychology, spirituality, and the development of community. He has published widely in these areas. George is an ordained United Church of Christ minister who has helped establish Christian base communities among the homeless in the inner city and teaches contemplative practices to men in a maximum-security prison. Currently he serves on the International Faculty of Contemplative Outreach, an organization dedicated to teaching Centering Prayer.

◇

A botanist I know (who does not take recreational drugs) believes that 30 million Americans took drugs between the 1960s and 1990s, and that the visions the drug users had while in that altered state account for the utterly new sea-change of attitude that we find today at the end of the century: a deep and reverent regard for our planet and for those others out in space, for our environment, for the rain forests and both wild and domestic animals, for the idea that the Earth itself—Gaia—is breathing, has consciousness, and that all living beings, all rocks and plants and sentient beings are inextricably entangled; that we humans are now evolving to a higher plane of divine consciousness.

SOPHY BURNHAM, *THE ECSTATIC JOURNEY:
THE TRANSFORMING POWER OF
MYSTICAL EXPERIENCE,* 1997

What I would like to do here today is first to describe briefly a theology of human liberation that is already radically transforming the church and, second, to discuss the place that entheogens may have to play in this theology. From reading the CSP entheogen mailing list on the Internet, I found that many writers have a rather conventional view of the church. I suspect that some of you may not be familiar with this radical redefinition of what it means to be a church. This theology of liberation begins by describing the context in which the person works, so I will begin by describing my context, including my social location. It is important for you to understand that the people I have served are not the comfortable—they are among the most shunned persons in our culture. This theology grows out of this work and at root requires involvement with people on the margins.

CONTEXT

I am both an ordained UCC minister and a psychologist. I have spent much of my adult life working among marginalized and oppressed people here in the United States. Much of my journey has been a process of uncovering my biases and presuppositions regarding my inner life and the systems within which we all are imbedded. My original research in infant and child development was undermined when I began one of the first infant care programs in the country. When I saw how few resources were available for basic well baby care, I found it difficult to continue the extremely expensive neonatal research that I had engaged in for the previous five years. During the next ten years I worked with seriously mentally ill persons in both inner city and ultra rural areas who were largely ignored by the larger culture. Here too I found that much of my work was applying bandages to the wounds of people who were victims of larger systems of oppression. One turning point for me was when I found that our mental health center was cycling court-ordered Native American clients through a thirty-day outpatient program for chemical dependency and then sending them home to reservation towns with rates of alcoholism that exceeded fifty percent. At the same time, my clinical work in altered states (biofeedback, hypnosis, meditation, guided imagery, etc.) resonated with a call to ministry to ask questions of the larger systems in which we are imbedded and to seek personal and systemic liberation.

Over the past seven years I have engaged in contemplative prayer and ministered with communities of the most victimized people in our culture—homeless and marginally housed people, many of whom are seriously physically or mentally ill. Beginning a street ministry and later encouraging small communities of faith to develop in what used to be called flop houses has come to be a contemplative practice of both inner and outer liberation that has transformed my life. Lee and Cowan describe the "dangerous memories" that are recovered in such a practice:

> . . . that there is a double composition to following Christ; the mystical and the political. There is not first the mystical and then the

political. . . . The political is of the substance of the mystical. (Lee and Cowan 1986, 12).

This ministry and hundreds of thousands like it all over the world provide a powerful new vision for the church. I believe that entheogens may have a place in such a contemplative/activist practice of being church. But first, let me describe how the choices made in my life have limited my exposure to entheogens. I believe that systemic social and legal pressure have split the inner work in which healthy aspects of the "psychedelic culture" engaged from the outer work of those of us involved in social action. This split has contributed to the continuation of what Robert McAfee Brown (Brown 1988, 23–33) has called the "great fallacy": that inner and outer transformations are falsely separated.

SPLIT BETWEEN INNER
AND OUTER ACTION

Since the mid 1960s I have been involved in political action in one way or another. Selective prosecution for the use of illicit substances was and is a fact of life for those who are politically engaged. In Georgia, where I began this work, several persons who were active in the civil rights and anti-war movements received unusually stiff prison sentences for possession of relatively small amounts of psychoactive substances. From the very beginning, I chose to not possess such materials, and to make it publicly known that this was and is the case. Organizations to which I belonged that were engaged in political action took similar stands in order to protect their core mission of seeking social and political change.

HEALING GROUNDED IN INNER WORK

I teach a course titled "Practical Theology of Mysticism." While my wife says that this is a triple oxymoron, I intentionally chose this title to subvert just such false separations. The contemplatives in our tradition provide us with numerous examples of how the inner work of contemplation leads to action and service. The contemplative experience leads one to deeply understand that the inner work and the outer work are fully intertwined.

Contemplative Activists

In fact, contemplative activists are some of the most effective agents for encouraging the liberation of individuals and systems in all of human history. They are persons whose inner practice overflows into the public sphere in exceedingly effective and powerful ways. They heal the split and expose the great fallacy through their prayers and actions. Consider this short list of persons of action in the twentieth century who have a contemplative awareness: Gandhi, Martin Luther King Jr., Thomas Merton, Mother Theresa, Thich Nhat Hanh, and the Dalai Lama are but a few. These people embody the contemplative potentialities of what it is to be human and to act effectively on these understandings.

While many of you here know much more than I do about contemplative understandings, this much I do know. These practices offer us ways to understand and transform ourselves and others, as well as the communities and larger systems in which we are imbedded. In the Western Christian tradition this means we become more fully the beings that God created us to be: fully human and compassionate servants of others. As we continue this conversion to compassionate beings, we act as models and agents of conversion for other individuals and systems. Others here described the place that entheogens have had and will continue to have in developing such understandings.

Activist Contemplatives

A powerful movement focusing on prayerful service has developed within the Christian church in the latter half of the twentieth century. Here too the split is healed and the great fallacy challenged. From beginnings in Latin America in small communities at the base of society new methods and voices developed. This way of engaging in practical action followed by formal reflection is called liberation theology.

It involves a radical engagement with the poor, reading scripture as it relates to the community today, engaging in worship, and then acting on these engaged understandings. This is not an isolated movement for the church. It is likely that there are now more than a million of these base Christian communities spread all over the world. There are parallel movements in other religious traditions.

WHY HIDDEN MEMORIES REMAIN HIDDEN

Why is it that we hear so little about this movement in North America? First, the movement is frequently portrayed in the North American context as only a theology of radical, and even revolutionary, social and political action. Culturally, we downplay, undercut, deny, and obscure the emphasis that liberation theology places on prayer and the interior life. Why is it that the North American power structure is so threatened by liberation theology that it needs to deny its roots in Christian theology and practice? Because these movements deeply challenge us and the current power structures from the vantage point of the grinding poverty of most people. The reaction by the government of the United States was predictable.

> In 1969 President Nixon sent Nelson Rockefeller to Latin America to investigate the situation. His report stated that the church there was changing into "a force devoted to change, by revolutionary means if necessary." (Boff and Boff 1987, 86)

Later this reaction escalated when advisors to President Reagan produced the Santa Fe Document, which states explicitly that "American foreign policy must begin to counterattack (and not just react against) liberation theology" (Boff and Boff 1987, 86).

Participant/writers in the Latin American context such as Leonardo and Clodovis Boff have clearly described the contemplative and sacramental core of this movement (Boff and Boff 1987, 94). They and others have strongly emphasized that Gospel values are the bedrock on which liberation theology is based. In the U.S., the government-sponsored view that liberation theology is only a radical political movement divorced from the church is the image that persists when this movement is acknowledged at all.

A second and perhaps even more significant reason that we have difficulty recovering these dangerous memories is that the process requires us to individually and collectively examine our own captivities, which are pervasive and largely unconscious. I am in agreement with Jacob Needleman that we are both material and spiritual beings, and that our culture has largely excluded the rich experience of the sacred from systematic awareness. He points out that since we have much more tangible material experiences, it is difficult to maintain the balance of the spiritual and the material. Thus the great fallacy persists in our individual and collective consciousnesses (Needleman 1991). The work of contemplative activists and of activist contemplatives in the church undermines this fallacy.

RADICAL OPENNESS

The world of contemplation and action results in a radical openness that can never be reversed. Several years ago, during a protracted solitary retreat in a place sacred to native peoples, I had a vision and caught a glimpse of God's face. This extraordinarily powerful experience combined a full-bodied, overwhelming sense of sacred awe with a complete sense of being one strand in the interpenetrating web of all of God's creation. I have never been the same. Through the Christian process of centering prayer I continue to experience God's presence and be reminded that you and I are not separate beings—that your liberation is my liberation. Seeking the liberation of all of creation is our collective task as human beings.

Others here have described how practices incorporating the sacramental use of entheogens have provided similar deeply engaged understandings of our connection with all of creation. Once we have such an experience, how can we not seek the liberation of all beings? I believe this is what the Gospels call me to do. This is what the sacred writings of other authentic traditions call us to do. This is the dangerous memory that challenges us and our culture into new ways of being. In the church, as the theologian Dorothee Sölle points out, structures of dominance are not amused when we recover these understandings. When we have the direct experience of God and God's intimate, ever-present nurture in creation, we don't need intermediaries to be gatekeepers between us and God. These are profoundly subversive understandings. To the extent that entheogens help us open to these understandings, such substances have a place in facilitating the full-bodied work of liberation.

These recovered memories of the Gospels challenge me to name, unmask, and engage systemic evil. These hidden memories are a call to individual and social liberation. The spiritual practices that underlie this action are central to sustaining this work. The practices provide ways to recover the memories and to sustain the story of transformation in human history. I urge all of you to help us sustain these hidden memories and together to seek the liberation of all of creation.

REFERENCES

Boff, L. and C. Boff. 1987. *Introducing Liberation Theology.* Mary Knoll, N.Y.: Orbis Books, 86, 94.

Brown, R. M. 1988. *Spirituality and Liberation: Overcoming the Great Fallacy.* Philadelphia: The Westminster Press, 233–330.

Lee, B. J. and M. A. Cowan. 1986. *Dangerous Memories: House Churches and Our American Story.* Kansas City, Mo.: Sheed and Ward, 12.

Needleman, J. 1991. *Money and the Meaning of Life.* New York: Doubleday.

Sölle, D. 1981. "Mysticism, liberation and the names of God." *Christianity and Crisis* 41: 179–85.

18

Consciousness and Asian Traditions

AN EVOLUTIONARY PERSPECTIVE

Roger Walsh

Roger Walsh, M.D., Ph.D., is professor of psychiatry, anthropology, and philosophy at the University of California, Irvine. His publications include the books *Essential Spirituality: The Seven Practices Common to World Religions* and (with Frances Vaughan) *Paths Beyond Ego: The Transpersonal Perspective.* A native of Australia, he has been a student of contemplative practices for over twenty years. His writings and research have received more than 20 national and international awards.

Indeed, isn't religion, above all—before it is doctrine and morality, rites and institutions— religious experience? Under the influence of Protestant theologian Friedrich Schleiermacher in nineteenth-century Europe and philosopher-psychologist William James in early-twentieth-

century America, many Westerners have come out in support of the priority of religious experience. And isn't religious experience in its highest form mystical experience, as in India, where it seems more at home than anywhere else? . . .

. . . First of all, we have to ask, what is "mystical experience," anyway?

Discussion of this matter has not quieted down since the appearance of Aldous Huxley's The Doors of Perception *in which he reported personal mystical experiences while taking drugs that approached the highest levels of religious thought and perception: the Christian beatific vision, the Hindu saccidananda or the Buddhist nirvana. Are all mystical experiences, then, fundamentally alike, regardless of whether one reaches them through asceticism and meditation and LSD or sex?*

HANS KÜNG, JOSEF VAN ESS, HEINRICH VON
STIETENCRON, AND HEINZ BECHERT, *CHRISTIANITY
AND THE WORLD RELIGIONS: PATHS TO DIALOGUE
WITH ISLAM, HINDUISM AND BUDDHISM*, 1986

I was asked to discuss Asian traditions and their implications for the subject of this conference. I will do that from an evolutionary perspective.

HUMAN EVOLUTION

About six million years ago humans and the great apes started to diverge. Today we still share 98 percent of our genetic material with the great apes, but that 2 percent makes a big difference. The earliest known human fossils date back some four million years—to *Australopithecus ramidus*. Over the next two million years, as various *Australopithecines* evolved, their brain size gradually increased up to about eight hundred milliliters. Then about two million years ago came the first humans, *Homo habilus,* and shortly after, *Homo erectus.* These early humans appeared in Africa and very quickly migrated around much of Europe and Asia. Very basic stone tools are the only evidence of any tool making for a period of some two million years of evolution. Finally, about half a million years ago, came *Homo sapiens.*

Then about 130 thousand years ago, *Homo neanderthalis* appeared. At this stage we have the first evidence of some religious sensibility, in as much as *Neanderthals* cared for the sick. They also buried their dead in ways that suggest some sort of symbolic ritual activity. This is pretty much all that we know about the religious activity and consciousness of the Neanderthals. But we do know that for one hundred thousand years, they did not change, and human culture did not advance.

The next major evolution was the appearance of modern humans, *Homo sapiens sapiens,* between one hundred and two hundred thousand years ago. These people started to migrate out of Africa and spread around the world perhaps one hundred thousand years ago. Around this time, we find a dramatic explosion in artifacts, tools, and other things that we think of as human and associate with human culture.

About thirty-five thousand years ago, something dramatic happened. We don't know what caused it, but the "great leap" forward began at that time. The best guess is that there was a language explosion. Suddenly, humans had everything from fishhooks and fishing nets, to ornamentation and art, to long-distance throwing weapons. This was also the beginning of extraordinary cave art—whole caves filled with dynamic animal figures.

In the cave of Trois Frères in France, you can see something quite interesting: a human figure with a buffalo head. One guess is that it depicts an early shaman. Along with other archaeological evidence, this suggests that shamanic practices go back perhaps fifty thousand years, to when Cro-Magnon or modern *Homo sapiens* were moving into Europe. At this stage in the evolution of shamanism we have, for the first time that we know of, the systematic alteration of human consciousness. As far as we can tell, shamans were the first people not only to devise a technology for transforming consciousness, but also to form an effective institution by which that knowledge was transmitted from generation to generation.

From this point on, human consciousness evolved in a new way. At first the evolution was biologically driven, then culturally and linguistically driven. With the advent of shamanism it became technologically driven.

SHAMANISM

Obviously, a key question here is: What is a shaman? There are five central features that define shamanism. First is the systematic induction of specific altered states of consciousness. Shamans do this by a variety of methods including physiological ones of fasting and exposure to the elements; psychological ones of set, expectation and ritual, and rhythmic approaches such as drumming. The drum is one of the most common instruments of the shaman.

Second, while in specific altered states, shamans experience themselves as separate from or freed from the body. Third, while out of their bodies, they travel as free souls or spirits to other realms. Fourth, in those realms, shamans reportedly meet other beings, spiritual beings, from whom they obtain information, power, or help. Fifth, they return to use what they have acquired for the benefit of others in their own culture.

Shamans appear to have used various entheogens systematically for tens of thousands of years. Over a hundred different psychoactive materials have been identified in archaeological digs. This indicates a tradition of consciousness alteration employing both entheogenic and external aids (such as rhythm and drumming) that has been used for tens of thousands of years around the world in practically all cultures, except certain island cultures.

EARLY INDIA AND
THE VEDIC TRADITION

I want to segue into the history of India. When I was asked to discuss Asia, I decided to focus on India just to keep it relatively simple and to keep a story going. So we've come up to a period of about four thousand years ago, at which time in India there were two distinct peoples, one dark-skinned and one light-skinned. At this time successive waves of invading light-skinned people, so-called Aryans, began to arrive in India. There are at least two theories of their origins. One idea, associated with Maria Gimbutus is that these people swept down from the Russian steppes. Gimbutus held that they were a sky-god-worshipping, warrior culture that pretty much decimated the matriarchal and more peaceful old European culture.

Linguistic and archeological analyses are opposed to this idea. These analyses suggest that peoples from Anatolia, which is now Turkey, were dispersed beginning about eight thousand years ago, primarily through farming. With the migration of these people came the spread of the Indo-European languages. They spread into India, bringing with them the Vedic tradition.

The Vedic tradition goes back at least four thousand years and has given us some of the world's oldest text, the Vedas. To summarize simply the Vedic tradition, it was a life attitude very much focused on this world, the celebration of life, the world, and its pleasures. Their cosmology was animistic and polytheistic. Various powers ruled the world, and heaven and earth were linked in what is sometimes called the law of correspondences: as above, so below. The main strategy of the Vedic peoples was to try to control the gods and other powers by tapping in to this macro-micro link. Their practices were focused primarily on ritual prayer and sacrifice. Although the Vedic people seem to have had some meditative practices, these were not central or clearly delineated.

At the heart of the Vedic tradition was the mysterious chemical substance soma. There are some hundred and twenty verses in the Rig-Veda referring to it in the most laudatory terms. For example, it is referred to as a plant, as rootless, leafless, blossomless, and from the mountains. As Huston Smith mentioned last night, the puzzle seems to have been solved by R. Gordon Wasson, who identified this as *Amanita muscaria,* or the fly agaric mushroom.

YOGA

The yogic tradition appears to go back at least three thousand years. Images found in the city of Moheno-Daro showing people seated in what look like yogic postures date back this far. The yogic tradition, which lies at the heart of Indian spiritual practices, is associated with a philosophy known as Samkhya, which is world negative, viewing the world as problematic. The world is seen as a place where each of us suffers. This view was formulated most precisely by the Buddha's First Noble Truth, which states that life is *dukkha.* This is often translated as "life is suffering," but it's an inadequate translation. *Dukkha* is a much more sensitive, profound term, implying a subtle existential dissatisfaction, an incapacity to obtain complete and enduring satisfaction in this world and through its pleasures, so it's a much more subtle term. It's not that life is all bad; it's not that all life is suffering. It's that life is problematic.

The yogic tradition presents a dualistic picture of the world. There is *purusha,* or consciousness, and there are phenomena. The universe is composed of these two major elements. The problem, as the yogis see it, is that pure consciousness—which by itself would rest in isolation, untroubled by anything—somehow becomes identified with matter, with phenomena, the world, the body, the mind. The mind itself is hyperactive, continuously in motion, as those of you who have a meditative practice or a yoga practice of some kind know only too well. The mind has a mind of its own. Attention wanders all over the place.

The yoga sutras, the classic sutras of Patanjali, begin with the line, "Yoga is the discipline of bringing the spontaneous activity of the mind to rest." Our usual state of consciousness is one in which our minds are continuously distracted and out of control. This leads to an entrapment of consciousness; the mind identifies with the body, with the world, and forgets its own nature. However, if the mind could be stilled, if attention could be stabilized, if we could free ourselves from the entrapment of successive waves of overpowering emotions, desires, and fears, then consciousness could once again come to rest. The mind could recognize that it is not the body and the world, and come to rest in its own being.

The goal for the yogic tradition, then, is one of liberation through mental training. Here we have a breakthrough, another evolutionary jump in the technology of consciousness. With the shamanic tradition there was a reliance on external aids—entheogens, drumming, music. However, yogis learned to alter consciousness without external aids. The method is a systematic, multidimensional, mental training program, or yoga. Yoga means yoking, the union of the small, individual self with the greater self. There are many elements to it and there are, of course, different types of yoga.

To jump ahead a little bit, in yoga we find the first demonstration of the general principle that there are common elements among traditions capable of authentic transformational, transpersonal development. There are seven common psychological elements. The first is an ethical foundation. The second is attention training, or stabilization. The third is emotional transformation, that is, the ability to reduce negative emotions such as anger, fear, and greed by transforming them into love and compassion. The fourth is a shift in motivation, moving up Maslow's hierarchy of needs, what traditionally was called purification. The fifth is an enhancement or clarifying of perception. The sixth is the cultivation of wisdom—insight into and understanding of the nature of mind and reality. Finally, there is service, which may take forms such as teaching, helping, or healing.

We find in yoga, with its emphasis on an ethical foundation, the yamas and niyamas. We find *pranayama,* the breath work to stabilize and control the mind. We find the emphasis on concentration, culminating in samadhi, the unwavering capacity to hold attention still. As you can see, there's been a major jump from the shamanic to the yogic practices.

ATMAN AND BRAHMAN ARE ONE

But this is by no means the end of the story. About two and a half thousand years ago, we have what's called the axial age, a term used to describe the fact that something truly profound happened for human consciousness. Around the globe, there was a breakthrough in religious consciousness. Think of the breakthroughs in Greece by Socrates and Plato; in China by Lao Tsu and the Taoists, in India by Mahāvīra, the Upanishadic sages, and of course the Buddha, and then a few hundred years later in the Middle East, by Jesus, among others. To put it simply, these breakthroughs constitute the recognition of a greater unity.

Perhaps the best way to describe this is through Vedanta, meaning "what follows after the Vedas." The Upanishadic sages were the people who embodied and taught the Vedantic tradition. In the Chandogya Upanishad there's a story of a youth, Svetaketu, who as a Brahmin child is sent out at age twelve to study. Twelve years later he comes back knowing everything, suffering from a kind of sophomoric inflation. His father says, "Svetaketu, you are conceited and arrogant and think yourself well-read, but did you ever ask for that knowledge by which one hears that which cannot be heard, sees that which cannot be seen, and knows that which cannot be known?" And Svetaketu says, "Well uh, actually no. Could you perhaps tell me about that?"

His father then proceeds to teach him through a series of exercises in which he is asked, for example, to dissect a seed until he can find nothing of the seed. His father says, "Yet from this nothing grows a great tree." He is asked to put some salt in water and come back the next day. The salt is dissolved and can't be seen, but there's a taste that pervades the water. The father's message is that there is a subtle essence at the heart of reality that cannot be seen, felt, or touched, but which is at the center of all things. And "tat tvam asi"—you are that.

For the shamans there were individual souls meeting other individual souls, and for the yogis there was still the individual release of consciousness. In the Vedic tradition, the self and the supreme reality are recognized as one. "Atman (individual consciousness) and Brahman (universal consciousness) are one" say the Upanishads. In the words of the Buddhist tradition, "Look within. You are the Buddha." In China the words were "heaven, earth, and human form one body." Later Jesus would declare, "The Father and I are one" and Mohammed would promise, "He who knows himself, knows his Lord."

THE NONDUAL

Even this isn't the end of the story. While the unity of self and God, or Atman and Brahman, had been recognized, there was still a divide between the divine and the world. Several hundred years later, there was a further progression.

Around the dawn of the Common Era, Nagarjuna in the East and Plotinus in the West initiated a new phase. Not only were the self and the divine recognized as one, but also the world and the supreme reality were recognized as nondual, of one essence. This is the central metaphysical recognition of both Advaita Vedanta and Mahayama Buddhism. It is expressed paradoxically in the words of the twentieth-century sage Ramana Maharshi: "The world is illusion, Brahman alone is real. Brahman is the world."

This evolution of consciousness in the Indian tradition (but not only in the Indian tradition) begins with the original shamans and their external technologies (including entheogens), which induce a sense of freedom from embodiment. The early yogis carry that freedom into the disentanglement of consciousness from phenomena and the world. The Vedantic tradition recognizes that the self and the divine are actually one, and the nondual traditions recognize that it is all one: all is the manifestation of the divine, and all is divine.

MAPPING STATES OF CONSCIOUSNESS

In terms of contemporary study, what can we make of this evolution? Can we map these states of consciousness more precisely? In the past couple of decades, with the development of the field of transpersonal psychology, the answer has been "yes." The transpersonal field has attempted to understand and map the different states of consciousness described in the various traditions. How do we do this?

One thing we can do is simply map out the different dimensions of experience that characterize different states. For example, how much control is there? How much awareness do people have of their environment during the altered state? Is their concentration distracted or enhanced? Are they aroused or calm? What's their dominant emotion? What's their self-sense or identity when they have an out-of-body experience? These are some key dimensions for mapping states of consciousness.

How would the shamanic journey of consciousness be described on this experiential map? Shamans have an increased ability to enter and leave altered states and to partly control their experience. They can be aware of the environment. They can at times interact with people around them while in their trance. Their concentration is enhanced but fluid; shamans can focus on different things at different times. They can be activated and aroused. Their emotions can be either pleasurable or painful according to the situation. Their identity is of a separate self-sense, but as a nonphysical soul. They have an out-of-body experience, and the content of the experience is an organized, coherent imagery that fits the shamanic worldview: for example, that there are spirits to be encountered and worked with and that there is a three-layered universe.

Let's compare that with the Buddhist and yogic traditions. Remember that these are very different practices. Yogic practitioners work, in the classic approach described by Patanjali, by fixing attention unwaveringly, first on an object such as the breath, and ultimately in consciousness itself. Yogis have extraordinary control over their mental faculties and capacities. Concentration is extreme. There is no out-of-body experience, in fact quite the opposite. Awareness of the environment may be totally lost, a state called "enstasis." Arousal may be dramatically reduced as they become very calm. Yogis may become lost in ineffable bliss. Their identity becomes a sense of unchanging consciousness.

The Buddhist meditator, using the classic vipassana, or insight, practice is having a very different experience. The vipassana practice consists not of fixing attention unwaveringly on one thing, but of allowing attention to move to whatever becomes predominant in the field of awareness, investigating it and exploring it as minutely as possible so as to cultivate the mind's sensitivity and precision. This allows practitioners to observe and understand mental processes, and by illuminating those processes, to reduce the distortions, to clear away the illusions, to see through them into reality. For Buddhist practitioners there is partial control; awareness of the environment is actually increased, as is concentration. Arousal can vary but usually decreases over time. The emotion may vary because the meditators are not controlling their attention; they are allowing it to follow whatever arises. The identity is deconstructed; that is, awareness is so precise that Buddhist practitioners are able to deconstruct the self-sense, or ego, into its constituent components of images and thoughts and so forth. There's no out-of-body experience, and again, the experiences that arise are seen very clearly, precisely, and minutely.

So we now have the capacity to differentiate very distinctly among states of consciousness. Because entheogens can elicit a huge range of states, there are many implications for research.

There are a variety of factors that determine how easily specific states are accessed with entheogens. Of course dose and type of entheogen will play a role. Then there are other factors, such as psychological health, developmental level, and prior psychological and contemplative experience, which have been clearly demonstrated to be major components. My guess is that we will find some of these states to be more easily accessible than others. For example, shamanic states would be more easily accessed than yogic samadhis because the latter require a degree of concentration that is probably very rare in entheogenic experiences. Of course, there's the possibility of breaking through to samadhi-like states, but my guess is that as we map the states that arise with entheogens, we'll find that some are easier to access than others. But of course, as Huston Smith said, stabilization is a crucial question. And to what extent can entheogens help one live a religious life as opposed to having religious experiences? I'm going to talk about this on the panel tomorrow so I'll save that discussion (see chapter 3).

A DEVELOPMENTAL PERSPECTIVE

The Asian traditions, like other contemplative traditions, emphasize that practice fosters psychospiritual development through a series of recognizable stages. This developmental perspective offers a valuable way of comparing experiences induced by contemplation and entheogens.

A graphic map of development is shown in the classic Zen ox-herding pictures. These are a series of ten pictures depicting a youth looking for an ox, finding it, taming it, and then transcending it.

The first picture is called "seeking the ox." This is an image of a person seeking the sacred. I did a three-month seminar on the ox-herding pictures with the Abbot Reb Anderson of the San Francisco Zen Center. I don't remember much about the seminar, but I do remember the first thing he said. He said, "Well, this is the first picture. Here we are with all our neuroses, our hang-ups, our craziness. If we could just totally accept ourselves the way we are, we'd be at picture ten, and we could all go home." Needless to say, we stayed there for three months.

The second picture is "finding the tracks." This is often interpreted as finding the writings or the stories of religions. It's not direct experience, but it can point us toward direct experience.

Then comes "glimpsing the ox." This is the first glimpse of the transcendent or sacred. It's a peak (or peek) experience. Based on many reports, it is clear that entheogens can elicit such experiences for some people at some times.

The fourth picture is "catching the ox." This is an image of a very powerful beast that does not want to be caught or tamed, and those of you who meditate will know that's a wonderful model of the mind.

Here is where we begin to see, from a developmental perspective, some of the limitations of entheogens as a psychospiritual tool. These limitations become particularly apparent with the fifth picture, "taming of the ox" and subsequent pictures. Mental training proceeds to a point, which is classically described in Buddhism as "effortless effort." The training continues, but it's almost automatic. It's not an active struggle anymore. This is portrayed beautifully in the sixth picture, "riding the ox home." The person has become a beginning sage, and the mind has a course of its own. The newly conditioned mind takes the person in the direction of the sacred goal, until the whole training process begins to be forgotten. The problem of training the mind is completely forgotten in the seventh picture, "ox forgotten, self alone." Beyond this, in "both ox and self forgotten," the breakthrough occurs into the dharmakaya of pure awareness. The separate self-sense is transcended, not as a transient peak experience or altered state but as an enduring altered trait.

These first eight pictures portray a developmental progression from the initial search to a temporary peak experience, followed by a prolonged mental training to stabilize an effortless and enduring altered trait. As I interpret the research, entheogens can offer the glimpses portrayed in the first three or four images, but by themselves entheogens are unlikely to produce later enduring stages.

With the eighth picture comes "the return to the source." This is the vision of nonduality, in which samsara and nirvana are one. The world is now seen as an emanation of the divine.

In the last ox-herding picture we have this wonderful image of a kind of rascal sage. The picture is called "entering the city with help-bestowing or bliss-bestowing hands." The sage wanders into the city and is totally indistinguishable from anyone else. There is no way to tell the sage by lifestyle or by the way he or she looks. Sages may drink: they may seem like anyone else. They have passed the so-called stench of enlightenment, but all that they do is directed toward helping and healing other people.

For this there are many metaphors. In the West the classic metaphor is Plato's cave: the person escapes into the light and sees the good, and is then impelled to return to the cave in order to help and heal and teach. In Christianity, the metaphor is the fruitfulness of the soul. The soul, having experienced the divine marriage, makes the supreme sacrifice of separating from the divine in order to return to the world and help those who have not yet had this experience. In Joseph Campbell's mythology, this is the hero's return. In Judaism, it is the movement from divestment of corporeality to worship through corporeality.

In Arnold Toynbee's work, the one common characteristic he found among those who had made the most contributions to humankind and its evolution was what he called "the cycle of withdrawal and return." These people tended to withdraw from the world for periods of time in order to turn inward, to face their deepest fears and anxieties and the existential questions of life as profoundly as they could. When they came to some deep, existential insight, they returned to society to offer what they had learned for the welfare of all. That is the culmination, in a sense, of the spiritual quest of each of the great traditions—the idea that one undertakes a discipline or practice; experiences for oneself; stabilizes that experience; and then brings the experience and understanding back to the world.

THE GLOBAL IMPLICATIONS

Certainly our world needs that understanding at this time. You know, it's extraordinary. In the past fifty years, the world's population has doubled. We have lost over half a billion people due to starvation. We have lost untold numbers of species, we don't even know how many. The world has spent over fifteen trillion dollars on weapons during that time. The global problems that we are facing—pollution, starvation, ecological degradation, overpopulation—are in each and every case a product of human behavior.

The state of the world now reflects the state of our minds. What we call our global "problems" are actually "symptoms" of our individual and collective mind states. If we are to be effective in transforming the crises we face, we must work, not only to reduce overpopulation and feed the hungry, but also to reverse the psychological states, limitations, and perceptual distortions that allowed us to create these things in the first place. We are going to have to work in both arenas, in the world and in ourselves, if we are to effect a healing.

If we look at the world and its insanity, we can see that it reflects our own insanity. A central element of this insanity is our belief in our separateness; that we are, as Alan Watts called it, "skin encapsulated egos." Therefore, our motivation is "me, mine, number one."

What contemplative practices train for, and what entheogens sometimes induce, are mystical experiences that embody a recognition of our unity—with all humankind, with all life, and with the cosmos as a whole. From this experience of unity, there arises spontaneously a compassionate concern for and desire to help others.

We are in a race between catastrophe and consciousness, and we do not know which will win. A key question of our time is whether we can create a critical mass of aware people in sufficient time. This will determine whether we create a sustaining and sustainable society or leave behind a planet that is polluted and plundered and poisoned. We have the power to do both.

So, where does this leave us? In summary, we can see that the entheogens very likely played a crucial role in both the birth and the maintenance of many spiritual traditions. Moreover, research suggests that in some circumstances, in some people, at some times, entheogens can elicit certain states, experiences, insights, and perspectives, which spiritual traditions have carried for millennia, though by themselves entheogens seem unable to stabilize these states. Other cultures have used and valued entheogenic substances more wisely than we have. Clearly there is much to be learned from further cross-cultural and historical research.

19

The Strengthening Aspects of Zen and Contemporary Meditation Practices

Kathleen O'Shaughnessy

Kathleen O'Shaughnessy has a thirty-year background in Soto Zen practice, psychosynthesis and gestalt therapy, movement as a means of expanding the capabilities of the human nervous system, the fragilities of nutritional healing, primary shamanic states (including plant-induced frames of mind), multiple and multilevel bodywork approaches to balance, and the practicalities of transpersonal crisis.

Meditation: Reflecting on Your Attitude toward Altered States

What is your relationship to unusual and altered states in meditation? As you read about these experiences, notice which ones touch you, notice where you are attracted or what reminds you of past experiences. How do you meet such experiences when they arise? Are you attached and proud of them? Do you keep trying to repeat them as a mark of your progress or success? Have you gotten stuck trying to make them return over and over again? How much wisdom have you brought to them? Are they a source of entanglement or a source of freedom for you? Do you sense them as beneficial and healing, or are they frightening? Just as you can misuse these states through attachment, you can also misuse them by avoiding them and trying to stop them. If this is the case, how could your meditation deepen if you opened to them? Let yourself sense the gifts they can bring, gifts of inspiration, new perspectives, insight, healing, or extraordinary faith. Be aware of what perspective and teaching you follow, for guidance in these matters. If you feel a wise perspective is lacking, where could you find it? How could you best honor these realms and use them for your benefit?

JACK KORNFIELD, *A PATH WITH HEART: A GUIDE THROUGH THE PERILS AND PROMISES OF SPIRITUAL LIFE,* 1993

A spiritual practice and a visionary substance (Zen and LSD) came into my life within two weeks of each other. I lived in a part of the country where support for either was simply nonexistent. This had the effect of driving me into deeper relationship with each. I soon realized that Zen is LSD . . . in slow motion. The same strata of mind are revealed. I began to think of consciousness as a bowl with a lid on it; no matter what tool is used to lift the lid (be it fasting, prayer, meditation, yoga, or entheogens), *the content of the bowl is the same.* Since I did not move in circles where sacramental substances were readily available, I became more and more absorbed in the lone and demanding practice of "zazen"—the sitting practice at the heart of Buddhism.

I readily saw that I had to bring my body into the picture as scaffolding for what was happening in my mind. I began teaching myself the mind/body systems of hatha yoga and the Arica gym. *The practices themselves* became my teachers, for no teachers (or students for that matter) were available in the Deep South during those years. When I began reading Buddhist texts eleven years later, I could see that they described a map of where I had been rather than of where I was going. This is why I trust the nature of the practices so completely. Because of this particular style of learning, I tend to lift the practices out of their cultural or even specific spiritual contexts and teach them purely as process of mind. What happens in the spirit evolves of its own accord.

Then I began to see that at the center of the major religions is a core of individuals who do *a* practice. The common denominator of *all* these practices is that *mind is engaged with an activity of the body in this moment.* The Sufi whirling dervish, the multi-chordal Tibetan chanter, the shaman amidst drum and rattle rhythms, the yogi at the outer edges of posturing, the Christian in repetition of prayer, the primal tribal dances, the finite weavings of mind and breath in Buddhist meditation all contain that common theme of mind/body/now. When the moment called "now" is touched, everything expands and paradoxically begins to merge with the Large Space. With the realization of that common theme, I could then explore *multiple* spiritual practices and remain true to my purpose.

Each practice calls you to its center experience of balance . . . a sweet and delicate equipoise. Once that equilibrium is experienced viscerally, it is mirrored into the emotions and the psyche. A deep yet flexible strength develops, which manifests in one's interactions with the textures and energies of everyday life. This is primary experience—one without words or mind projections.

The mind is trained through meditation to see and experience finite detail, which in turn shifts the entire perceptual base of the nervous system. Life decisions and choices are now made from this broader base of perception. You quite simply see more clearly and in greater detail; thus action is taken according to the unique ingredients of individual situations. Rules are not necessary.

Consciousness converges with the self as a landing tern touches the outspread feet of its shadow on the sand; precisely, toe hits toe. The tern folds its wings to sit; its shadow dips and spreads over the sand to meet and cup its breast.

ANNIE DILLARD,

AN AMERICAN CHILDHOOD

Much later, and in the midst of my own transpersonal process, I began to work with Stan and Christina Grof for a span of several years, coordinating and facilitating in their month-long programs at Esalen Institute. I became intimately knowledgeable regarding the beauties and perils of the transpersonal journey and how best to support it. I worked with LSD in a sheltered (some would say covert) way with self-selected individuals who were carrying terrifying layers in their psyche. These included second-generation holocaust survivors and people who were near death. Clearly, the substance was a healer. What I could also see clearly was that those who had had at least some meditation experience stood stronger in and gained more understanding from the sessions. I began to think of this focused training of the mind as an important adjunct and follow-up to the substance-expanded experiences and made the decision to teach it.

My own inner explorations at this point had turned toward the *visionary plants* exclusively when I became ill with Epstein-Barr virus. I had to give *all* of my energies to educating myself in nutritional healing and to maintaining enough physical strength to continue earning a living. I could no longer tolerate *any* chemical, mind-manifesting or otherwise, and I became allergic to all fungi. As my health improved over a seven-year period, I experienced the alchemical aspects of food—its effects on emotions, organ meridians, mental acuity, and physical energy. I could also sense that my guiding principles were funneling me exclusively toward the dimethyltryptamine-containing brews for personal ritual.

A botanist, Terence McKenna, pointed me down many avenues for understanding DMT. It rang true when he said that when we were a foraging species, testing the edibility of plants in untouched forests, we took DMT in through our diet and this was how the brain and nervous system developed. With the advent of agriculture, these plants disappeared from our diet, and the visionary aptitude of the human neocortex has yet to develop. That would seem to have been "the fall from The Garden"—the juncture at which man became separated from nature. Our evolutionary possibilities have been stunted.

With some of these ideas and this background, I began to reflect on the wisdom of a culture that could encourage strengthening of the mind and body through proven systems and substances, with which we can mark our development and life transitions.

1. The use of traditional spiritual practices to train ourselves as better observers with stronger bodies, enabling us to experience that visionary epicenter with more clarity and physical stability.
2. To return dimethyl-tryptamine to our diet. To plant DMT-containing plants in our gardens.
3. To homeopathically potentize DMT (or other mind-expanding substances) so they can be taken in unmeasurable, energetic doses on a regular basis. Homeopathic remedies are now potentized in multiple levels by a company in Germany, resulting in a product said to act as a harmonic in the body. Entheogens, managed in this way, could slide through laws and borders.
4. The use of diet as internal clearing, with emphasis on enzymes with a broad pH ratio, chlorophyll (these first two are very basic healing substances), life-enhancing foods, and traditional Chinese herbs.
5. To train in proven energetic practices such as Tai Chi, Chi Gong, the yogas, and an effective contemporary movement meditation form called "Continuum" that is designed to expand the capacity of the nervous system and brain.
6. To regularly ingest herbs or supplements such as ginkgo biloba, gotu kola, co-enzyme Q-10, and a co-enzymatic form of vitamin B_6 called P5P (which I have found intensifies imaging in dreams and gives

a crystalline quality to my thinking). A diet of bright green, without fat, salt, or chemicals. In short, biochemical enhancement to the ultimate.

7. To use entheogenic rituals at crucial junction points in life such as puberty, onset of adulthood, marriage, mid-life, and certainly in preparation for death.

8. And last, to use the sacramentals collectively at important planetary events such as the solstice and equinox.

Who could ever tire of this heart-stopping transition? This deliberate emergence into a Place so broad that breath suspends and the inner eye squeezes in an effort to miss nothing of the streaming beauty. And to laugh and laugh at the irony of a life taken so seriously. Then to bring this visceral understanding and weave it finitely into the meat and potatoes level of everyday existence. Who could ever tire of it when the sum of these moments at the edge and in the presence of ourselves is the very best we have?

I begin my sixty-seventh year in April. I desire to live these years restored to the world of sacramental plants and to the family of people who have remained clean with them and true to them. It is important for me to remain in contact with a world that makes sense and for which I have great love, as I move toward my own final expansion.

Can we meet on this plane in a collective way called religion? Could we begin collectively to pave a morphogenic avenue? And, finally, from Sri Aurobindo:

Can we hope that this body, which is at present our means of terrestrial manifestation, will have the possibility of progressively transforming itself into something that will be able to express a higher life, or will we have to abandon this form totally in order to enter into another that does not yet exist upon the earth? Will there be continuity or will there be an abrupt appearance of something new? Will there be a progressive passage between what we are now and what our inner spirit aspires to become? Or will there be a break—in other words, will we be forced to abandon this present human form and wait for the appearance of a new form—an appearance whose process we do not foresee and which will have no relation to what we are now?

And again, this question:

Will the human species be like certain other species that have vanished from the earth?

20
Transpersonal Counseling

SOME OBSERVATIONS REGARDING ENTHEOGENS

Frances Vaughan

Frances Vaughan, Ph.D., is a psychologist in private practice in Mill Valley, California, author of *Shadows of the Sacred, Awakening Intuition,* and *The Inward Arc,* and coeditor of *Paths Beyond Ego: The Transpersonal Vision.* She was formerly on the clinical faculty at the University of California Medical School at Irvine and currently serves as a trustee of the Fetzer Institute.

❖

[P]rofound religious experience is always moving and probably the most captivating and shattering experience known to man. When I say "shattering" I mean that the experience shatters certain fundamental assumptions about life which stand in the way of a broader and more humane view.

WALTER HOUSTON CLARK,
CHEMICAL ECSTASY, 1969

INTRODUCTION

I would like to give a testimonial for Myron Stolaroff's protocol, because I had the privilege of being one of the subjects in his research with entheogens at the Foundation for Advanced Study in 1965. I was happy to meet Myron at the Vallombrosa conference for the first time and to have the opportunity to express my gratitude to him for making that experience possible for me.

More than thirty years ago, I had the good fortune to attend a lecture by Huston Smith in which he spoke about the phenomenological identity between the natural mystical experience and the entheogenic experience. There I met Jim Fadiman, who asked if I would like to be a subject in the research project, under Myron Stolaroff's direction, at the Foundation in Menlo Park. After careful screening, we were given a high dose of LSD combined with mescaline. Then we relaxed and listened to selected music, wearing earphones and eyeshades, under the supervision of a well-trained psychiatrist. That experience changed my life.

I had unwittingly prepared for this by studying comparative religions, humanities, and philosophy at Stanford as an undergraduate. I realized that although the research project experience had not changed my worldview, it affirmed what I understood about religion and philosophy, particularly existentialism. I had written a senior thesis on the concept of freedom in Gabriel Marcel's work, but now I felt I understood freedom in a new way. Although I cannot begin to express the full depth of that profound mystical experience in words, one insight can be encapsulated in the words, "The truth shall make you free." Another revelation was that love is at the heart of the universe, or that God is Love. Since then, my spiritual journey has been partly about learning to live with awareness of love and freedom.

Soon afterward I went back to graduate school and earned a degree in clinical psychology in an effort to understand more about my experience and how the mind works. When research with entheogens became virtually illegal, some of us who were interested in this research looked for other ways of working with the psyche. I became interested in depth psychotherapy, and this has occupied my professional life for most of the past thirty years. During this time I have learned much about a variety of altered state experiences from the people I have worked with, who have shared their struggles, hopes, and fears.

In the sixties many of us believed (or hoped) that the world was really changing, and that if everyone could have an entheogen experience the world would be transformed. We soon learned that this was not the case, and that not everyone benefits from the use of entheogens. Certainly one's perception of the world can be altered, but unless a person has the psychological maturity to integrate such experience, it can be problematic.

DISCERNMENT

I think we should consider the following questions regarding the use of entheogens: What is wise use of these powerful substances? What are skillful means for the use of these tools that profoundly alter consciousness? Who benefits, and who is at risk?

I think the importance of set and setting, the training of the guide, the psychological health of the subject, and the intention of the people involved should be carefully considered. If they were, I doubt that we would see so many problems stemming from misuse, or that we would have so much remedial work to do in transpersonal counseling.

Psychologists are not necessarily trained to work in this area. When I studied the psychology of C. G. Jung, I found that analytical psychology was not a big enough container for the full range of potential experiences. Then I began to explore transpersonal psychology, where the spectrum of consciousness is more encompassing. Transpersonal psychology does not hinge on the insights of any one single person, but draws on the work of a number of people. I have been particularly inspired by the work of Ken Wilber and Stanislav Grof. What I have found useful in my clinical practice is having a cognitive framework that helps people make sense of their non-ordinary experiences, whether or not they are entheogen induced. While some experiences may be interpreted in the context of a particular religion, they do not necessarily have to fit into a religious framework in order to be understood. For me, the transpersonal field has provided a broad psychological and spiritual context for understanding what is happening in the psyche, be it in dreams, ordinary waking life, or nonordinary states of consciousness.

SPIRITUALITY AND RELIGION

I think the distinction between spirituality and religion is very important. I refer to spirituality as a subjective experience of the sacred, whereas religion usually refers to an organized institution that provides a creed, a code of ethics, and community rituals for believers. Religion may or may not provide a supportive structure for a person's spiritual life. Spirituality is by no means the exclusive property of any religion. It occurs inside religions and outside of religions, as a natural impulse that exists in the hearts and minds of people everywhere. Spirituality may be theistic or nontheistic or polytheistic. For example, it is polytheistic in Hinduism and shamanism; theistic in Christianity, Judaism, and Islam; and nontheistic in Buddhism. I have found this awareness to be helpful in counseling people, whether or not they have a religious worldview.

The difference between a pastoral counselor and a transpersonal psychologist has sometimes been attributed to disillusionment with formal training. The pastoral counselor, disillusioned with religion, turns to psychology—often psychoanalysis—for answers, while the transpersonal psychologist, disillusioned with conventional psychology, turns to spirituality for answers. The work of pastoral counselors is certainly valuable but does not usually extend to counseling in relation to psychoactive substances. While pastoral counselors work within a particular religious framework, I would define a transpersonal psychologist as someone who works in an ecumenical spiritual context that is not limited to one particular religious orientation.

THE SHADOW SIDE OF ENTHEOGENS

I want to mention some of the problems that I have observed associated with the use of entheogens. If we evaluate the experience in a developmental framework, we see that while it may facilitate change and alter perceptions of self and others, it does not necessarily contribute to psychological maturity or to increased compassion or tolerance in an enduring way. In other words, the entheogenic experience does not necessarily advance a person's cognitive or moral development. In my work, I attempt to help people understand and integrate their experiences in an effort to realize their healing potentials. When people fail to integrate an experience, there are at least two types of pitfalls: 1) they may repress the experience, deny it, and pretend that it never happened; or 2) they may become addicted to the experience and more interested in repeating it than in changing the quality of their lives. Finding a way that enables a person to use these sacramentals in a manner that enhances psychological development and spiritual growth is both a challenge and a responsibility.

There could be value in having entheogens available electively in the training of psychologists and other mental health professionals and divinity school students. I think some of those who want to be priests, pastors, or counselors might benefit significantly from having direct experience of these altered states. This might foster their own growth and enhance their empathy and understanding of what other people may go through in the growth process. For anyone struggling with psychological addiction, there is much work to be done in finding ways of reducing dependency on altered states.

PREPARATION

Counseling sessions were of value to me, and I think could be of value to others, in preparation for the deep experience. We were given psychological tests and encouraged to read Alpert, Leary, and Metzner's rendition of *The Tibetan Book of the Dead*. All this contributed to providing a supportive set and setting. In this context, viewing these experiences as tools for psychological and spiritual growth seemed vitally important.

In my work as a psychotherapist I have emphasized growth-oriented therapy rather than a medical model of cure for pathology. Growth-oriented work is a process where these substances can sometimes be valuable. Entheogenic experiences seem to be potentially helpful for people who benefit from "uncovering" types of therapy, but certainly not everyone benefits from them. I have also seen entheogens exacerbate pathologies such as narcissism or borderline conditions. Obviously, not only healthy people are drawn to the use of these substances.

This brings us to another issue that needs to be addressed: Who are the best candidates? When does the potential benefit outweigh the risk, and *vice versa*? I remember reading in the literature—and it is true in my experience—that people who benefit most from the entheogenic experience are those who have a strong, healthy ego. It is easier to transcend a healthy ego than a weak ego. For people who need structure-building therapy, psychoactive substances would probably be contraindicated. These questions need to be addressed in developing guidelines for skillful and wise use of these sacramentals. Like any powerful tool, the entheogens can be enormously beneficial, and high risks are also associated with them.

CONCLUSION

Two things that have been useful for me, and could be useful for others doing inner work, are having a source of inner guidance and finding the ability to trust oneself. This may involve learning to trust your intuition, or learning to pray or focus attention as in meditation. Traditional spiritual practices can be beneficial for this learning. I like the definition of an atheist as a person of no invisible means of support! In transpersonal counseling, clients are encouraged to find the inner resources that are best suited to them.

Perhaps our continuing dialogue can help us discern more clearly: When is an experience with entheogens appropriate? How is it appropriate? For whom is it appropriate? What are the best ways of initiating people into a wider view of other dimensions of reality? And—something that has been mentioned before—what is the purpose? Clarifying intentions can make a significant difference to the outcome.

21
The New Psychotherapy
MDMA AND THE SHADOW

Ann Shulgin

Ann Shulgin is married to Alexander Shulgin and has participated in his past research into the effects of new psychedelic drugs. Before 1985, she did work as a lay therapist for several years, using mostly MDMA for both individual and marital problems, as well as for the spiritual growth of certain individuals. She co-authored the books *PIHKAL* and *TIHKAL* with her husband, and is engaged with him in the writing of a third book, as yet unnamed. Ann has four children and five grandchildren and loves spinach, earthquakes, and thunderstorms.

❖

Although many words could be written, two quotations summarize the essence that the author of this dissertation wishes to communicate. Henri Bergson observed that, "Mankind lies groaning, half crushed beneath the weight of his own progress." Paul Tillich formulated "the question our century puts before us" as follows: "Is it possible to regain the lost dimension, the encounter with the Holy, the dimension which cuts through the world

of subjectivity and objectivity and goes down to that which is not world but the mystery of the Ground of Being?"
WILLIAM ALAN RICHARDS, "COUNSELING, PEAK
EXPERIENCES AND THE HUMAN ENCOUNTER WITH
DEATH" (DISSERTATION), 1975

Modern psychotherapy utilizing psychoactive drugs probably began in the early 1960s. MDMA (methylenedioxymethamphetamine), now known on the street as "Ecstasy," first came to the attention of certain members of the mental health community because of the efforts of one man—now dead—an elderly psychologist whom I shall refer to as "Adam."

Adam had been quietly giving mind-expanding drugs to many carefully selected patients and friends for years to help them in their psychological and spiritual growth. He discovered the power of MDMA in 1972, through my husband, Sasha Shulgin, who had unearthed the original 1912 German patent and made the compound in his laboratory. He introduced Adam to it as a possible antidepressant.

Having tried the drug himself, Adam—who had been on the verge of retirement—started a new practice, devoting himself almost entirely to training innovative and courageous psychologists and psychiatrists across the country, and eventually Europe, in the use of MDMA in therapy. At the memorial service after his death, one of his closest friends told me, "I think that, all in all, Adam trained around four thousand people around the world in the use of MDMA, just in that last dozen or so years."

He began by giving the drug to the therapists, because—in his opinion—no therapist has any business giving a consciousness-altering drug to any other person unless he, the therapist, personally knows its effects. That rule was honored by all who followed Adam in this kind of work, and it still holds. It applies not only to MDMA, but to any other psychoactive drug that is used.

This rule applies most particularly to the drugs called hallucinogens, psychedelics, entheogens, or entactogens (MDMA is an entactogen). "Entheogen" means awakening the God within; "entactogen" means touching the self within.

MDMA became a favorite tool of psychotherapists because it can be given safely to people who are too emotionally fragile to benefit from mescaline, psilocybin, LSD, and similar drugs. There is no loss of control with MDMA, and it produces none of the dramatic visual changes associated with psychedelics, effects which can be disturbing and do not necessarily contribute to the quality of the inner experience.

The general structure of a drug-assisted therapy session had been evolving since the 1960s, and when MDMA became available and proved itself to be, indeed, "penicillin for the soul," there was already a considerable body of experience on which to base the new therapy.

Here, I will give a very brief overview of certain aspects of this kind of work, whether it is done for problem solving or for spiritual growth. For instance, how does therapy with MDMA or another psychoactive drug differ from the generally accepted forms of psychotherapy and hypnotherapy?

If you are the therapist, remember that, before any drug is ingested, a contract must be made—verbally, face to face—with the client, keeping in mind that you are speaking not only to his conscious mind, but also to the listening unconscious.

The contract includes the following rules. The exact wording is open to change, at the therapist's discretion. The content, however, must remain intact.

1. All sexual feelings are allowable; they can and should be discussed, but will not be physically acted out here.
2. Feelings of hostility and anger are allowable; they can and should be talked about, but must not be acted out against me or my possessions, except in a manner agreed to between the two of us.
3. If you (the patient) should see the friendly death door and know, that by stepping through it, you can be done with this life, you will NOT do so during this session. You will not end your life in such a way, when you are here with me, because such an act would cause me great injury, and you will not injure me, as I will not injure you.

4. You will swear to abide by these rules, without exception and without reservations.

Rule 1 is self-explanatory.

Rule 2 requires an additional note to this effect: The therapist should, of course, make it possible for the patient to express his anger, to indeed act out feelings of rage and desire to kill—if and when such feelings arise in response to unburied memories—by supplying such things as old sheets or pillows to pound or tear, and by coming to an agreement with the client as to when, how, and where (the therapist may have a special room set aside for this purpose). All this will be carefully explained to the client after the contract has been agreed to.

Rule 3: The wording of this rule may sound cold and uncaring, but the patient's reaction will be a sudden shock of understanding that what is being talked about is literally a matter of life and death, and his unconscious mind will register the fact that whatever may happen during the coming session, there are rules that must be followed.

The death door is an actual experience that most explorers in the world of the human psyche will eventually encounter. It takes many forms, all of them gently welcoming, and its message is "Here is the way back home, when you decide to return." It does not seduce or entice; it's just there. If it appears to a deeply depressed patient, it may mean escape from pain and desolation, and without the contract, the temptation to go through might be overwhelming. Some people have given in to the temptation and been sent back, but we have heard of one—and there may be more—who stayed on the other side of the opening. The therapist in such a case faces not only his patient's death, but also the legal and professional disaster that results from it.

Rule 4 speaks for itself.

There are other differences: any session using one of these drugs will take a minimum of six hours (with MDMA), and often as long as eight to twelve with other substances. The duration of the session depends not only on the kind of drug used, but also on whether a critical psychological or spiritual problem is being worked through.

Many times, in my experience, the most important emotional confrontations or spiritual battles begin to happen at what should have been the falling-off of the drug effects, during the last hour or so of the session.

Most sessions with a patient or client involve some intense work that is begun and ended well within six hours and often earlier. However, if a last-minute vital struggle takes place, one of the most important rules of drug-assisted therapy is that the therapist—no matter how tired he might feel—MUST NOT cut short the session. He must stay with the client, continue working with him, until the breakthrough has been achieved.

The human psyche has its own private and personal schedule for growth, and will take important steps in its own way and in its own time. The therapist is there to help the process, to devote himself—heart, soul, and insight—to guiding and supporting the hard work his client is doing.

When the CLIENT, on the other hand, decides he is too tired to work further, that is the signal that his psyche is closing the door and telling everyone, "Sufficient unto the day," and it is only then that the therapist should begin bringing the session to a close.

MDMA is an entactogen, and some people call it an entheogen. It is an insight drug, and one of the ways it enables insight to function in its user is that it removes the deep-seated fear most of us feel when we face our own Shadow—to use the Jungian term—or dark side.

In place of fear, in almost every user, there arises a peaceful acceptance of whatever is encountered, and an unaccustomed compassion for himself; in other words, an acceptance of all the aspects of his own nature, giving and selfish, kind and vengeful, loving and despicable.

I have often described this experience of unconditional self-acceptance as "being held in the loving hands of God," and it can be considered, in and of itself, one of the most healing experiences that any human being can have.

Once he has felt—possibly for the first time in his memory—such absolute validation of the totality of who he is, old habits of defensiveness fall away.

There is less need to protect himself against his own Shadow, his dark side. The therapist should remind him that it's there in him, as it is in every other human being, to serve a purpose, and that purpose is self-protection and survival. Not just survival of the physical body, but also of a self-image constructed by the unconscious to enable him to get through life with some degree of self-acceptance.

MDMA will enable him to consider changes he may need to make in himself, without accompanying guilt or self-rejection.

The degree of insight achieved in any session using MDMA or other drugs—such as 2C-B, which is relatively short-acting—depends first of all on the willingness of the patient to face and acknowledge his dark side or Shadow, the repressed, closed-off, long-denied aspects of his nature.

Putting it in Buddhist terms, he is being asked to confront the demons known as the guardians of the gate, and the prospect of seeing what he unconsciously believes to be the core—the essence—of himself as a series of horrendous, malignant, totally unacceptable entities, can bring about a state of fear that has no parallel in ordinary life.

No person can be asked to do the work of confronting his Shadow without being told by his therapist, in advance, that what he will see and feel is not—NOT—the whole truth about who he is, but only one important and essential part.

There should have been a great deal of discussion—before any drug ingestion—not only about the nature and function of the Shadow, but also of the need to feel compassion for the innocent child he had been, and to understand why and how that child developed certain habits of behavior and emotional response to his environment, in an effort to survive in a world he wasn't equipped to deal with or control.

It is in this preliminary discussion that the experience and persuasiveness of the therapist comes into play. He himself MUST have had this kind of emotional and spiritual journey, before he asks a client to undergo it.

He must have felt that stomach-churning fear of opening up a view of his core Self that he simply could not have lived with, if it had been, indeed, his true nature. And he should have been guided by a therapist or friend who knew how to lead him through this terrifying territory and out the other side. Only a therapist who has undergone this process of self-confrontation can speak with unmistakable authority and believability to a client who is struggling with intense, deep fears.

All these explanations and reassurances must have taken place before the client makes a final decision about taking a therapeutic drug. It is essential preparation, because without it, the drug session might be wasted.

When the unconscious psyche anticipates the possible destruction of a needed and long-nurtured good self-image; when the Survivor hears footsteps outside the massive door that has guarded his monster aspect from view for most of his life, one result may well be a complete lack of response to the drug. No insight, no images, no nuthin'.

Or there may be the eruption of an acute anxiety state, which thoroughly blankets any other effects and distracts the attention of everyone involved.

There are other ways in which drug-assisted therapy (or spiritual growth guidance) differs from ordinary analysis or psychotherapy.

It is essential that the therapist lay aside all preconceived theories and belief systems, either psychological or spiritual, as much as possible. His attitude must be that of a student, learning a new part of the universe, seeing it for the first time. The client is a new world, unlike any other he has previously encountered, and the therapist must be ready to learn a language of symbol and imagery peculiar to that world.

He has to keep his eyes and ears open and all his antennae alert, so that he might begin to get a glimpse of the emotional and spiritual structure and rules of survival that inform life in this unique human landscape.

What the therapist should remember is that the client's psyche contains a part that is a self-healer, and that it is a component of what might be called, for lack of a better term, his higher Self. I prefer to call it the Overseer. He should tell the client of the existence of that healer within, because by doing so, he will help activate it.

There is another rule that I believe must be observed by any therapist undertaking this kind of journey with a patient or friend. He has to be able to feel something very close to love for the person he is guiding. There should be real caring, and it cannot be simply an intellectual concern for the client's welfare; it must be deeper than that, at the gut level.

Real caring, like love, cannot be forced, as we all know, and the therapist should have sufficient insight of his own to be aware of what his feelings toward the client really are.

If there is hostility or apprehension, he must be prepared to do the necessary insight work to discover the reason for those feelings, to work on whatever projections may be involved, and if he cannot completely resolve them, he should direct the client to another therapist. I'm not talking about such feelings as momentary irritation or impatience; those can come naturally in response to many things, and they don't negate basic love or caring.

It is in connection with this ability to affirm and care about his patient that the therapist's own past training with the substances becomes important. If he has sufficient experience of his own with these tools, he will have (he should have) taken certain spiritual steps, which will have brought him to specific places within himself. One of these is the often referred-to "participation mystique," in the words of the great anthropologist Eliade, and it usually happens in the first drug session, if it is conducted, as it should be, in quiet natural surroundings.

He will have felt the sense of kinship with every living thing, and he will have known—again this is gut knowing, not intellectual knowing—that every animal, plant, and human being is related to him. He will have sensed that everything alive carries within it the God-essence, a spark of the Great Spirit, and that indeed we are all highly individual parts of one living, conscious Being.

What may have appealed to him before as nothing more than a beautiful, poetic concept will suddenly have taken the form of reality, and the profound impact of this realization will have become part of him for the rest of his life.

That is why, once he has had the privilege of being in this place in his soul, he will find it possible to feel true caring, even love, for a client who is preparing to open himself to himself. He will know that this person he is working with is, in the deepest sense, his parent, his brother, and his child.

Since I've touched upon the experience of confronting the Shadow, I should add that there is one important way in which drug-assisted exploration differs from, for instance, Jungian analysis, when it involves facing and acknowledging the Shadow.

A Jungian analyst will encourage his client to see his Shadow as clearly as he can—see what shape it takes, sense what its qualities are—and then to continue working on understanding its origins and its functions. Eventually, it will transform into an ally of the whole, integrated, conscious Self.

It may not sound like a dramatically important difference, but a therapist working with MDMA, psilocybin, or a similar drug will gently help his client to take one additional step, when he has full view of his Shadow, which, by the way, usually, but not always, takes the form of a large, powerful animal.

He will urge the client to first face, then enter into, the dark figure he is meeting; he must work to get inside the beast's skin and look out through its eyes.

It is here, at this point, that a battle may have to be fought, because not only does the conscious man have to fight his own revulsion, shame, and fear of this forbidden aspect of his psyche; the mind may project upon the Shadow an equal resistance to being seen or touched.

Some people seem to be able, once they have acknowledged the Shadow, to step right into it. Others must fight to get there, with strong, patient, loving support and encouragement from the therapist.

The first response to successful merging is usually astonishment at an unaccustomed absence of fear of any kind. The second is a growing appreciation and then frank exhilaration at the sensation of power—immense, fearless power—that characterizes this creature.

This stage of getting to know the Shadow from the inside may take more than one session, but many times I have seen the work completed in one day.

As the client learns to accept and understand his Shadow and its primary goal, a transformation will begin.

Ultimately, the Shadow will take its place as a devoted ally and protector, available when needed to the whole Self, respected and validated by the conscious mind, even though it will never be entirely housebroken or have good table manners. In other words, the final goal is identical to that of the Jungians.

A final, sad reminder:

Since the Controlled Substance Analogue Enforcement Act of 1986 was passed, this kind of therapy and spiritual journey, using these priceless tools, has been illegal in the United States.

Despite thousands of years of spiritual training using visionary plants in native cultures worldwide, modern governments have, with very few exceptions, attempted to repress the use of consciousness-opening plants and chemicals by classifying them alongside dangerous narcotics and stimulants as addictive—which they are not—and without social value.

You might blame an almost universal ignorance on the part of lawmakers, as well as most of the general public, about these substances and their appropriate uses.

I blame something else: an intense unconscious fear of the hidden depths of the human psyche, and an unacknowledged certainty that the Shadow is, indeed, the final terrible, rock-bottom truth about the nature of man. This belief, in most of us, has been nurtured in a thousand ways by family and culture, and too often by institutional religion.

It will be up to us—and others who feel as strongly as we do—to find out how to turn this around in our own nation. In many other countries, in Europe and South America, a change in attitude seems already to have begun.

It seems to me that if the human species is to survive much longer on earth, this kind of spiritual journey, this kind of understanding and transformation of the dark side of the soul will have to be seen as a necessary part of that human survival.

22

The Birthing of
Transcendental Medicine

Rev. Karla A. Hansen, M.Div.

Rev. Karla Hansen, M.Div. (1940–2001), received her BS in Biology with minors in Chemistry and Spanish. She graduated from Western Michigan University in Kalamazoo with a Certificate in Secondary Education. She taught in secondary education in Baldwin, Michigan, where earlier she had codirected a laboratory in a medical facility set up under the "War on Poverty." She was a Certified Medical Technologist by the American Association of Clinical Pathology and served the medical laboratory field in various capacities, including administrative. In 1980, in a career change, she received her Master of Divinity at Starr King School for Religious Leadership at the Graduate Theological Union in Berkeley and was ordained by a Unitarian Universalist congregation. Following ordination in 1981, she worked on issues of social justice including religious freedom, which is where she first encountered psychoactive sacramentals in the Native American Church. She was a pastoral counseling minister serving the breast cancer community and was an advocate of the use of and continued research on entheogens with people diagnosed with life-threatening conditions.

❖

The greatest impact this acid trip had on me was to entirely alter my view of death. This has affected the way I live. I grew up adamantly agnostic, pragmatic, a skeptic about anything religious or spiritual, with a down-to-earth orientation. I scorned notions of god, of life after death. I dismissed the possibility of psychic phenomena and denied that dreams might be an important part of life. In college the only spiritual philosophy I ever accepted was Emerson's view of the Over-Soul. If I had been asked to draw a picture of death I would have drawn a black box; that is all. Now I have tried drawing pictures of death in which I am fusing into the horizon, feeling ecstasy. My sense was, and is, that the strong beam of light from the setting sun on the ocean horizon will pull me into its orange warmth, and I will sink into a "beyond."

NATALIE ROGERS, *EMERGING WOMAN: A DECADE OF MIDLIFE TRANSITIONS*, 1980

A MINISTRY— FROM CALAMITY TO OPPORTUNITY

The Chinese character for calamity is the same as that for opportunity. It could easily become a symbol for both my life and my ministry. In 1993 I became part of a sorority that I did not seek to join, but which I deeply value. It is the sisterhood of those diagnosed with breast cancer. I didn't know that I would survive. So far I have. In the early wake of the horrific physical and emotional trauma that I was experiencing first hand, I started to envision helping other women seize the spiritual opportunities that any life-threatening diagnosis can present. Thirty percent of the women diagnosed with breast cancer do not survive. This sorority and their families live with this fact every day. Living in the moment, quality of life, loving, legacy, mortality, and sometimes immortality—these life priorities suddenly shifted from the abstract to the concrete. Ultimately, in the midst of the physical and psychic suffering, this far-from-gentle "initiation" brought me many gifts, new directions, and much love.

For me, this experience shattered the illusion most people live with: that cancer and death happen to someone else. It made me deeply aware of the meaning of the psalmist's words I had repeated at so many funerals, "through the valley of the shadow of death." I had always known this intellectually. Now I know it emotionally. I found no evil in this valley, but I did meet fear, and I vowed that I would transform this fear into something sacred.

Central to the turning point was designing a ritual with spiritual sisters, a group I had celebrated with for six years. The ritual provided the setting for each of us to share the impact of my diagnosis from our own unique perspective. This healing rite became the model for rituals for other women facing similar or other difficult diseases. The healing had begun and so had the new ministry.

The next phase in my journey through the "valley" began when I met two very special women with metastasis who became not only my friends, but also my teachers. I shall always be indebted to them for inspiring me with their courage and wisdom. I have them to thank for calling me to and training me for this new ministry and the future.

It was early in my chemotherapy when I first heard about Jane. She was living with the third occurrence of cancer, from breast to lungs and to bone. When a mutual church acquaintance first suggested that we meet, I felt a new but genuine reluctance, a feeling very unlike me. I knew it had nothing to do with this phenomenal woman I came to know and love—and lose. She was an experienced sister in this sorority and she had been in this excruciatingly vulnerable place I now found myself. She had moved into the beginning stages of terminal illness. She reached out to me first, and a very special relationship evolved. We accompanied each other through the next two and one-half years, and I was able to see her through her death at home.

A year after my diagnosis and a little less scared, I met Ann when she joined our Kaiser support group for those of us diagnosed for the first time. She had been diagnosed with metastasis to the bone and had been told she had three months to live. There was no support group for such women at Kaiser. Initially, our group provided support for her, but it ultimately became unworkable, as the other group members, who were getting well, avoided Ann and the real fear haunting us all. Any of us could become like her.

When Ann left the group, I eventually made a trepidatious phone call to her, shakily offering support. I began to transcend my fears for the moment. What unfolded was another deep and loving friendship. Under the care of my oncologist, she went well past the three-month "sentence." Several years later a test revealed that she did not have bone cancer! We celebrated the joy of her reprieve from bone metastasis and death and shared our anger at a medical system that could have made this kind of mistake, causing unnecessary suffering. We were gratified that the mistake was in her favor. Tragically, because the doctors had all focused on the misdiagnosis of cancer, she did not get the proper attention to other serious conditions and she died at age fifty-three, three months after her "reprieve."

One afternoon when a failing sister returned from her final trip to her doctor, I had homemade fish chowder ready. The broth unexpectedly became the sister's last physical nourishment. Her mother lingered longer than usual at a shift change, joining me for supper, finally letting someone care for her, too. Her daughter took a long-distance phone call from a friend, the leader of her metastatic support group and the president of the local Y-Me chapter. We heard her say, "I'm getting close to the end." I felt a silent sad communion between her mother and me as the dreaded truth became audible for the first time.

When the last moment came, I was not there. Shortly after, I arrived and covered the stilled body of our sister with our church caring quilt, which represented many of the names of the congregation to which we both belonged. Later I assisted her mother in reverently letting go of the body, opening the doors and the garden gate for the funeral directors. This was not expected so soon. This sister was only forty-seven.

When I started this journey into the valley of the shadow of death and this unexpected sorority, I had no idea what I would learn about ministering to the terminally ill. My fears began to dissolve in the face of these women's courage, and their stories would touch on a vision I had had for a long time. In my view, it would herald a new era of pastoral care for the dying. I renewed my vow to transform the fear and the loss into something sacred.

HEALTH RIGHT

In the unfolding of this new direction in my ministry, I had occasion to renew my interest in some medical research. A month before my entry into seminary in 1977, I had a fortuitous meeting with Dr. Stanislav Grof at a transpersonal psychology conference. He was a psychiatrist who had pioneered the field of LSD psychotherapy in Czechoslovakia. Dr. Grof showed slides of the religious artwork done by clients who had undergone this type of treatment. Over two decades of research had determined these substances to be "entheogenic"—inducing genuine mystical experience. Some researchers thought they "should be considered sacramentals because they can mediate contact with transcendental realities." I learned that these catalysts had everything to do with spirituality and healing.

Dr. Grof was invited to continue his research in Spring Grove, Maryland (1967–73), at the Maryland Psychiatric Research Center. Researchers there had focused on psychiatric patients, until, in 1965, an unforeseen and tragic event first shifted their attention to the needs of dying patients. A professional member of the team, a woman in her early forties, was diagnosed with terminal breast cancer. She had undergone a radical mastectomy, and subsequent surgery had revealed inoperable metastasis to the liver. Although still ambulatory, she was in considerable distress, unable even to breathe deeply without severe pain. She was fully aware of the gravity of her condition and was becoming increasingly depressed and distraught over her steadily worsening course. While not directly associated with the research projects, she was conversant with the nature of the work. Since over a hundred psychiatric patients had been treated by that time with LSD-assisted psychotherapy without serious side effects, she requested treatment. The limited but encouraging research observations, coupled with the clinical investigative experience, led to a decision to proceed with the treatment of this woman. Two weeks later Gloria described her experience and the changes that it brought.

> Mainly, I remember two experiences. I was alone in a timeless world with no boundaries. There was no atmosphere; there was no color, no imagery. Suddenly I recognized that I was a moment in time . . . Again in the void, alone without the time-space boundaries, life reduced itself over and over again to the least common denominator. I became poignantly aware that the core of life is love. At this moment I felt that I was reaching out to the world . . . to all people . . . but especially to those closest to me. I wept long for the wasted years, the search for identity in false places, the neglected opportunities, the emotional energy lost in basically meaningless pursuits.
>
> As I began to emerge, I felt joy, not only for myself but also for having been able to use the experience of these people (the treatment team). Later, as members of my family came, there was a closeness that seemed new. That night, at home, my parents came, too. All noticed a change in me. I was radiant, and I seemed at peace, they said. I felt that way too.
>
> What has changed for me? I am living now, and being. I can take it as it comes. Some of my physical symptoms are gone . . . the excessive fatigue, some of the pains. I still get irritated and yell. I am still me, but more at peace. My family senses this and we are closer. All who know me well say that this has been a good experience. (Grof and Halifax 1974)

The researchers administered MMPIs to the patient one week prior and two weeks subsequent to her LSD session. The retesting indicated a significant reduction on the depression scale and a general lessening of pathological signs. She returned to work and appeared in relatively good spirits. Shortly after the 200-mcg session, the patient went on a vacation with her husband and children. Five weeks after the date of the session, upon the development of ascites, the patient was rehospitalized. She died quietly three days later (Goldberg et al. 1973).

This pivotal single session catalyzed a whole new field of research with the terminally ill, shifting the focus of the therapy from psychiatry to thanatology. Tragically, the research and the use of these transcendental medicines were stopped in the 1970s, in spite of their promising results as indicated by Gloria's experience. Although limited research has been reinstituted, and the women I mentioned above wanted to participate, they were too ill to travel to the research sites. Had this research restriction been changed, these women would have been well served in their greatest hour of need, and they could have contributed to the legacy of the research.

Although there are many respectable advocates for assisting the dying in this way, to this day there is no provision for a "compassionate use policy" by any of the medical professions or the government. However, I was encouraged recently by Dr. Neal Goldsmith, a social psychologist and consultant at Tribeca Research Incorporated in New York. He specializes in "research utilization" (i.e., overcoming resistances to the implementation of valid research into policy and practice). In a recent conversation he stated:

> The clinical research on the use of psychedelics with the dying is perhaps the best data we have and should have been implemented long ago. The Spring Grove group had the longest-running and, perhaps, the most methodologically sound research program in this area.

Dr. Goldsmith recently presented this research to seventy hospice workers and staff at The Memorial Sloan Kettering Cancer Institute, where it was, in his words, "unusually well-received."

In the future, as this promising research expands and improves to take the medicine to the patient's bedside, I hope it will offer non-toxic, adjuvant therapy that would be as helpful to my new sorority sisters as it was to Gloria, whenever the diagnosis comes or whatever the prognosis might be. This research has implications for anyone who comes face to face with fear in the universal "valley of the shadow of death," in which we all, and always, live. One day each of us will see the end coming and, if we are lucky, have the opportunity to face it with peace instead of fear.

LAST RITES

As early as 1958, philosopher Aldous Huxley contacted Canadian psychiatrist Dr. Humphry Osmond. Osmond was the physician and scientist who coined the word "psychedelic," meaning to him "mind-manifesting." However, looking at its Greek roots, its meaning is closer to "to make the soul visible or clear." Osmond cited as a benefit of the new word that it was "uncontaminated by other associations." The "psychedelic sixties" changed that. A group of scholars headed by Carl Ruck noted in 1979 that "psychedelic" "has become so invested with connotations of the pop culture of the 1960s that it is incongruous to speak of a shaman's taking a 'psychedelic' drug." They proposed the new term "entheogen," based on the Greek "entheos," meaning "god within."

Through his research Osmond had introduced Huxley to mescaline, the psychoactive ingredient of the peyote cactus used in the Native American Church, and to several other entheogens. Huxley's interest in the subject was born of both his early experiences with mescaline and his experience with the death of his first wife, Maria, of cancer in 1955. During her final hours he used a hypnotic technique to bring her into touch with her memory of ecstatic experiences that had occurred spontaneously on several occasions in her life.

Later, in a letter to Osmond he wrote:

My own experience with Maria convinced me that the living can do a great deal to make the passage easier for the dying, to raise the most purely physiological act of human existence to the level of consciousness, and perhaps even of spirituality.

In another letter in February 1958, Huxley was quite explicit about his idea of seriously considering the use of entheogens with the dying. He reinforced his earlier letter by referring to "yet another project—the administration of LSD to terminal cancer cases, in the hope that it would make dying a more spiritual, less strictly physiological process." His second wife, Laura, mentioned on several occasions, "last rites should make one more conscious rather than less conscious, more human, not less human." In 1963, when Huxley himself was dying of cancer, he asked Laura to administer last rites to him with d-lysergic-acid two hours before his death, practicing what he had preached.

Huxley spoke to a great human need—the need for "the living to make the passage easier for the dying." Since the time he expressed his wisdom, this need has been answered in part by the hospice movement, the involvement of transpersonal psychologists, and the formation of professional organizations in the field of thanatology. Yet it was over two decades after Huxley proposed the concept of this kind of "spiritual last rites" that they became initiated though the fortuitous session with Gloria that changed the focus of the research at Spring Grove.

Dr. June Singer, a transpersonal psychologist and psychotherapist, in speaking of Grof and Halifax said:

> Physician and medical anthropologist join here in recreating an old art—the art of dying. They have assisted persons dying of cancer in transcending the anxiety and anger around their personal fate. Using psychedelics, they have guided the patients to death-rebirth experiences that resemble transformation rites practiced in a variety of cultures.

In *The Human Encounter with Death,* Grof and Halifax reported that those who had gone through death-rebirth sequences in their entheogen sessions often described a very radical change in their attitude toward death.

Deep experiences of cosmic unity and of other certain transpersonal forms of consciousness seem to render the matter of physical death irrelevant. The fact that these experiences can have profound transformative influence on individuals for whom the prospect of physical death is a matter of months, weeks, or days suggests that they deserve serious attention.

In the 1977 foreword to Grof and Halifax's book, Dr. Elisabeth Kübler-Ross wrote that the book "is the latest of many recent publications in the newly evolving field of thanatology. It is, however, a quite different kind of book—one that belongs in every library of anyone who seriously tries to understand the phenomenon we call death." Unfortunately, the book is out of print.

IT IS ALL ABOUT SABBATH

In Genesis, God's resting on the seventh day gave birth to the concept of Sabbath—taking extended time out periodically to reflect on the inner life and to relate to the transcendent. When I was a Methodist youth, I sang the old hymn "Take Time to be Holy" with vigor and passion. I was a fervent Christian at the time, believing what I was taught, but I had absolutely no idea what I was singing about. I was in my early forties and had earned a Master of Divinity degree before "divinity began to master me." I finally had an experience that would teach me the meaning of taking time to be "holy."

Sometime during my seminary training, a classmate gifted me with a copy of *Maria Sabina: Her Life and Her Chants*. For the uninitiated, Maria was the Mazatec curandera (healer) who revealed the secret of the sacred mushroom rite (velada) in 1955 to Gordon Wasson and his wife Valentina, a pediatrician. Fortunately, I later met someone trained in Maria's healing rites, and I was able to experience directly this ethnobotanical spiritual practice. There are hardly words to express what I felt. I had teachings, inklings, and faith—and loss of faith—but never any direct experience that matched the words I had known only as concepts.

I "beheld" a genuine awareness of the transcendent that I had previously only heard or read about. I felt a "peace that passes all understanding" that gave meaning to St. Paul's words. I discovered a wellspring of joy and a sense of well-being that I did not know was possible. I felt a deep feeling of gratitude, thanksgiving prayer, grace—and love. After a few sessions, I felt very humbled by the process and developed a profound respect for this Mazatec medicine woman who had devoted her life to "curing." She became my Patron Saint.

Maria Sabina's sacramental "medicine" eventually yielded up its secrets in a modern chemical laboratory. The active ingredient was synthesized and found its way into a traditional Christian church in North America. On Good Friday of 1962 in Marsh Chapel at Boston University, two ministers conducted a scientific experiment. The Rev. Dr. Howard Thurman preached a two-hour Good Friday service in the main chapel upstairs while his gentle, truth-filled voice reverberated through the speakers into the basement chapel. There the Rev. Dr. Walter Pahnke, a physician and minister, administered psilocybin (the active ingredient of the sacred mushroom) to ten of the twenty carefully screened young theological students who had never before partaken of this kind of indigenous communion. The results of the experiment are reported by two participants in other chapters of this book, but, essentially, the experiences of those young men had long-lasting, positive effects on their lives.

This unprecedented moment in "Protestant America" became known as the "Miracle of Marsh Chapel." This was a historic marriage between science and religion that these two unique clergymen, one a mystic and the other a physician, presided over with great enthusiasm. Rev. Thurman shared in his sermon that day that he had always referred to "Good Friday as Dark Friday." Judging by what was reported in a twenty-five-year follow-up study of the "subjects" who became "communicants" in this Chapel experiment, it was genuinely a "Good Friday." A ray of light and hope shone out of that historic "miracle" moment. A new church was conceived that day, with parentage from the best of both American Protestant tradition and Mexican Indian healers. This new church has been gestating in the womb of the spiritual catacombs of our times. Perhaps it is time for this church to begin to "show" itself to churches much in need of renewal and to a culture gravely in need of healing.

PROFESSION FOR THE FUTURE

I named these plant chemicals transcendental medicine—medicine for the soul—soon after I experienced them. I studied Stan Grof's research and Maria Sabina's life, and I had my own personal experience. I then learned about the Native American Church and the Good Friday experiment. Since first meeting Dr. Grof twenty years ago, I have had a lengthy reflection on these "medicines." I have learned sacred stories from people in pulpits, pews, teepees, and from naturalists outside religious structure. I have concluded that these "medicines" are effective in the hands of healers. They have been shown to be safe and efficacious by both ancient indigenous practice and the contributions of modern science.

When I titled this chapter "the birthing of transcendental medicine," I was referring not only to the coining of a new term but also to the birthing of a new tradition—the practice of transcendental medicine. I say "new" with qualification. It is not a new practice to some indigenous peoples of Mesoamerica. It has been practiced for centuries, albeit not without continued persecution by both governmental and ecclesiastical authorities—mostly Christian. I say "new" because the revelations mentioned above have come from sciences, which have been leading us into more mysterious realms than are found in mainstream religions.

I was invited to present on a liturgical panel at the Psychoactive Sacramentals Conference at Vallombrosa Center and to help conduct an "entheogen-compatible liturgy." I was both encouraged and surprised by the conference. It was a reunion of many I had read and/or met, including Stan Grof. It was an opportunity to hear the story of Rick Doblin's follow-up study to Dr. Pahnke's Good Friday experiment. The biggest surprise was the presentation of two of the original experiment participants, one being Dr. Huston Smith and the other a ministerial colleague in my denomination, Rev. Mike Young.

Mike and I belong to a spiritual community that "affirms and promotes the free and responsible search for truth and meaning." The living tradition we share also draws from "direct experience of that transcending mystery and wonder, affirmed in all cultures, which moves us to a renewal of the spirit and openness to the forces that create and uphold life." Both of these values invite a free and responsible discussion of transcendental medicines. As a spiritual descendant of the American Transcendentalists, I feel my naming of the substances is befitting. I hope that the dialogue opened at Vallombrosa will lead to the birthing of a new pastoral care tradition both within my spiritual community and beyond it.

There are many details to be worked out, but there are also many models to draw from as to who should preside over this professional practice, who should train for it, and how. The tradition is passed on in indigenous cultures by apprenticeship. In the Native American Church the leader is called the "Peyote Chief" or "Road Man" and has three liturgical assistants. In Mazatec Mexico the officiant is called curandera—healer—and is sometimes accompanied by apprentices. In the development of such a practice, the model of internship seems appropriate, since it is used in both medical and ministerial training. Mike Young has suggested a poet-liturgist as the practitioner, an idea that resonates deeply with me.

As to who would serve in this new field, it could be physicians and/ or psychiatrists, but I think few would be interested. More likely, interested practitioners would be drawn from a pool of pastoral counselors, transpersonal psychologists, and hospice nurses, to name the most obvious. They would undergo an internship/apprenticeship with specialized courses in both liturgy and pharmacology. As to who would have jurisdiction—religion or science—it could be both, as in the "Miracle of Marsh Chapel." As to who sponsors the training and develops the accrediting process, I would hope it would be enlightened seminaries with the transdenominational support of the Council on Spiritual Practices.

The nature of government involvement is yet to be determined. For now, there will have to be a shift from prohibition to regulation, as there is with the Native American Church. It is my view that these sacramental medicines should be removed from their present scheduling, where these "entheogenic" substances clearly do not belong. They could be placed in a new category to be co-administered by interested spiritual communities and, conceivably, the Office of Alternative Medicine under the National Institute of Health.

I started this chapter with a description of my ministry, revealing the testimony of one of my "sorority" sisters. Gloria made history with her story and left us a great legacy, but the Glorias of today are denied the same opportunity to access these transcendental medicines. Yet this denial can be overcome, transforming calamities into opportunities for healing and spiritual growth—even unto death. In the words of the Rabbi Hillel, "If not us, who? If not now, when?" It is my prayer that the legitimate practice of Transcendental Medicine will be made so.

Karla Hansen died on May 12, 2001.
May her prayer be answered.

REFERENCES

Goldberg et al. 1973. *Psychopharmacological Agents for the Terminally Ill and Bereaved.* New York: Foundation of Thanatology.

Grof, S., and J. Halifax. 1974. *The Human Encounter with Death.* New York: E. P. Dutton.

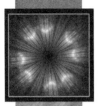

23

The Judicial
Architectonics of
Psychoactive Sacramentals

Richard Glen Boire

Richard Glen Boire, J.D., is director of the nonprofit Center for
Cognitive Liberty and Ethics.

*For law enforcement officers engaged in the
protection of youth from the harmful effects of
"drugs," it may be very difficult, given their
training, to distinguish what appears to be
harmful use of street drugs from the responsible
use of entheogens in spiritual practices. But it
is fundamentally the mission of the law to draw
distinctions. Legislators who earn the most respect
write laws that draw careful and appropriate
distinctions between the permitted and the
proscribed. The respect accorded lawyers and
judges is, in part, recognition of their wisdom in
hearing the evidence and making the judgments—*

oftentimes subtle—that maintain the full protection of the
Constitution and its guarantees when they are warranted.
ERIC E. STERLING, "LAW ENFORCEMENT AGAINST
ENTHEOGENS: IS IT RELIGIOUS PERSECUTION?"
IN *ENTHEOGENS AND THE FUTURE OF RELIGION,* 1997

It is well documented that some plants and substances are capable of eliciting religious cognition in some people when used knowledgeably. However, religiously motivated users of controlled entheogenic substances who are arrested for possessing such substances, many of which are outlawed under federal and state law, are faced with an arduous task. They must navigate an extremely difficult and often poorly defined maze of judicial requirements just to gain the right to present evidence that their use of a controlled substance was for religious purposes. In a previous essay, I discussed the practical aspects of the "compelling state interest test" as it is applied to sacramental use of entheogens by individuals (see "Entheogens and the Free Exercise Clause: Practical Legal Aspects for Individuals," *The Entheogen Law Reporter,* no. 28, 1994). Here, I plot with a more theoretical focus the legal landscape that must be crossed in order to trigger application of that test.

THE SUPREME COURT'S DEFINITION OF RELIGION

The threshold issue for any court considering a claim that a defendant's possession of an illegal entheogen was for "religious purposes" is whether or not the person's asserted belief system can be defined as "religious." For better or worse, the Supreme Court's view of religion is ever changing and, at present, poorly defined.

From the late 1800s to the mid 1900s, the Court's definition of religion was decidedly theistic. If a person's belief system was not focused upon a Supreme Being, the belief system was not considered "religious" and received no free exercise protection. From 1960 through 1970, however, the Supreme Court began to expand its view of religion, reaching its broadest definition in a number of cases interpreting the federal Selective Service Act. In a 1965 case, for example, the Court drew upon the writings of Paul Tillich, John Robinson, and David Muzzey to define religion as a "sincere and meaningful belief which occupies in the life of its possessor a place parallel to that filled by the God of those admittedly qualifying for the [conscientious objector] exemption . . ."

Since 1970, however, the Court has compressed its view of religion, distinguishing *religious* beliefs from *philosophical* beliefs. The distinction was outlined in a 1972 case, where the Court reversed the criminal convictions of several Amish parents who withheld their children from school in violation of a Wisconsin law. The convictions were reversed after the Court determined that the parents' actions, though in violation of a criminal law, were indeed premised upon religious beliefs as opposed to personal philosophy. Seeking to distinguish between the two, the Court remarked:

> [I]f the Amish asserted their claims because of their subjective evaluation and rejection of contemporary secular values accepted by the majority, much as Thoreau rejected the social values of his time and isolated himself at Walden Pond, their claims would not rest on a religious basis. Thoreau's choice was philosophical and personal rather than religious, and such belief does not rise to the demands of the Religion Clauses.

The Supreme Court's shifting definition of religion leaves religiously motivated entheogen users in a difficult spot. Many entheogen users sincerely consider their use of entheogens religious, yet they do not believe in a Supreme Being. Such nontheistic religious users of entheogens run a danger of having a court classify their belief system as a "philosophy" unprotected by the First Amendment. In contrast, religious users of entheogens who have a theistic orientation (as does the Native American Church) are more likely to survive the threshold inquiry necessary to present a religious defense.

BELIEF VERSUS PRACTICE: THE SUPREME COURT'S DUALISTIC VIEW OF RELIGION

Even if a religious user of a controlled entheogen succeeds at having his or her "drug-taking" accepted as religious, the journey to acquittal is still just beginning. Since a landmark case in 1878 holding that Mormons are free to *believe* whatever they want to believe but aren't allowed to *practice* polygamy, the United States Supreme Court has analyzed potential free exercise violations by dividing religion into two components: religious *belief,* and religious *conduct.*

The cases show that the Supreme Court's concept of "belief" is extremely limited and abstract. Belief, as the court has used that word, means a purely internal mental experience. The court views the Free Exercise Clause as protecting only that interior space—"the mental operations of persons," to use the court's words—from governmental interference. As the court has explained, "Congress was deprived of all legislative powers over mere opinion, but was left free to reach actions which were in violation of social duties or subversive of good order. . . . Laws are made for the government of actions, and while they cannot interfere with mere religious belief and opinions, they may with practices."

Essentially, the Free Exercise Clause, as interpreted by the court, only gives absolute protection against a sort of governmental "religious-thought-police." Religious *conduct* receives far less protection. Under a 1963 Supreme Court ruling, conduct, even if motivated by religious belief, is subject to a balancing test that in essence protects such conduct only when it is consistent with, or causes no harm to, a "compelling governmental interest." In cases involving religious use of illegal entheogens, the courts have routinely described the government's compelling interest as "the protection of individual health and social order."

To my mind, the belief/conduct binary is roughly analogous to human-created distinctions: ends versus means, inside versus outside, mind versus body, nonmaterial versus material, or spirit versus flesh. While these distinctions can probably be defended linguistically, they are not mandated, as even a passing knowledge of Taoism makes clear.

In fact, the belief/conduct distinction entails a dualistic view of religion that is decidedly Protestant in nature and particularly Pauline. The Supreme Court's reified distinction between religious belief and religious conduct preordains that certain types of religion, including entheogen-based religions, will almost never receive complete protection. As Ludwig Wittgenstein wrote, "A picture held us captive. And we could not get outside it, for it lay in our language and language seemed to repeat it to us inexorably."

In the 117 years since the court invented the belief/conduct doctrine, only one free exercise case has succeeded at opening up the conceptual apartheid. In the 1972 Amish case discussed earlier, the court found that for the Amish community, religious belief and conduct were inseparable. Most legal commentators have opined that the court's finding in that case is limited to the facts of the case and is almost impossible to extend to facts outside the Amish community.

The court's belief/conduct distinction is a conceptual hierarchy that entails a one-way causality. This formula fails completely when applied to an entheogen-based religion. The court has viewed religious beliefs as causing or directing the subject's conduct. For example, the Mormon's belief in polygamy causes the conduct of seeking to marry multiple spouses. In contrast, the causal vectors at play in an entheogen-based religion move in the opposite direction: from conduct (incidental to ingesting the entheogen) to religious experience (during the entheogen experience) to the religious belief (having experienced the Godhead, one now believes it). For religious users of entheogens then, prohibiting the conduct entirely prevents the belief or "mental operation" that is the sine qua non of all entheogen-based religions. Apropos is Albert Hofmann's comment in an entirely different context: entheogens operate "at the borderline where mind and matter merge."

CONCLUSION

The analysis routinely employed in religious free exercise cases is structurally flawed in application to entheogen-based religions. The flaws construct a hostile and uphill terrain for any religiously motivated user of a controlled entheogen. For such people, the ultimate success of a general free exercise defense thus rests on unifying existing jurisprudential binaries, something that can only be accomplished by educating the court with respect to the unique qualities of entheogenic sacramentals within the religious context.

24

On Nomenclature for the Class of Mescaline-Like Substances

AND WHY IT MATTERS

Compiled by Robert Jesse

Robert Jesse, convenor of the Council on Spiritual Practices, was trained in engineering at the Johs Hopkins University. He has consulted in the software industry and worked in several capacities for Oracle Corporation, most recently as a vice president of business development. In 1994, he left Oracle to devote himself to the Council's work.

———————◆———————

1957 I have tried to find an appropriate name for the agents under discussion: a name that will include the concepts of enriching the mind and enlarging the vision. . . . My choice, because it is clear, euphonious, and *uncontaminated by other associations*, is psychedelic, mind manifesting. [emphasis added]

HUMPHRY OSMOND, "A REVIEW OF THE CLINICAL
EFFECTS OF PSYCHOTOMIMETIC AGENTS"

Other Associations with the Word "Psychedelic"

The conical lamps contain a watery fluid and the "lava." When the "lava" is warmed, it becomes less dense and rises, then cools and slithers its **psychedelic** way to the bottom.

KAREN FREEMAN, "IN KITSCH, A SOLUTION,"
THE NEW YORK TIMES, JANUARY 13, 1998

Gidget goes global in this witty world tour of surfwear, tunics, saris, and sarongs, done in gold mesh, bandana prints, denim, and beaded chiffon. While some of Sui's fans may miss her grunge and Gothic motifs, most will savor this **psychedelic** pu pu platter for polyglot hipsters.

BOB MORRIS, "LET'S GO: FASHION SPRING '98,"
THE NEW YORK TIMES, FEBRUARY 1, 1998

I can't believe what I've gotten myself into. Imagine this: a roomful of doctors, lawyers, financial consultants, and filmmakers, all cross-legged on cushions, staring intently at a middle-aged man and woman who are talking about wee-wees and hoo-hoos amid tropical foliage and a **psychedelic**-purple backdrop.

CAL FUSSMAN, "LIKE A VIRGIN; TANTRIC SEX SEMINAR,"
ESQUIRE, MARCH 1998

Step into the headquarters of Diesel S.P.A. in northern Italy, and you are greeted by two life-size cutouts of North Korean soldiers, who warn, "No Jeans!" The walls are **psychedelic**; the plastic chairs are iridescent; the receptionists are deeply cool. The place seems more like an MTV set than like a major clothing corporation.

"READY TO RUMBLE," *NEWSWEEK*, MARCH 30, 1998

But, like in-laws from different cultures, my New York City Barbies have never met their suburban sisters. The Midwest gals are a bit out of date, still clad in **psychedelic** pants suits and beauty parlor bouffants.

SUSAN SHAPIRO, "BARBIE MOVES TO THE VILLAGE,"
THE NEW YORK TIMES, APRIL 5, 1998

Investigators discovered a room containing whips, chains, and pornographic videos in the house, where a couple who described themselves as sado-masochists were the hosts of the party, the authorities said. The girl's father, 34, of Camden, is suspected of leaving Samantha unsupervised while he smoked PCP, a **psychedelic** drug, Mr. Solomon said.

CHERRY HILL, "INQUIRY INTO A DROWNING
OF A GIRL DURING A PARTY," *THE NEW YORK TIMES*,
MAY 29, 1998

"A lot of advertising equates products with drug experiences," says Thomas Frank, the author of *The Conquest of Cool,* a scintillating history of the modern ad biz. Whether it's a soft drink like Fruitopia trading on **psychedelic** packaging or a stylish new car promising its owner escape and speed or a Nike shoe bestowing enhanced physical powers, the ubiquitous message of the advertising medium is Get High.

FRANK RICH, "JUST SAY $1 BILLION,"
THE NEW YORK TIMES, JULY 15, 1998

The music's late-60s roots showed clearly. . . . A younger guitarist, Joe Karafiat, has joined the longtime Plastic People; he wailed above the riffs with **psychedelic** squiggles, and occasionally added quick-scrubbing 70's funk chords.

JON PARELES, "ECHOES OF 1968 CZECHOSLOVAK
ROCK AND STRUGGLE," *THE NEW YORK TIMES*,
JULY 20, 1998

The **psychedelic** tinge of much of this work also calls to mind a certain kind of special-effects art associated with 1960's poster and album cover graphics. Two concave paintings done in Day-Glo by an artist named Yek fit this description. . . .

HOLLAND COTTER, "PAINTING FROM ANOTHER PLANET,"
THE NEW YORK TIMES, JULY 24, 1998

They are hardly the only reminders of mainstream America's plunge into The Haight, a neighborhood that threw open its **psychedelic** arms to the hippies and misfits whose Summer of Love more than 30 years ago became part of the national conscience.

MICHAEL JANOFSKY, "WAYWARD YOUTH TRY PATIENCE
OF HAIGHT-ASHBURY," *THE NEW YORK TIMES*,
AUGUST 9, 1998

With its sky-blue ceilings and lavender-and-lime walls, the space "has a whimsical storybook feel," says Tarantino. That's what you'd expect from a designer who cites *The Brady Bunch* and her "**psychedelic** hippie parents" as influences.

ANNE-MARIE O'NEILL, ". . . INSECT-SHAPED HAIR CLIPS,
RINGS AND TIARAS HAVE HOLLYWOOD ABUZZ,"
PEOPLE, AUGUST 31, 1998

"It would seem an absurdity to blend fashion and Parmesan, and yet in the history of our family, it makes sense," Luigi says, selecting a small piece of cheese and urging me to try one. The cheese has a rather rugged, melted consistency, and the flavor ricochets across the taste buds. "It's **psychedelic** Parmesan," I tell Luigi. "It is like acid," he says.

JAMES SERVIN, "WHO IS MAXMARA? ITALIAN
WOMEN'S CLOTHING MANUFACTURER,"
HARPER'S BAZAAR, OCTOBER 1998

Are you sorry you tossed that Bob Dylan poster? You know, the one with his face in silhouette and his hair a tangle of **psychedelic** spaghetti; the one that came folded up in the "Best of" album, which you tacked to your wall and then threw out after senior year?

DAVID W. DUNLAP, "WHEN WALLS TALKED TO YOU,"
THE NEW YORK TIMES, OCTOBER 23, 1998

Most communes of the 90s are not free-love refuges for flower children, but well-ordered, financially solvent cooperatives where pragmatics, not **psychedelic**s, rule the day. "Hippie communes of the 60s were high on idealism with little sense of self-discipline or direction," Mr. Norwood said.

ANDREW JACOBS, "YES, IT'S A COMMUNE. YES, IT'S ON STATEN ISLAND," *THE NEW YORK TIMES*, NOVEMBER 29, 1998

1968 [T]oday the word "psychedelic" is so well known that it is commonly used in advertisements. But its meaning has become more clouded as its fame increased. What is psychedelic? A style of lettering on posters? The deafening throb of a rock band? Kaleidoscopic light effects that tire the eyes? Or anything at all that one wishes to sell? The psychedelic fashions will pass, and the word "psychedelic" may have to go with them. It may have lost its ability to refer to an elusive and precious state of consciousness. Say "psychedelic" and you hear the glib voice of the salesman, the hypocritical tones of the mystifier, the rationalizing chatter of the dissipated and purposeless. But this was not what Humphry Osmond meant by the word. "Psychedelic" was a good word. A sick society has degraded its referent and thus the name. We need a new name and a new concept.

LISA BIEBERMAN, *PHANEROTHYME: A WESTERN APPROACH TO THE RELIGIOUS USE OF PSYCHOCHEMICALS*

1979 All languages grow together with the peoples who speak them, borrowing or inventing terms to keep pace with what is new, and retiring others when they are no longer needed. When the recent surge of recreationals use of so-called "hallucinogenic" or "psychedelic" drugs first came to popular attention in the early 1960s, it was commonly viewed with suspicion and associated with the behavior of deviant or revolutionary groups . . .

Out of the many words proposed to describe this unique class of drugs only a few have survived in current usage. It is the contention of the authors who have subscribed their names to this article that none of these terms really deserve greater longevity, if our language is not to perpetuate the misunderstandings of the past . . .

[N]ot only is "psychedelic" an incorrect verbal formation, but also it has become so invested with connotations of the pop culture of the 1960s that it is incongruous to speak of a shaman's taking a "psychedelic" drug.

We, therefore, propose a new term that would be appropriate for describing states of shamanic and ecstatic possession induced by ingestion of mind-altering drugs. In Greek the word "entheos" means literally "god (theos) within," and was used to describe the condition that follows when one is inspired and possessed by the god that has entered one's body. It was applied to prophetic seizures, erotic passion, and artistic creation, as well as to those religious rites in which mystical states were experienced through the ingestion of substances that were transubstantial with the deity. In combination with the Greek route *gen,* which denotes the action of "becoming," this word results in the term we are proposing: *entheogen.*

CARL A. P. RUCK, JEREMY BIGWOOD,
DANNY STAPLES, JONATHAN OTT, AND R. GORDON WASSON,
"ENTHEOGENS"

1980 Entheogen *nov. verb.*: "God within us," those plant substances that, when ingested, give one a divine experience, in the past commonly called "hallucinogens," "psychedelics," "psychotomimetics," *etc.*, to each of which serious objection can be made. A group headed by Greek scholar Carl A. P. Ruck advances "entheogen" as fully filling the need, notably catching the rich cultural resonances evoked by the substances, many of them fungal, over vast areas of the world in proto- and prehistory. . . . We favor the adoption of this word. Early Man, throughout much of Eurasia and the Americas, discovered the properties of these substances and regarded them with a profound respect and even awe, hedging them about with bonds of secrecy. We are now rediscovering the secret and we should treat the "entheogens" with the respect to which they were richly entitled. As we undertake to explore their role in the early history of religions, we should call them by a name unvulgarized by hippy abuse.

R. GORDON WASSON, *THE WONDROUS MUSHROOM:*
MYCOLATRY IN MESOAMERICA

1993
A recent book dismissed *entheogen* as "a clumsy word freighted with theological baggage" (T. K. McKenna 1992), the author having failed to appreciate its non-theological sense, and being apparently unaware of the use of the word in ancient Greece. Incongruously, the word was dismissed for its supposed "theological baggage" in a book entitled *Food of the Gods!* . . .

Entheogen has been used by many leading experts in the field, including J. Bigwood, M. D. Coe, J. L. Díaz, W. Doniger (O'Flaherty), W. A. Emboden, A. Escohotado, J. Fericgla, P. T. Furst, J. Gartz, G. Guzmán, J. Halifax, A. Hofmann, F. J. Lipp, B. Lowy, D. J. McKenna, E. MacRae, B. R. Ortíz de Montellano, C. A. P. Ruck, R. E. Schultes, R. G. Wasson and others; though some, such as W. La Barre and A. T. Shulgin, have shunned it (La Barre 1988). Entheogen has appeared widely in print in English, German, French, Italian, Portuguese, and Spanish. . . .

JONATHAN OTT, *PHARMACOTHEON: ENTHEOGENIC DRUGS,*
THEIR PLANT SOURCES AND HISTORY

1994
Ethnobotany, rather than anthropology, pioneered the study of that remarkable class of plants—the botanical hallucinogens—employed by the shamans of some Native American peoples to facilitate the ecstatic trance that is an indispensable component of shamanism. . . . [A]ll plants are regarded as having souls or spirits, but the so-called hallucinogens are of a different order. Their users credit their extraordinary effects, which science knows to be due to certain alkaloids, by themselves or in combination, to supernatural

power. The plants are sacred, and at least some are personified as deities that must be treated with care and propitiated with offerings, lest
they turn their powers against those who use them. Because of these
special qualities, some students of the phenomenon have proposed to
do away with *hallucinogen* and replace it with *entheogen,* a compound
term that means "containing deity" or "the god within," thus conveying
more accurately what is meant in the indigenous universe.

PETER T. FURST, "AN OVERVIEW OF SHAMANISM"

1997 Once, when a journalist casually referred to peyote (a
classic entheogen) as a drug, a Huichol Indian shaman
replied, "Aspirin is a drug, peyote is sacred."

ROBERT FORTE, IN THE INTRODUCTION TO
ENTHEOGENS AND THE FUTURE OF RELIGION

2000 Nomenclature has been a problem. . . . The word
"psychedelic" is etymologically innocuous, liter-
ally meaning "mind-manifesting," but it is dated, tagged to "the psychedelic sixties" when recreational use of the drugs took over, and thus
clearly inappropriate when speaking of shamans, Eleusis, and the Native
American Church. We need a word that designates virtually nonaddic-
tive mind-altering substances that are approached seriously and reverently, and the word "entheogens" does just that.

HUSTON SMITH,
CLEANSING THE DOORS OF PERCEPTION

REFERENCES

Bieberman, L. 1968. *Phanerothyme: A Western Approach to the Religious Use of Psychochemicals.* Cambridge, Mass.: See www.csp.org/docs/phanerothyme.
Forte, R. 1997, 2000. *Entheogens and the Future of Religion.* San Francisco: Council on Spiritual Practices, Introduction. New Edition: *Entheogens and the Future of Religion.* Rochester, Vt.: Park Street Press, 2012.

Osmond, H. "A Review of the Clinical Effects of Psychotomimetic Agents." *Annals of the New York Academy of Sciences,* March 14, 1957.

Ott, J. 1993. *Pharmacotheon: Entheogenic Drugs, Their Plant Sources and History.* Kennewick, Wash.: Natural Products Co., 104–5.

Ruck, C. A. P., J. Bigwood, D. Staples, J. Ott, and R. G. Wasson. "Entheogens." *Journal of Psychedelic Drugs,* vol 11, nos. 1–2, January–June 1979.

Seaman, G., and J. S. Day, eds. 1994. *Ancient Traditions: Shamanism in Central Asia and the Americas.* Niwot, Colo.: University Press of Colorado and Denver Museum of Natural History.

Smith, H. 2000. *Cleansing the Doors of Perception.* New York: Tarcher/Putnam.

Wasson, R. G. 1980. *The Wondrous Mushroom: Mycolatry in Mesoamerica.* New York: McGraw-Hill, xiv.

25

An Entheogen Idea-Map—Future Explorations

Thomas B. Roberts

Thomas B. Roberts, Ph.D. (Stanford), is an emeritus professor of Educational Psychology now teaching *Psychedelic Studies* in the Honors Program at Northern Illinois University. His major publications include the reference-resource, *Religion and Psychoactive Sacraments: An Entheogen Chrestomathy* (www.csp.org/chrestomathy), *Psychedelic Horizons, Psychedelic Medicine* (2 vols), and *The Psychedelic Future of the Mind* (forthcoming 2012). He was the Program Chair of the Vallombrosa Conference that inspired this book. His home page resides at niu.academia.edu/ThomasRoberts.

There is a central human experience, which alters all other experiences . . . not just an experience among others, but rather the very heart of the human experience. It is the center that gives understanding to the whole. Once found, life is

263

altered because the very root of human identity is deepened.

WILSON VAN DUSEN,

LSD AND THE ENLIGHTENMENT OF ZEN

Our minds are larger, more complex, and capable of a wider range of experience and thinking than we usually realize. Many of these neglected thoughts and experiences occur in states of consciousness other than our usual awake state, and entheogens are one among many ways to explore this new (or rediscovered) territory. On a map of the world of ideas, where are these entheogenic lands located? The first section of this chapter, "Multistate Mindview and the Singlestate Fallacy," situates entheogens within a multistate consciousness paradigm. What opportunities do entheogens offer religion and the life of the mind? The next section, "Questions for Religious Studies Today" surveys some of the entheogenic heartland, and "Growing Intellectual Interest" maps ideas being traded across nearby disciplinary borders. Taking a long look forward, the last section, "An Entheogenic Future," shows us that this idea-map includes unknown lands for future entheogenic explorers to chart.

MULTISTATE MINDVIEW
AND THE SINGLESTATE FALLACY

I find the following imaginary conversation a good way to teach the concept of a multistate mind.

Imagine that a friend of ours has just bought a powerful new computer and is telling us about it.

"What are you going to use it for?" I ask.

"I'm going to play chess with it," he answers.

"Are you going to use it to write, check your spelling, and use the thesaurus?" you ask.

"No," he responds, "I'm going to play chess."

Another friend asks, "You're going to send e-mail, aren't you? You can communicate around the world on the Internet and find information on the World Wide Web."

"No!" he insists, "I'm going to play chess!"

"What about bookkeeping, making spreadsheets, and tracking your financial records?" asks another friend, who is an accountant. "You're going to use it for these, aren't you?"

"NO! NO!" our friend shouts angrily, "I'm going to play chess!"

We can all recognize that our friend is under-utilizing a powerful resource for processing information.

In the realm of our minds, you and I and most of the people we know resemble our friend. We make the mistake of processing information in only one way—one of our "mental programs," so to speak. We use our minds when we think about our religious beliefs, participate in religious activities, or use ethical standards to judge others and ourselves, yet we habitually access only one group of thinking processes—just like our friend (and his computer). This habitual "program" is our ordinary, awake state, but it is only one of many possible states.

I call this error in thinking—that our minds function well in only one mindbody state—the "singlestate fallacy." We wrongly assume that all useful abilities reside in our ordinary, awake mindbody state. Recognizing this error can lead to major shifts in theology and philosophy. Both modernism and postmodernism grant unquestioned, privileged hegemony to the cognitive processes of our ordinary mindbody state. The multistate paradigm suggested and expressed in this book can release us from the constrictions of the singlestate fallacy, opening us intellectually to many mindbody states and their various cognitive processes. As we shall see, our habitual way of thinking about religion is as limited as our chess-playing friend's view of computers.

Moving beyond the singlestate assumption does not mean we must discard all singlestate theology and philosophy (and everything we have learned so far). As our view of the mind expands to encompass new states and vistas, our ordinary state remains an important part of the larger view—just as our ideas of religion expand to include old and new ideas.

How does a multistate perspective change our view of religion? This volume gathers reports from religious explorers who have used entheogens specifically to investigate this question. But it is not a book of answers. It is more a book of partially answered questions, or rather, a book of partly formulated questions or inklings of questions.

In their spiritual quests, the explorers who contribute to this book have studied many religions and mindbody psychotechnologies (including widely varied forms of contemplative prayer, meditation, singing, chanting, breathing, fasting, sleep deprivation, and withdrawing "into the desert," among other practices). While these disciplines do not always produce shifts into religious mindbody states, intensive practice for prolonged periods often does. Various spiritual practices also incorporate the use of martial arts, yoga, diet and exercise, dream analysis, psychoactive substances, hypnosis, focused attention, and sensory overload and deprivation to achieve religious mindbody states. These psychotechnologies are familiar to students of religion. In *Psychoactive Sacramentals* [*Spiritual Growth with Entheogens*] we focus on entheogens—psychoactive plants and chemicals used in a religious context—and the questions that arise with their use.

Where do mindbody psychotechnologies come from? People invent them, import them from other cultures, and rediscover and update traditional practices. I believe the recent explosion in mindbody psychotechnology, as well as our growing willingness as a culture to explore its possible benefits, will greatly benefit human civilization. Mindbody psychotechnologies are tools for transformation, potentially as powerful as the invention of agriculture, the rise of monotheism, the invention of the printing press and movable type, and the combination of observation and reason into science. Why do I have such large-scale expectations? All of these inventions and discoveries enlarged the idea of what it means to be human, and brought about changes that continued to grow and flower for decades. Similarly, the multistate perspective achieved with the use of mindbody psychotechnology has the potential to redefine what it means to be human. To realize our full potential as humans, we must utilize our ability to achieve multiple mindbody states, and we must utilize the religious and spiritual capacities of these states.

COMMON MISCONCEPTIONS

Entheogens are part of a large family of mindbody methods that, until recently, most of Western culture has largely ignored. Certainly, some uncritical writers have lauded entheogens with unquestioned enthusiasm; others, in ignorance, have damned them vehemently. I hope that this collection of essays will help overcome both polemics with a more balanced view and realistic tone. Before we consider how entheogens can enrich religion and religious studies today, and before we speculate about their long-term benefits for human civilization, I would like to dispel four common misconceptions about entheogens.

First, taking an entheogen does not guarantee a spiritual (or primary religious) experience. Like religious retreats and other opportunities for spiritual experience, entheogens sometimes produce the desired effect and sometimes do not. If someone takes an entheogen and does not have a primary religious experience, it does not mean that entheogens never produce such experience. Not having a spiritual experience (especially the first time) is common, especially among people whose worldviews are seriously threatened by the idea of an entheogen-induced mystical experience. Through careful preparation, including attention to the location, guides can increase the likelihood of a primary religious experience. However, even people who are well prepared and open to the experience may be disappointed.

The second misconception is the belief that all mindbody psycho-technologies are entheogenic. People who lack education or experience in mindbody psychotechnologies may sometimes misinterpret the reports of entheogen-experienced mindbody explorers. Clearly, dreams, meditation, contemplative prayer, and LSD have very different effects. They are by no means equated.

Similarly, not all shifts in mindbody states will result in primary religious experience. This third misconception seems particularly common among adolescents or others who lack education about mindbody states and psycho-technologies. There are many mindbody states, and while some have a powerful sacred element, most do not.

The fourth misconception is the assumption that entheogen use is an easy path—that entheogenic experiences are always ecstatic, beautiful, or pleasurable. Some critics of entheogen use believe that entheogen-induced mystical experiences are "unearned" and therefore not valid. Although some beginning explorers may have had only pleasurable experiences with entheogens, I don't know anyone who is moderately experienced and still maintains this. The entheogenic path holds hellish emotions, terrible thoughts, and psychological suffering; anyone embarking on this road must be willing to experience the dark night of the soul. The best descriptions I know are Grof's portrayals of the perinatal parts of our minds, particularly Basic Perinatal Matrices II and III.

People may under-report the unpleasant aspects of entheogenic experiences for two reasons: (1) strongly negative experiences often resolve themselves into strongly positive ones; and (2) negative experiences may be unresolved and still too frightening to face.

As you read this book, you may find yourself thinking, "Entheogens might be all right for some people, but not for me." In this case, you are probably right. People who benefit from something naturally want to share their discovery with others, and people are especially enthusiastic about the topic of religion. This is why we have evangelists of all stripes trying to convert others to their religious practices. With entheogenic experience, however, the initial enthusiasm matures into a realization that this practice, like religious practices such as monasticism, Pentecostal enthusiasm, or the study of sacred texts, is not appropriate for everyone.

QUESTIONS FOR RELIGIOUS STUDIES TODAY

With these misconceptions corrected, let's consider the question: What opportunities do entheogens offer religion and the life of the mind? The experiences and observations that underlie this book invite renewed study and discourse on religion. Do we take for granted certain religious ideas and thinking processes that are actually artifacts of our usual mindbody state? How do theology, religious history, mysticism, meditation, prayer, sacraments, ecumenism, sacred texts, ethical standards, and other standard religious topics appear from an entheogenic perspective?

Can entheogens help us become more spiritually intelligent? First, let's consider intelligence. Cognitive psychologist Robert Sternberg defines intelligence as "mental self-management." Surely, then, someone who can select from a larger repertoire of thinking skills has a higher level of mental self-management (intelligence, that is) than someone with a more limited selection. For example, Kary Mullis attributes the insight that lead to his invention of the PCR process (for which he won the Nobel Prize) to a cognitive skill that he developed during LSD trips. In Western culture, we have largely developed the cognitive abilities of only our ordinary, awake state. When we add the cognitive abilities that reside in other mindbody states, our repertoire of thinking skills—our intelligence—is greatly increased.

Entheogens commonly produce states that enhance our ability to have spiritual experiences—for example, the primary religious experiences that Brother David describes in the introduction of this book. Remembering that Sternberg's definition of intelligence is "mental self-management," I find myself stunned by the implications of this question: since entheogens open the door to increased mental self-management in the spiritual domain, have we actually discovered a way to increase spiritual intelligence? With proper selection, preparation, teacher training, and follow-up, could we design a program to increase spiritual intelligence? I believe it is a moral, spiritual, intellectual, and social duty to examine the feasibility of this idea.

Two illustrations from current intellectual trends—consciousness and postmodernism—show how entheogens and a multistate paradigm reframe existing topics. While the study of "consciousness" has appeared in various disciplines, singlestate assumptions usually limit exploration to the consciousness of our ordinary state. For example, when philosophers ask questions about consciousness, they typically mean self-reflexiveness (knowing that we know). But how do identity (self), reflexiveness (a cognitive process), and self-reflexiveness vary from mindbody state to mindbody state? What about transcendent states, where we lose our sense of self? Entheogens can turn these questions from speculations into empirical experiences.

To most people who are even moderately experienced with entheogens, concepts such as awe, sacredness, eternity, grace, transcendence, dark night of the soul, heaven, and hell are more than theological ideas; they are experiences. How to understand them is the hard question. Did people's experiences (entheogenic or not) produce these ideas, or do people's ideas and expectations produce the experiences? The answer is probably a mixture of both. Taking a radical postmodern stance in *Mysticism after Modernity,* Cupitt claims that there is no such thing as experience prior to language, stating, "Language goes all the way down." In other words, there is no experience or knowledge about experience without language. Grof, on the other hand, reports that entheogenic experience overrides cultural set and language-based expectations.

> The other important consequence of the shocking emotional and physical encounter with the phenomenon of death is the opening up of areas of spiritual and religious experiences that appear to be an intrinsic part of the human personality and are independent of the individual's cultural and religious background and programming. In my experience, everyone who has reached these levels develops convincing insights into the utmost relevance of the spiritual and religious dimensions in the universal scheme of things. Even hard-core materialists, positively oriented scientists, skeptics, and cynics, and uncompromising Marxist philosophers suddenly became interested in a spiritual search after they confronted these levels in themselves. (Grof 1976, 95–96)

If radical postmodernists were to take several massive, overwhelming entheogen doses, to what extent would their presession thoughts determine their experiences? Afterward, would they still maintain "Language goes all the way down"?

The multistate paradigm leads us to ask another question: Even if language comes first in our ordinary, awake state, does this mean that language comes first in all other mindbody states? Entheogens, along with other mindbody psychotechnologies challenge our singlestate assumptions about our minds, and they present a research technique for gathering empirical evidence on consciousness studies and postmodernism.

This book also raises questions about the ethical side of religious development. Many people believe they have ethically benefited from entheogen-induced mystical experiences, and among the entheogen-experienced people I have talked with, this is a common perception. It certainly makes sense that ego-transcendent experiences may decrease egocentric motivation, such as the addictive desires for ownership, consumption, wealth, power, and fame. Furthermore, research on the effects of mystical experiences, whether entheogenic or not, confirms a personal transformation toward social responsibility, an ecological perspective, and spiritual concerns. Thus, to many of this book's authors, it is a humane, social responsibility to explore entheogenic possibilities. Is there a moral imperative to do so?

In addition to a social responsibility, is there a parallel spiritual responsibility? Some people say there is a moral obligation to develop oneself spiritually. If so, doesn't this entail a spiritual moral obligation to systematically investigate the claims of people who report that entheogens aided their own spiritual development such as their ability to understand sacred texts? Does this make our neglect of entheogens' religious possibilities a spiritual omission?

These topics and questions describe some landmarks in the territory of religious studies, while trade in entheogenic ideas crosses borders with adjacent disciplines, too.

GROWING INTELLECTUAL INTEREST

After years of neglect, new scholarly interest in entheogens is reopening long-delayed questions in disciplines adjacent to religious studies.

This section notes some cross-border trade in entheogen-related ideas. To start with, the overall intellectual landscape has changed. Looking at how entheogens might influence theology in her 1966 book *The Mythmakers,* anthropologist Mary Barnard wrote, "Looking at the matter coldly, unintoxicated and unentranced, I am willing to prophesy that fifty theo-botanists working fifty years would make the current theories concerning the origins of much mythology and theology as out of date as pre-Copernican astronomy." "I am the more willing to prophesy," she laments, "since I am, alas, so unlikely to be proved wrong."

In the intervening decades, new developments in mind-body studies provide a nurturing context for Barnhard's theo-botanists. There was little knowledge of mindbody psychotechnologies in 1966, but today, interest in meditation and psychopharmacology, to name only two, is burgeoning. In fact, the study of mindbody psychotechnologies has accumulated into an unrecognized discipline of its own, one that includes religion and extends far beyond it. This new, gestating academic discipline might be called "mindbody studies" and includes contributions from archeology, anthropology, and history; sociology, psychology, and human relations; medicine, pharmacology, and mental health; music, literature, painting, film, and art criticism; biology, chemistry, and botany; philosophy, science, and, of course, religious studies. What are some of the leading contributions to entheogenic and mindbody studies?

At the 1998 meeting of the Society for Neuroscience, biologist David Nichols began his address to the Serotonin Club with the following suggestion. "A significant number of the people in this room tonight, and indeed a significant percentage of serotonin researchers worldwide, first gained their interest in serotonin through some association with psychedelic agents." Unfortunately, hiding the entheogenic source of one's intellectual curiosity is widespread throughout many professions and disciplines. I believe this is a great disservice to the truth and integrity of many academic, religious, and secular institutions.

Much evidence of the growing interest in entheogens comes from professional organizations and periodicals. *The Journal of Transpersonal*

Psychology (published by the Association for Transpersonal Psychology, founded in 1969 by Abraham Maslow) includes articles on mystical experience and entheogens, two of the group's primary interests. The journal's periodic reviews and summaries of research on mystical experience reveal a surprisingly large number of instruments, surveys, and other tools for assessing transpersonal (including primary religious) experience. Other professional organizations and publications that support entheogenic studies include the Society for the Anthropology of Consciousness (founded in 1980), the *Journal of Economic Botany* (a report from the fields of ethnobotany and ethnomycology, founded by R. Gordon Wasson and R. E. Schultes), and the *Journal of Consciousness Studies*.

The dialogue between religion and science is an exciting advance in the intellectual world. In *Why Religion Matters,* Huston Smith points out that there are now ten centers devoted to the study of religion and science, hundreds of college courses on the topic, and several new journals that carry on this dialogue. I would like to suggest that the dialogue between religion and science must include discussion of entheogens, including the insights and challenges they produce and the opportunity they present of joining science and religion into an experimental religious phenomenology. As William James reminds us in *The Varieties of Religious Experience,* "No account of the universe in its totality can be final which leaves these other forms of consciousness quite discarded." The same can be said for religion.

Since 1994, I have been compiling an online resource of books, special topical issues of journals, and dissertations on entheogens. When I began, I expected to find several dozen books, but to my surprise (and I believe, beyond the expectations of others in the field) *Religion and Psychoactive Sacraments: An Entheogen Chrestomathy* has grown to include over five hundred items. New publications continue to stream in, and entheogenic classics are being republished. Clearly, academic interest is just not a relic of the 1960s.

In evaluating these publications on religious experience, mysticism, spiritual development, or twentieth-century religion for scholarly thoroughness, I use an informal (and admittedly biased) method. Where appropriate, does a writer reference Huxley's *Doors of Perception,* Pahnke's Good Friday Experiment, Wasson's thesis on entheogenic contributions to religion, Grof's work with LSD-occasioned transcendence, and Hood's *Mysticism Scale?* These are key works that I consider touchstones for entheogenic and religious studies. Huston Smith's *Cleansing the Doors of Perception* (published in 2000) is the most recent addition to my mental checklist. Sometimes I extend the list to include other authors, topics, and works—for instance, the Native American Church's use of peyote, or the ayahuasca churches of Brazil. Without a doubt, expecting references to all of these is too high a standard. But for preliminary assessments, this quick rubric helps me estimate whether authors are informed about the entheogenic aspects of their professions or are still stuck back in 1966 with Barnard's theo-botanists.

Entheogens provide Departments of Religious Studies and nearby disciplines, as they exist today, many opportunities to trade ideas and to expand their inquiries into additional mindbody states. How might these opportunities develop if we look further into the future?

AN ENTHEOGENIC FUTURE

Will twenty-first-century seminaries, theology departments, and divinity schools offer courses in myco-theology and entheogenic hermeneutics? Will religious studies programs offer laboratory courses in experiential mysticism? This is not likely. However, if intellectual interest in a multistate paradigm continues to grow through this century, then perhaps by the twenty-second century such courses will be widely offered. Each chapter in this book seeds questions and nourishes discussions for entheogen-informed futurists.

An entheogen research agenda or a university seminar on entheogens might begin with any one of the following questions:

- Do humans have an innate spiritual nature? What parts do biology and culture play in this? Can entheogens help activate and develop our spiritual nature?

- Are entheogen-assisted primary religious experiences authentic? What criteria should be used to measure authenticity? Who should decide the answers to these questions?
- Can we build a strong bridge between science and religion if we omit entheogenic girders from our materials?
- Is sacredness a quale? During some entheogenic states, sacredness seems to reside in any number of objects, thoughts, or emotions. Can sacredness be attributed (or misattributed) to any handy object, or any passing thought?
- As entheogenic experiences become more readily accessible, will theologians be able to develop clearer descriptions and more complex typologies of them? For example, how might Wilber's typology of nature, deity, and formless/nondual mysticism be further elaborated?
- Might entheogens democratize unitive states and access to primary religious experience? If so, what might religion become?
- Can entheogenic peak experiences, though only temporary states, be converted into permanent personal traits and continued spiritual development?
- Did entheogens play a significant role in the origins of religions— shamanic, ancient, and modern? Were the 1960s a period of "Great Awakening," as Ellwood and McLoughlin claim?
- Can entheogens be useful in specialized mental health treatment or pastoral counseling—for instance, with alcoholics or hospice patients?
- Do entheogens make it possible to study mysticism experimentally? How might they be instructive to carefully selected and prepared seminarians and advanced students of religion? Might entheogen-induced primary religious experiences help those in religious professions rededicate themselves to their calling?
- Do entheogen-induced mystical experiences boost the immune system or have other healthful effects? If so, how might this relate to reports of spiritual healing?
- Who is most likely to benefit from entheogens, and who is not?

How should people be screened and prepared for their sessions? What kinds of follow-up are most useful?

• What regulatory issues and legal hurdles do entheogens face? In a country dedicated to freedom of conscience and that believes in the separation of church and state, how might current laws accommodate the use of entheogens?

This book looks mostly at entheogens used alone. But what if entheogens are combined with meditation, contemplative prayer, ascetic practices, chanting, or other mindbody practices? Perhaps twenty-first-century mind-body inventors will develop methods to sequence psychotechnologies or combine them into new technologies. Might they invent new, unknown mindbody states? What abilities might we discover or create in these states? What will we learn about the human mind? What will we learn about the varieties of religious experience?

In *About Religion,* Mark Taylor notes that the distance between the Haight-Ashbury and Silicon Valley is "not as great as it initially appears." Many of us have heard of leaders in the information revolution using psychoactives as aids for creative problem solving at work and for personal development at home. This is not a surprise, since technologies that come of age together often marry. The outcome of this entheogenic-electronic union remains to be seen and is certainly one of the most fascinating mysteries of the new millennium. Biotechnology is also maturing in concert with entheogenic studies. Electronic technologies, psychotechnologies, and biotechnologies—each of these embodies paradigmatic shifts in information processing that will contribute to a hybrid generation of new ideas and practices.

In the twentieth century, the tycoons of the Industrial and Retailing Age spent millions of dollars establishing foundations and charities to benefit society. Will the billionaires of the Information Age do the same? As writings in this book indicate, the opportunities for entheogen-informed foundations to positively impact religion, health, and education are huge.

REFERENCES

Alcoholics Anonymous. 1984. "Pass It On": *The Story of Bill Wilson and How the A. A. Message Reached the World*. New York: Alcoholics Anonymous World Services, Inc., chapter 23.

Association for Transpersonal Psychology. 1969. P.O. Box 3049, Stanford, CA 94309.

Barnard, M. 1966. *The Mythmakers*. Athens, Ohio: Ohio State University Press.

Council on Spiritual Practices. 1997. "States of Unitive Consciousness: Research Summary." www.csp.org/docs/unitive_consciousness.html.

Cupitt, D. 1998. *Mysticism after Modernity*. Malden, Mass.: Blackwell Publishers.

Ellwood, R. 1994. *The Sixties Spiritual Awakening: American Religion Moving from Modern to Postmodern*. New Brunswick, N.J.: Rutgers University Press.

Doblin, R. 1991. "Pahnke's 'Good Friday Experiment': A long-term follow-up and methodological critique." *The Journal of Transpersonal Psychology* 23(1): 1–28.

Eleusis: Journal of Psychoactive Plants and Compounds 1998. http://users .lycaeum.org/~eleusis.

Forte, R., ed. 1997, 2000. *Entheogens and the Future of Religion*. San Francisco: Council on Spiritual Practices.

Grinspoon, L., and J. Bakalar. 1979, 1997. *Psychedelic Drugs Reconsidered*. New York: The Lindesmith Center.

Grof, S. 1976, 1993. *Realms of the Human Unconscious: Observations from LSD Psychotherapy*. New York: E. P. Dutton. 1993 edition published by Souvenir Press (Educational and Academic): London.

———. 1980, 1994. *LSD Psychotherapy*. Alameda, Calif.: Hunter House.

Grof, S., and J. Halifax. 1977. *The Human Encounter with Death*. New York: E. P. Dutton.

Heffter Research Institute. 1998. http://heffter.org.

Hood, R. W. Jr. 1975. "The construction and preliminary validation of a measure of reported mystical experience." *Journal for the Scientific Study of Religion* 14(1): 29–41.

Hood, R. W. Jr., Morris, R. J., and P. J. Watson. 1993. "Further factor analysis of Hood's Mysticism Scale." *Psychological Reports* 73(1): 1176–78.

Journal of Consciousness Studies. 1993. Richmond, Va.: Imprint Academic/ Virginia Commonwealth University.

Lukoff, D., and F. Lu. 1988. "Transpersonal psychology research review: Topic: Mystical exerience." *The Journal of Transpersonal Psychology* 20(2): 161–84.

Lukoff, D., R. Turner, and F. Lu. 1992. "Transpersonal psychology research review: Psycho-religious dimensions of healing." *The Journal of Transpersonal Psychology* 24(1): 41–60.

———. 1993. "Transpersonal psychology research review: Psycho-spiritual dimensions of healing." *The Journal of Transpersonal Psychology* 25(1): 11–28.

Lukoff, D., R. Zanger, and F. Lu. 1990. "Transpersonal psychology research review: Psychoactive substances and transpersonal states." *The Journal of Transpersonal Psychology* 22(2): 107–48.

MacDonald, D. A., L. LeClair, C. J. Holland, A. Alter, and H. L. Friedman. 1995. "A survey of measures of transpersonal constructs." *The Journal of Transpersonal Psychology* 27(2): 171–235.

McLoughlin, W. G. 1978. *Revivals, Awakenings, and Reform: An Essay on Religion and Social Change in America, 1607–1977.* Chicago: University of Chicago Press.

Multidisciplinary Association for Psychedelic Studies and *MAPS Bulletin* 1986+. www.maps.org.

Nichols, D. E. 1998. "From Eleusis to PET scans: The mysteries of psychedelics." *Bulletin of the Multidisciplinary Association for Psychedelic Studies* 1(4): 50–55.

Pahnke, W. N., and W. A. Richards. 1969. "Implications of LSD and experimental mysticism." In Charles Tart, ed., *Altered States of Consciousness.* New York: John Wiley & Sons. Several reprint editions exist.

Passie, T. 1997. *Psycholytic and Psychedelic Therapy Research 1931–1995: A Complete International Bibliography.* Hannover, Germany: Laurentius Publishers.

Riedlinger, T. J., ed. 1990, 1997. *The Sacred Mushroom Seeker: Essays for R. Gordon Wasson.* Portland, Ore.: Dioscorides Press. Paperback edition: Rochester, Vt.: Park Street Press.

Roberts, T. B. 1989. "Multistate education: Metacognitive implications of the mindbody psychotechnologies." *The Journal of Transpersonal Psychology* 21(1): 83–102.

———. 1999. "Do entheogen-induced mystical experiences boost the immune system?" *Advances in Mind-Body Medicine,* 15: 139–47. www.csp.org/docs/roberts-immune.html.

Roberts, T. B., and P. Hruby. 1994–2001. *Religion and Psychoactive Sacraments: An Entheogen Chrestomathy.* www.csp.org/chrestomathy.

———. 2002. "Toward an entheogen research agenda." *Journal of Humanistic Psychology,* vol. 42, no. 1, 71–89.

Roberts, T. B., and R. N. Jesse. 1997. "Recollections from the Good Friday Experiment: An interview with Huston Smith." *The Journal of Transpersonal Psychology* 29(2): 99–104.

Ruck, C. A. P., and D. Staples. 1994. *The World of Classical Myth: Gods and Goddesses; Heroines and Heros.* Durham, N.C.: Carolina Academic Press.

Rudgley, R. 1993. *Essential Substances in Society: A Cultural History of Intoxicants in Society.* New York: Kodansha International.

Serotonin Club. 1988. http://146.9.4.210.

Smith, H. 2000. *Cleansing the Doors of Perception: The Religious Significance of Entheogenic Plants and Chemicals.* New York: Tarcher/Penguin Putnam. Deluxe limited edition available from the Council on Spiritual Practices: www.csp.org/CDP.

———. 2001. *Why Religion Matters: The Fate of the Human Spirit in an Age of Disbelief.* San Francisco: HarperSanFrancisco.

Society for the Anthropology of Consciousness. 1980. www.ameranthassn.org/sac/index.htm.

Steindl-Rast, D. 1997. "Explorations into God." In R. Forte, ed., *Entheogens and the Future of Religion.* San Francisco: Council on Spiritual Practices. New Edition. *Entheogens and the Future of Religion.* 2012. Rochester, Vt.: Park Street Press.

———. 1988. "Thoughts on mysticism as frontier of consciousness evolution." In Grof, S., and M. Livingston Valier, eds. *Human Survival and Consciousness Evolution.* Albany, N.Y.: State University of New York Press.

Sternberg, R. J. 1988. *The Triarchic Mind: A New Theory of Human Intelligence.* New York: Penguin.

Stolaroff, M. J. 1997. *The Secret Chief: Conversations with a Pioneer of the Underground Psychedelic Therapy Movement.* Charlotte, N.C.: Multidisciplinary Association for Psychedelic Studies.

Tart, C., ed. 1969, 1990. *Altered States of Consciousness: A Book of Readings.* New York: John Wiley. Several other editions exist.

———. 1991. "Influences of previous psychedelic drug experiences on students of Tibetan Buddhism: A preliminary exploration." *The Journal of Transpersonal Psychology* 23(2): 139–74.

Taylor, M. C. 1999. *About Religion: Economies of Faith in Virtual Culture.* Chicago: University of Chicago Press.

Wasson, R. G., S. Kramrisch, J. Ott, and C. A. P. Ruck. 1986. *Persephone's Quest: Entheogens and the Origins of Religion.* New Haven, Conn.: Yale University Press.

Wilber, K. 1999. "Spirituality and developmental lines: Are there stages?" *The Journal of Transpersonal Psychology* 31(1): 1–10.

Epilogue

Ought it to be assumed that in all men the mixture of religion with other elements should be identical? Ought it, indeed, to be assumed that the lives of all men should show identical religious elements? In other words, is the existence of so many religious types and sects and creeds regrettable?

To these questions I answer "No" emphatically. And my reason is that I do not see how it is possible that creatures in such different positions and with such different powers as human individuals are, should have exactly the same functions nor should we be expected to work out identical solutions. Each from his peculiar angle of observations, takes in a certain sphere of fact and trouble, which each must deal with in a unique manner.

WILLIAM JAMES,
THE VARIETIES OF RELIGIOUS EXPERIENCE, 1902
WWW.CSP.ORG/DOCS/JAMES-VARIETIES

About the Council on Spiritual Practices

The Council on Spiritual Practices (CSP) is a collaboration among spiritual guides, experts in the behavioral and biomedical sciences, and scholars of religion dedicated to making direct experience of the sacred more available to more people. There is evidence that such encounters can have profound benefits for those who experience them, for their neighbors, and for the world.

CSP has a twofold mission: to identify and develop approaches to primary religious experience that can be used safely and effectively, and to help individuals and spiritual communities bring the insights, grace, and joy that arise from direct perceptions of the divine into their daily lives.

The Council on Spiritual Practices has no doctrine or liturgy of its own.

www.csp.org

CSP CODE OF ETHICS FOR SPIRITUAL GUIDES

[**Preamble**] People have long sought to enrich their lives and to awaken to their full natures through spiritual practices including prayer, meditation, mind-body disciplines, service, ritual, community liturgy, holy day and seasonal observances, and rites of passage. "Primary religious practices" are those intended, or especially likely, to bring about exceptional states of consciousness such as the direct experience of the divine, of cosmic unity, or of boundless awareness.

In any community, there are some who feel called to assist others along spiritual paths, and who are known as ministers, rabbis, pastors, curanderas, shamans, priests, or other titles. We call such people "guides": those experienced in some practice, familiar with the terrain, and who act to facilitate the spiritual practices of others. A guide need not claim exclusive or definitive knowledge of the terrain.

Spiritual practices, and especially primary religious practices, carry risks. Therefore, when an individual chooses to practice with the assistance of a guide, both take on special responsibilities. The Council on Spiritual Practices proposes the following Code of Ethics for those who serve as spiritual guides.

1. [**Intention**]Spiritual guides are to practice and serve in ways that cultivate awareness, empathy, and wisdom.

2. [**Serving Society**] Spiritual practices are to be designed and conducted in ways that respect the common good, with due regard for public safety, health, and order. Because the increased awareness gained from spiritual practices can catalyze desire for personal and social change, guides shall use special care to help direct the energies of those they serve, as well as their own, in responsible ways that reflect a loving regard for all life.

3. [**Serving Individuals**] Spiritual guides shall respect and seek to preserve the autonomy and dignity of each person. Participation in any primary religious practice must be voluntary and based on prior disclosure and consent given individually by each participant while in an ordinary state of consciousness. Disclosure shall include, at a minimum, discussion of any elements of the practice that could reasonably be seen as presenting physical or psychological risks. In particular, participants must be warned that primary religious experience can be difficult and dramatically transformative.

Guides shall make reasonable preparations to protect each participant's health and safety during spiritual practices and in the vulnerable periods that may follow. Limits on the behaviors of participants and facilitators are to be made clear and agreed upon in advance of any session. Appropriate customs of confidentiality are to be established and honored.

4. [**Competence**] Spiritual guides shall assist with only those practices for which they are qualified by personal experience and by training or education.

5. [**Integrity**] Spiritual guides shall strive to be aware of how their own belief systems, values, needs, and limitations affect their work. During primary religious practices, participants may be especially vulnerable to suggestion, manipulation, and exploitation; therefore, guides pledge to protect participants and not to allow anyone to use that vulnerability in ways that harm participants or others.

6. [**Quiet Presence**] To help safeguard against the harmful consequences of personal and organizational ambition, spiritual communities are usually better allowed to grow through attraction rather than active promotion.

7. [**Not for Profit**] Spiritual practices are to be conducted in the spirit of service. Spiritual guides shall strive to accommodate participants without regard to their ability to pay or make donations.

8. [**Tolerance**] Spiritual guides shall practice openness and respect toward people whose beliefs are in apparent contradiction to their own.

9. [**Peer Review**] Each guide shall seek the counsel of other guides to help ensure the wholesomeness of his or her practices and shall offer counsel when there is need.

OTHER BOOKS IN THE
CSP ENTHEOGEN PROJECT SERIES

Cleansing the Doors of Perception: The Religious Significance of Entheogenic Plants and Chemicals
By Huston Smith

Entheogens and the Future of Religion
Edited by Robert Forte

Religion and Psychoactive Sacraments: An Entheogen Chrestomathy
Edited by Thomas B. Roberts and Paula Jo Hruby
Published online at www.csp.org/chrestomathy

The Road to Eleusis: Unveiling the Secret of the Mysteries
Twentieth Anniversary Edition
By R. Gordon Wasson, Carl A. P. Ruck, and Albert Hofmann

Index